NAVAJO WOMEN
OF MONUMENT
VALLEY

Preservers of the Past

Robert S. McPherson

Robert S. McPherson is Professor of History Emeritus at Utah State University—Blanding Campus and author of numerous books about the history and cultures of the Four Corners Region.

Other books of related interest by the author:
Traditional Navajo Teachings, A Trilogy
> *Volume I: Sacred Narratives and Ceremonies*
> *Volume II: The Natural World*
> *Volume III: The Earth Surface People*
> (University Press of Colorado)

Traders, Agents, and Weavers: Developing the Northern Navajo Region
> (University of Oklahoma Press)

Both Sides of the Bullpen: Navajo Trade and Posts of the Upper Four Corners
> (University of Oklahoma Press)

Viewing the Ancestors: Perceptions of the Anaasází, Mokwič, and Hisatsinom
> (University of Oklahoma Press)

Under the Eagle: Samuel Holiday, Navajo Code Talker
> (University of Oklahoma Press)

Dineji Na'nitin: Navajo Traditional Teachings and History
> (University Press of Colorado)

Navajo Tradition, Mormon Life: The Autobiography and Teachings of Jim Dandy
> (University of Utah Press)

Along Navajo Trails: Recollections of a Trader, 1898-1948
> (Utah State University Press)

A Navajo Legacy: The Life and Teachings of John Holiday
> (University of Oklahoma Press)

Navajo Land, Navajo Culture: The Utah Experience in the Twentieth Century
> (University of Oklahoma Press)

The Journey of Navajo Oshley: An Autobiography and Life History
> (Utah State University Press)

Sacred Land, Sacred View: Navajo Perceptions of the Four Corners Region
> (University Press of Colorado)

The Northern Navajo Frontier, 1860-1900: Expansion through Adversity
> (University of New Mexico Press)

CONTENTS

INTRODUCTION

Women of the Desert

Monument Valley is the iconic homeland of the Navajo. Its scenery is painted upon pottery, woven into rugs, plastered on billboards, etched into signage, marketed in print, and photographed during all seasons. Known to the Diné as "Treeless Area or Valley Amidst the Rocks" (Tsé Bii' Ndzisgaii), this land did not permanently become theirs until 1934, although they were certainly present by the 1500s and possibly as early as the 1100s–1200s AD. Regardless of this tentative dating in the distant past, there is no denying their ownership and involvement with this area in the historic present. Now, hundreds of thousands of tourists descend upon the valley each year, fascinated with the rock formations, captivated by scenic vistas, and curious about the people who live here. There is plenty to inform them, since the Navajo are among the most researched and best documented of all of the American Indian tribes in the United States. Their religious and philosophical beliefs, often referred to as traditional teachings, are complex and profound, serving as the basis for a unique worldview. Their earlier lifestyle was harmoniously adapted to the landscape and a desert economy. And their sense of kinship coupled with a pragmatic view of survival allowed them to weather many of the storms of life that would have crushed and then buried other people. That life was never easy, but was often filled with personal significance.

Today, there are elements that confront this traditional lifestyle. The dominant society's education challenges many of the beliefs and practices serving as the core of Navajo teachings. Science butts heads with religion, modern conveniences replace old ways, and the sterile homogenized American lifestyle is supplanting an existence foreordained by the holy people. Both views have their benefits, but who wants to return to traversing with horse and wagon a wind-blown trail winding through sand dunes when a straight, paved highway dotted with convenience stores dispensing gasoline and doughnuts makes travel so much easier? Why stare at starvation and hope that one's garden will produce sufficiently when grocery stores stock recently arrived goods in refrigerated units and food aisles bulging with cans and packages awaiting to be opened? Who wants to struggle learning the Navajo language when most people speak English and all of the telecommunication platforms and social media use it to send their messages? Even at home, the vast majority of parents use the English language to communicate with their children on a daily basis. And when someone is sick, hospitals and clinics, dispersed on or near the reservation, provide an additional, if not alternative, way of handling sickness when compared to ceremonies that are often expensive and can last for nine days or nights. Elements of the twenty-first century have infiltrated every aspect of traditional Navajo life.

One could surmise that those teachings and experiences of the past now hold little value for the rising generations. What was, does not fit now. There is nothing to learn when so much is out-of-date and irrelevant in a push-button, instantaneous world composed of plastic, computer chips, and chrome. However, many children, youth, and adults admire and adhere to the "elderlies" who lived in such a different world as that of today. Many young people, while recognizing the difference between now and yesteryear, understand that their roots come from the same soil and that white hair and declining bodies can also be a receptacle of wisdom and cultural insight. Many Navajos cling to traditional beliefs for their personal, familial, and tribal identity in an attempt to escape the foreign and sometimes cloying world of modern America. Where their roots were planted in the past is quiet and has a calmness that comes with reassurance that difficult times can be survived. Down where those roots grow, it is serene when compared with the winds blowing aloft. This book is about those roots and the soil that made them possible.

In the early 1990s I had the opportunity to both teach and interview Navajo people in Monument Valley, Utah. This provided a chance for me to meet many of its residents and to ask questions concerning the Navajo experience in this corner of their vast reservation. After obtaining ethnographic permits from the tribe, I set out to talk to many of the older residents about their life in this beautiful but sometimes harsh landscape. Many of them ranged in age between seventy and ninety, placing their births sometime between the early 1900s and the late 1920s. These dates are important because they mean that those interviewed were raised at a time when their elders were conversant with the stories of the Long Walk era (1858–68) as well as having themselves witnessed the golden age of the trading post, the trauma of livestock reduction (1930s), the flourish and decline of uranium mining (1950s–60s), and the evolution of many locally inspired events and changes—introduction of the movie industry, development of tourism, expansion of transportation, and a growing wage economy's impact on individual and family values. Just as important was the effect all of this had on those who had earlier survived in an agricultural and livestock economy. How did these changes that made men the dominant providers interface with a matrilineal society where the home, garden, and much of the livestock was traditionally owned and controlled by the women of the household? These shifting dynamics encouraged cultural change that challenged many of the precepts of traditional Navajo lifestyle.

Male versus Female

Anthropologists and other types of social scientists had previously raised questions about shifting cultural norms in different parts of the reservation, but none had concentrated major efforts in the Monument Valley area, which has its own unique set of circumstances. One reason for this is that the Utah portion of the reservation, when compared to the preponderance of Navajo land ownership and population residing in New Mexico and Arizona, is relatively small. The main focus of the tribe has always been on its burgeoning growth and economic activity in these two states. There were, of course, many similarities among Navajos in all three regions, but each area of the reservation has its own set of stories and circumstances that give uniqueness to the experience of those living there. Traditionalists recognize this and give latitude as to how people in each geographical territory may have their own way of explaining a story or of dealing with idiosyncrasies in ritual practices. While the whole remains similar, there often are slight differences.

When one looks at the extensive research examining Navajo life, it soon becomes apparent that Navajo men—whether concerning historical activities, autobiographies, cultural practices, or philosophy—dominate the scene. There are a number of reasons for this. Men, when compared to women, lived more varied lives. Traditional Navajo society teaches that everything (yes, everything) has a divine role assigned to it by the holy people (gods) at the time of creation. Part of this responsibility is defined by sex, since tangible and intangible entities, animate and inanimate objects, and man-made or natural things are either male or female. Even the human body shares this division, with the left side of a person being the male side and the right the female. If one were to philosophically bisect an individual, that means that the left eye, ear, nostril, lung, arm, hand, and so forth are to perform male functions related to the tasks assigned during the creation of the world. War, hunting, politics, ceremonies, and leadership become the domain of males while female functions such as making offerings, providing things that nurture, advocating for peace, and living a gentle existence are performed using the right hand and the powers associated with the right side. Extending this philosophy further, there are trees that are male and others that are female; the same is true with water, clouds, rocks, hogans, ceremonies, and the list goes on. The Navajo universe is a highly classified and orderly world that speaks to the values of those who reside within it.

While there was a rough equality between men and women, men served as the main repository for many of the teachings embedded in the narratives that frame the creation of the Navajo universe. Ceremonies are the physical enactment of what occurred in the myths and stories during that time, just as sandpaintings are portrayals of elements and incidents that call forth these powers to heal. In general, it is the medicine men who provide both the narration and ritual activities necessary for invoking assistance from the gods. Women, on the other hand, often heal through herbs and a limited amount of ceremonial performance. Men also use plants and herbs while both men and women may hold powers of divination—star gazing, crystal gazing, wind listening, and hand trembling being four of the most common types to be discussed later. Knowledge of any of these healing practices can benefit those who understand and control their powers, but they can also be harmful and dangerous if certain procedures are not followed. Since men are considered more capable in handling these spiritual elements, they are the ones most likely to interact with the holy people in effecting a cure.

This same principle of men being involved in the more physically challenging arenas of life such as war, politics, hunting, and long-distance travel is also true, while the role of a woman in traditional society is the polar opposite. Women remained home, tended children, raised gardens, gathered plants, herded livestock, wove blankets and rugs, and supported their husband's activities. There are exceptions to some of this, but generally speaking, they were the support arm of men, and only tangentially involved in the ceremonial and more active side of the life of their husband. Indeed, in writing this book, I called upon the experiences of eighteen women to provide a sense of what daily life was like for those living in the Monument Valley area between the 1920s and 1990s. Explanation of each of their lives paralleled those of their peers without much exception. Far less dramatic than those of their male counterparts, there is little doubt that they played a huge role in supporting the ritual and activity aspects of what their husbands had to accomplish, but they remained primarily in the background.

The matrilineal nature of Navajo culture forms solid bonds between females from birth to death. This mother has the responsibility to teach her daughters life skills, such as grinding corn, and respect for their heritage. The hogan behind them is their domain. (Used by permission, Utah State Historical Society)

This is one reason why there are more autobiographies about Navajo men than women. Medicine men, for instance, have garnered much more attention because of their understanding of not only ritual performance but also the embedded philosophy behind its many intricacies. They live in a fascinating world that explains why things occur from a religious perspective, far apart from those interpretations of the scientific community. Much of this is based in the creation narratives that provide insight into dominant forces at work beneath exterior appearances. Most traditional women are aware of portions of these explanations and may even know

a full account of some narratives, but an oft-heard response, when asked
a question about some aspect of ceremonialism, is to refer to a medicine
man who can give a complete answer. In the areas of more concern to
women, such as herbal medicine, conducting the female puberty ceremony
(kinaaldá), tools and equipment of the home (habeedí) such as the weaving
loom, fire poker, stirring sticks, and so forth, as well as birthing practices,
there is a much greater understanding. At times, women make a clear dif-
ferentiation between the teachings of males and females, and keep the
knowledge for their sex separate.

Navajo Women in the Literature

For those wishing to delve into female Navajo autobiographies of any
length, there are few. The most significant, detailed one is by Charlotte J.
Frisbie, *Tall Woman: The Life Story of Rose Mitchell, A Navajo Woman, c.
1874–1977*.[1] When added to Frisbie's *Food Sovereignty the Navajo Way:
Cooking with Tall Woman*, there are almost a thousand pages of information coming from a single Navajo woman, most of which is told in her
own voice.[2] The same is true of Kay Bennett's *Kaibah: Recollection of a
Navajo Girlhood*, in which the author describes early memories of her life
between 1928 and 1935.[3] Somewhat sanitized in its approach, omitting
the sheer drudgery punctuated by fear and hardship many Navajos felt at
this time of livestock reduction and turmoil, the book provides an accurate
picture of the high points of her daily life. Autobiographical teachings of a
Navajo woman dispersed through a limited life history is found in *Walking
Thunder: Diné Medicine Woman*.[4] This pastiche of short cultural insights
and personal experiences introduces the reader to profoundly important
and lengthy topics in a cursory fashion. Interesting and insightful on one
hand and far too brief on the other, the book offers a starting point for
more detailed study.

Leaving behind those who lived a traditional life associated with the
teachings of the pre–livestock reduction, World War II, and Cold War
eras, there are two notable autobiographies of Navajo women who speak
of more modern times. The best is *The Scalpel and the Silver Bear: The First
Navajo Woman Surgeon Combines Western Medicine and Traditional Healing*
by Lori Arviso Alvord and Elizabeth Cohen Van Pelt.[5] Alvord, the main
author, is half Navajo and searching for her roots. She finds them in working on the Navajo Reservation as a surgeon in some of the Indian Health
Service hospitals, in which she learns to combine aspects of Navajo and
Anglo healthcare. In terms of traditional teachings, what is presented is

accurate but superficial. The second book, *Beyond the Four Corners of the World: A Navajo Woman's Journey* recounts the difficult life of a woman, born in 1952, who grew up on the reservation, attended boarding school, and then struggled to find her place in the modern world.[6] Vacillating between a cursory understanding of traditional beliefs, generic Christianity, Mormonism, and Native American Church religion, Ella Bedonie's experience typifies the confusion and discord that many young people feel today. Interspersed within the autobiography are sections of traditional teachings that orient the reader to the general Navajo cultural experience.

Mention should also be made of some non-autobiographical works that explain female activities in a traditional and modern context. With one exception, that of Ruth Roessel in *Women in Navajo Society*, none of these female authors are Navajo.[7] Roessel was an older woman when she wrote her book, was steeped in traditional culture, and was eager to compare contemporary life to things of the past. She lived through much of what she teaches. The same is true of anthropologist Gladys Reichard, a prolific author who wrote *Spider Woman: A Story of Navajo Weavers and Chanters*.[8] In 1930 she lived with a Navajo family and wrote about her experience of learning how to weave and participating in their activities. The book is an excellent ethnographic study of daily life, including conversations, ritual practices, and Navajo thought. Maureen Trudelle Schwarz has made two important contributions concerning traditional culture in *Molded in the Image of Changing Woman: Navajo Views on the Human Body and Personhood* and *Blood and Voice: Navajo Women Ceremonial Practitioners*.[9] The former is based primarily on excerpts from interviews dispersed throughout, is organized topically to examine Navajo worldview, and has a heavy anthropological orientation. The latter follows the same format as a study of elderly Navajo women who take on the practice of being a chantway singer, which is usually the domain of men. While neither book is biographical in nature, there is a lot of personal testimony that gives the reader an insider perspective of Navajo thought.

Brief mention is made of three recent works, all of which center on contemporary issues of Navajo women against a backdrop of traditional practices that are challenged. Anthropologist Louise Lamphere fostered a four-decade friendship with Eva Price and her daughter and granddaughter living at Sheep Springs, New Mexico. Lamphere's *Weaving Women's Lives: Three Generations in a Navajo Family* examines not only the circumstances of these three females, but also that of the author as they come together to look at the past and compare it to the present.[10] Change, adaptation, and loss of traditional teachings underlie much of their story.

Perhaps no one provides a more positive example of not only surviving these changes but actively fomenting for some of them than Annie Wauneka (1918–97). Moving from her childhood in the sheep camps to the role of an activist who challenged a number of traditional beliefs, she bridged both cultures and encouraged the entrance of many practices of the dominant society. As an advocate for modern education, she also broke from the tradition of a woman not being involved in politics by serving on the Tribal Council for twenty-five years; she united medicine men and Anglo doctors to combat the ravages of tuberculosis; she used the Navajo language in radio broadcasts that encouraged modern ways; and she also fought against the evils of alcohol. Carolyn Niethammer's *I'll Go and Do More: Annie Wauneka, Navajo Leader and Activist* illustrates the potential power and acumen that strong women can attain in advancing a modern agenda.[11]

The final selection, *Reflections in Place: Connected Lives of Navajo Women* by Donna Deyhle, moves the reader in the opposite direction, looking at three generations of Navajo women and their struggles in education through purported racism.[12] Focusing on southeastern Utah, the book discusses the difficulty of students who follow traditional culture but are enrolled in a school system that is both intentionally and unintentionally at odds with those values. While I cannot speak to every person's experience, the schools in Monument Valley are highly sensitive to providing culturally relevant information and are supportive of student traditional practices. That does not mean that there is no cultural loss, but only that some of it may be self-imposed.

The Work at Hand

Where does that place the book you are about to read in this literature, and what is its purpose? Many of the texts cited above are carefully crafted and set in fine prose. I have chosen to take a slightly different approach by maintaining the voices of the women interviewed. There has been limited editing of their translated information, rather than an entire rewriting. During my days of interviewing, I found that there was a general pattern set by those sharing their experiences. Some discussions were quite short, others—two in particular—were long—in one instance extending over three days. But most of them followed the traditional practice of starting in the beginning, meaning that they reverted to the time of creation before getting into more contemporary events. This is a typical Navajo quality since all of the "rules," functions, and assignments of spiritual entities were given at this time. Storytellers follow the same pattern by outlining the connection between past and present, and so I have adopted a similar approach. To maintain an autobiographical presence, I have also limited the amount of interpolation so that the speaker's voice comes through without interruption. Endnotes and other academic modus operandi are kept to a minimum. My editorial goal was to have the elders' content and Navajo expression presented clearly to readers young and old.

A note is in order on the translation and spelling of specific names and terms found within the text. Shortly after the interviews were completed, Marilyn Holiday, Susie Yazzie's daughter, performed most of the translating while the words were still fresh in her mind. Since she was from Monument Valley, had Navajo as her original language, knew many of the people and places, spoke and wrote English well, and spoke Navajo fluently, she was a natural choice. There were some terms—for plants, ceremonial objects, and practices—that required the specialized knowledge of practitioners that she was unable to translate. Thirty years later, when I began focusing intently on the materials, I turned to Clayton Long and Charlotta Nez Lacy, two professional Navajo linguists, to unwrap the meaning and spelling of some of those terms. They did an excellent job, but there were still a few words that remained unknown. My goal was to have as much Navajo language in the text, with the correct spelling, as possible, and so they worked to ensure it happened. At the same time, where there are words that were unclear either in translation or spelling, I have put a question mark to identify them. To many readers, this will not make a difference as they continue to ride through the English text, but for those interested in the Navajo language, I have done the best that I can, and any errors are mine.

In using a number of personal manuscripts and various experiences, I wanted to avoid having these stories sound like a kaleidoscope of interviews. To satisfy the need of having a coherent picture while allowing a variety of voices to share their thoughts, I have chosen to use two lengthy interviews, those of Susie Yazzie and Ada Black, to be the central focus. Their narratives take the reader through different events and teachings characteristic of what many of their peers encountered, but avoid repetition by making Susie's and Ada's thoughts representative. Context, additional explanation, and excerpts from the other interviews are given in a preceding chapter, preparing readers for what they will encounter. Thus, the other women's voices augment what the two featured speakers share about those early days of Monument Valley. What becomes evident is the

Susie Yazzie with her daughter, Marilyn Holiday, the day of the interview, November 10, 2000. Susie, soft-spoken and gentle, was eager to preserve her history and culture, not only for her family, but also for other generations. Her faith in the future and wisdom from the past were rooted in her traditional beliefs. (Photo by author)

importance of the values and beliefs that allowed these women to endure the adversity that made existence so difficult.

There are places where one may be offended by the opinions a speaker shares. For instance, Susie's discussion of homosexuality, life in old age, or concerns with the younger generation may appear harsh. Navajo elders were well-known for speaking their minds, using graphic language, and driving home a point with which others may take issue. No offense is meant. What is said is a function of that person's experience, training, and values accumulated during their lifetime. Susie, for example, mentions that she does not know about the teachings concerning homosexuality, yet there is an extensive body of lore that discusses its role in Navajo culture and how it should be viewed and respected. Still, as times change, not everyone has been given this information. Susie, Ada, and others said what they thought according to their worldview; we, as readers, need to give them latitude to express those beliefs, regardless of our own values nurtured during the first quarter of the twenty-first century.

For those who have studied Navajo culture, they will encounter aspects of a familiar landscape with some different twists and unexpected turns. The women interviewed were asked to share their life history and thoughts, but were not approached as expert specialists with knowledge beyond their own personal experience. Indeed, many were shy, sometimes reticent, because they were unsure of some aspect of a topic. Navajo culture has a way of handling this. When a person has heard an individual talk about something but was not present to witness the event, that speaker will use the word "jiní" meaning "it is said." If they participated in the event and have personal knowledge of it, then that type of understanding would be clearly stated. Both Susie and Ada sprinkled their explanations liberally with "it is said" to the point that I removed some of them just to avoid the repetition. Their desire for accuracy was evident.

Still, they often spoke of things that they had been taught or heard, much of which was based in an oral tradition. Incompletely remembered ceremonial songs and prayers, narratives told around the fire at night, well-preserved gossip, or inaccurate accounts of events may lead a reader to fact-checking and a loss of credibility for the speaker, in a world insistent on written documentation and ironclad proof. This is not to discredit the oral tradition; indeed, at times it has proven to be more accurate than information committed to paper. But there is room for misinterpretation, misinformation, or faulty recall that scholars might note. Even between Susie and Ada there were differences in events and opinions, even though they shared similar backgrounds. Their understanding of the creation story, for instance, is tied to local geography as well as the broader Navajo world. Incidents and the holy people involved in them may vary. Consider that even accounts given by medicine men differ, with no two being exactly the same.

How, then, should this book be understood? Imagine, for a moment, you are a tourist in Monument Valley and want to catch a glimpse of the world as understood by a Navajo elder. You stop your car some distance from their hogan, wait for a few minutes to make sure they are prepared to receive you (that is the polite thing to do, rather than honking or rushing up to their door), and then start across the open yard. A couple of camp dogs bark as they alert to your footsteps crunching in the lately fallen snow, but then fall silent as the door opens and a yellow beam of light shines across the ground with a welcoming figure beckoning for you to enter. The young woman motions for you to remove your coat and have a seat in front of the fifty-five-gallon barrel cut in half with a stove pipe leading all the way to the smoke hole and cold night air above. The waves of heat coming from the metal radiate warmth while the light from the fire within flickers shadows against the cedar log wall of the hogan. Seated across from you to the west—the place of honor—sits a gray-haired woman, bent with age, holding her cane. She does not speak much English, and so it is the duty of her granddaughter to translate for her. You are comfortable but eager to hear what this older woman wishes to say.

Stop for a moment. You are here to listen to her experiences and wisdom, not test her accuracy against a book written by an anthropologist analyzing the various accounts of some narrative. What this elder is sharing is deeply personal and at the core of how she thinks and why she acts. Her life in a high desert environment, her worldview, and her feelings about the Navajo and their interaction with the holy people are what you have come to learn about. She is willing to share this, understanding that those times will never return and that she is part of a past that is slipping away. Even more important is handing this information on to her granddaughter, who lives in a world far different from hers. This is an opportunity, more motivating than anything else, to instill her teachings into a generation that needs and wants to understand its heritage before too much of it is lost. The single most motivating factor for sharing any of this is for the young people to understand the stories in order to build character and better prepare for a very different future. In some instances, it will be just as challenging but different from the world she lived in decades before. She begins, "It is said. . ."

CHAPTER ONE

Traditional Teachings

Foundations from the Past,
Formulas for the Present

A Universe of Power

Navajo culture rests upon a foundation of religious narratives and experience. As one reads the life stories of two traditional Navajo women and hears the thoughts of others, it becomes readily apparent that there are two spheres in which the People operate—one physical, the other spiritual—both of which are real, that interface with each other and influence various outcomes. Unlike the world of today's dominant society that thrives on understanding and manipulating solely the physical universe for man's benefit, the Navajo ponder the intangible and believe that what is seen in the physical world has been foreordained and organized and is now controlled by the holy people or gods, who have ultimate command of what takes place in both realms. Many answers to issues, explanations of events, healing of the sick, and solving problems are found by appeal to these powerful supernatural beings. Echoing through the words these women share is a connection through faith that remained paramount in their lives.

To understand this motivating belief system, one must turn to its origin—the creation and settling of this world by the holy people and their helpers. All was made spiritually before it existed physically, each sacred being inhabiting a different form that ranged from humans and animals to rocks and water. Everything tangible or intangible has what is known as a spirit, but which the Navajo refer to as The Inner Form that Stands Within (bii'gistíín). If the outer structure encasing this form were removed, it would have human qualities capable of thinking, speaking, acting, and controlling its special powers assigned to it by the gods. These first existed in three or four different worlds (depending on the version of the creation story) beneath the level of the Glittering World, in which we exist today. There are many different versions of what took place during the emergence and shortly after the holy people arrived here.[1] These narratives explain how each of these worlds had its own color, starting at the lowest level with black, then blue, yellow, and white before reaching the one we now inhabit. Each also had its own set of creatures that grew in complexity as one ascended—beginning with ants, insects, and other small creatures in the Black World—and culminating with all elements of the animal kingdom and the physical creation of man in the Glittering World. Every level provided new prototypes for what would exist on this level, fostered experiences and teachings that emerged with each being as it moved to the next stage of existence, and opened doors to a growing sophistication. Many of these new experiences taught control and what not to do. Indeed, the reason these beings migrated from world to world was because they had done things incorrectly.

When Susie Yazzie begins her narration about the waters covering the earth, it is just after the people were expelled into this world because Coyote, the trickster, had stolen a water baby. The water monster, angry at her loss, flooded the world beneath this one, forcing its inhabitants to crawl through a tall reed into the sky and reach the bottom of today's land, something that Ada discusses at length. Once these fleeing creatures entered upon this level, they found themselves on a small spit of land surrounded by water that needed to be drained. There are a number of different accounts telling how this was accomplished. One mentions how four holy beings, each setting off in one of the cardinal directions with a big knife, carved a channel through which the water could flow off the land and into a river system leading eventually to the ocean. Another tells of four colored rocks that whirred and buzzed like saws through the surrounding land formations, while Susie tells of a holy being, Badger, who dug a hole that drained the water. Regardless of the version, the land became exposed, leaving behind the rock formations of Monument Valley and the Four Corners region.

Gladys Bitsinnie, living on Douglas Mesa at the northern end of Monument Valley, offered additional details that confirm Susie's beliefs. Gladys said:

My father and grandfather told me about the different rock formations. There are holes in them, almost as if they had been made by man, but they are old and were formed when the rocks were mud. Past Kayenta, there is a place called Ndeelk'id (Long House Valley, literally "Side of the Hill"). We were traveling by there and my father talked about it. The rocks looked like they were stairs, and he said that they were from the time of the mud. All different kinds of wildlife, like big lizards, were around this place. One was called Tsé Adah'ayi'dziiłtaałii (One Who Kicks Anything in Its Path Down a Canyon) and another Anáá' Yee'ághánii (One Who Kills with Its Eyes). The holes in the rocks were their tracks, it is said. There were several ceremonies that he knew that had prayers, songs, and rituals that went along with them. The coyote stories are all related to that.[2]

Sally Manygoats from Navajo Mountain agrees and connects their presence and power to the five-night Shootingway ceremony (Na'at'ohjí), first held in the world beneath this one at a time when the men and women were separated. There are two forms of this ritual—one that is male and the other female—the latter being created at this time when the holy people emerged into this world. Locust, who led the people here, blew in all four directions and made the waters run to the east, south, west, and north, creating the canyons awash with wet earth. "Mud was left behind, so the beings uncovered by the disappearing water ran in different directions. Today on the rocks you can find strange tracks. This happened during the days of creation and is how the female Shootingway ceremony came about. When a man is dying from the effects of lightning and this ceremony is performed for him, he will be healed. If a woman is affected by lightning, then a male Shootingway is performed for her and she will be healed."[3]

Speaking of rock formations, Gladys offered that Alhambra near Mexican Hat was actually a group of young children turned into stones while the one known as the Bear and Rabbit at the north end of Monument Valley was once alive at the time that animals were like people. They were dancing and turned to stone. Nearby there is a small hill called White Mountain (Dził Łigai) that looks like a forked stick hogan with white on top; it is included in some of the ceremonial songs and connected to the four sacred mountains of the Navajo. Corn pollen offerings were left there.[4] As with the four major mountains, these other formations "sit there sacredly and are powerful. They were placed there from the beginning by White Shell Woman and are connected to the activities of the holy people."[5]

Other local rock formations are part of the creation story and hold power. For instance, Betty Canyon, speaking of the Oljato-Monument Valley area, felt that most places were sacred. "My father used to put his holy offerings at 'Organ Rock' and the 'Gray Ridge' just west of here. Also, around Train Rock, medicine man John Holiday and several others have done so for many years, which keeps our community at peace and in good health."[6] Near Navajo Mountain are rock formations with holes in them that are believed to be the home of the Holy Wind (Níłch'i Diyinii). Sally Manygoats from that area said, "When there is going to be wind, the people would say it sounded like the wind is coming in from the mountain. You could really hear it, and then two days later it arrived. It seemed very loud as it came to its home. This place will remain sacred as long as people still sing and pray the songs and prayers relating to it. Medicine men used to make offerings there a long time ago. That was why they lived in harmony for many years, receiving much rain and having plenty of vegetation all around."

The power of the physical universe does not end with those elements on the earth, but as Susie points out, even the heavens are connected. Star lore, divination, ceremonial interaction, agriculture, and many other beliefs and activities tie the Navajo to the holy beings in, on, and above the earth. Various stars and constellations have their own teachings and powers to guide the People. Sally Manygoats believed that the holy beings placed the Pleiades (Dilyéhé) to help in planning for and predicting the future. With one side longer than the other, it appears twisted, while its movement in the sky foretells such events as when to plant crops and hold specific ceremonies, and gives the time of night that medicine men should perform a particular part of a ceremony. It is said that when the Pleiades moves on a different path, that will indicate that things have gone wrong and the end of the world is approaching. There are also the Big and Little Dippers or Male and Female Revolving Ones that move about Polaris, said to be a fire around which this man and woman rotate during the year. Orion (Átsé'ets'ózí) carries with it a story that teaches that cousins should never intermarry. "You do not marry your cousin, it is said. This is why Orion is put up there. If you make your cousin your wife, it will affect one side of your body by drying it up and making it crippled. Your hands will become

Prominent rock formations throughout Monument Valley have stories of their origin and what they represent, while many hold powers that provide specific aid. These spires, known as the Three Sisters, are said to be holy people who argued to the point that they turned to stone. Some people say it is a mother leading two daughters. In either case, they are part of an integrated landscape of traditional teachings. (Used by permission, Utah State Historical Society)

like claws."[7] Although the stars are light years away, their influence on the earth surface people is immediate.

The Long Walk Era

The earliest Navajos in the Southwest were hunters and gatherers, living off of the land and leaving behind little for the archaeological record. Arriving perhaps as early as 1100 or 1200 AD, these people adapted to their environment, leading what must have been a difficult life. Not until the arrival of the Spanish in the 1500s and the establishment of towns in the 1600–1700s were these Native Americans identified as a group different from their Puebloan neighbors and noted for specific qualities, one of which was raiding both Indian and Euro-American camps and settlements. Their mobility, warrior culture, and adaptability made them well suited for the tasks at hand. Although there were times of peace buttressed by weak alliances, the general tenor of events framed the Navajo as an aggressive rival of the Spanish (1600–1821) and Mexican colonists (1821–48). Livestock theft, slave expeditions, ambushes, and raids characterized the flow of events on both sides, until the United States received the Southwest, California, and other lands after the Mexican War (1846–48). At first the Navajos felt like they had gained a new ally to wage destruction against the defeated Mexicans, but the U.S. government had other ideas, feeling responsible for protecting all of its citizens and non-citizens alike. This led to a twenty-year period of broken treaty agreements, continued conflict, and growing animosity against the Navajo, who followed their patterns from the past.

By the mid to late 1850s, with the American Civil War (1861–65) looming in the East and a series of broken treaties with the Indians in the West, the government determined that its best course of action was to defeat their Navajo charges. A scorched earth policy that involved neighboring tribes often at odds with the Navajo, as well as New Mexican volunteer units and U.S. soldiers, united to launch a concerted effort to defeat their enemy. The culmination of this undertaking resulted in approximately half of the Navajos being sent to Fort Sumner, also known as Bosque Redondo, for four years (1864–68) of incarceration and bare-bones survival. This was one of the two most difficult times in Navajo history, comparable to World War II in the Anglo psyche.

This is also where Susie starts her historical narrative. Old enough to have known people who had survived the Fort Sumner experience or who remained with those who escaped capture, she was well aware of both circumstances. Many who had lived in the Monument Valley area fled to Navajo Mountain and the Kaibeto region in order to band with other refugees and defend their family and friends. Those who remained in their original areas became increasingly susceptible to attack, capture, and enslavement, making this a time of serious trauma. Most families even today pass down narratives of those who went into captivity or those who remained free but impoverished. Since the Navajo people followed local leaders and shared clan affiliation, there was little unity and communication found in their governance. Each faction decided what was best for itself, leading to fragmented efforts with some leaders seeking peace while others encouraged war with each entity following its own path. That is why, when fighting erupted, there were those caught by surprise and mystified as to what was taking place. Others understood very well why they were now confronted by a more unified enemy.

All of the narratives derived at this time stress how the Navajos had to be vigilant and ever ready to grab a few possessions and then commit to either fight or flight at a moment's notice. Sally Manygoats recalled asking her father why the Long Walk era occurred and was told, "Many white men used to roam our land, then one day, for some unknown reasons, our people said they were going to become our enemies. From that time on, the people left their homes and livestock behind, hiding from the Anglos. Sure enough, they had become our enemies. They ransacked every home, killing off the people, but kidnapping the young girls."[8] Susie's account graphically describes what Navajos in Monument Valley encountered.

David Holiday, an old resident of this area, shared his family's story and what happened to his female relatives, which ties in nicely with Susie's account.

> Shortly before Fort Sumner, Ch'ah Łibáhi' (Gray Hat) and Hastiin Stł'inii (Husky Man) were living at the foot of Nakai Nikíhooniiłkaad (Where the Mexicans Chased Them Upward) on the east side of Hoskininni Mesa. Nádlohbaa' (Happy Warrior) and her sister Baa' Yázhí (Short War Woman) were living there also. The Mexicans and Utes attacked them unexpectedly and Ch'ah Łibáhi' was wounded. That is how the Mexicans managed to capture Nádlohbaa' and Baa' Yázhí as well as some of their livestock. They took them toward Chinle, building a brush corral each night they camped, where they guarded the women and animals. It took them four days to get to Chinle. On the fifth night, Nádlohbaa' awoke and found all the sentries sleeping. She was tied by a rope to her sash so she first rolled, loosened, then untied it. There was a guard between her and Baa' Yázhí, so she could not release her. She ran until she got some distance away before the Utes missed her and started looking. She crawled behind a waterfall to hide. One of the Utes spoke Navajo, saying, "Hágo, shik'is" (Come here, my friend) as he walked about. When all was quiet, she started again. It took her three days, traveling at night and hiding during hours of light, to get back. This happened just before Fort Sumner. Baa' Yázhí did not return until after Ft. Sumner. She had a baby by a Mexican while she was gone and was pregnant at the time she returned. She had the second child shortly thereafter.[9]

Gladys Bitsinnie was also curious about these events happening close to home, inquiring about specific places near Monument Valley. One site she asked about was a place on top of Black Mesa, questioning why it was called "Tsiiits'iin Łání" (Many Heads). Her father answered,

People say that incident occurred during one of the enemy raids. A wedding was taking place up on Black Mesa, with the groom coming from Navajo Mountain. A couple of men had ridden their horses in from Dennehotso, Arizona, to attend the wedding, and the enemy (white men) tracked their two horses leading to the event. At dawn the next morning, when some of the visitors went to fetch their hobbled horses, the enemy attacked, killing everyone at the wedding. Those who were looking for their horses heard the guns and took off running. They later found that everyone had been shot to death and then burned and their homes destroyed. That is how the name originated.[10]

Gladys wondered how the white men of those days compared to those she knew, and felt that they must have been mean and full of hate. These stories are a very real part of how these events are now viewed.

When asked about those who were captured or surrendered, Gladys did not feel like their situation was any better. The Long Walk, covering hundreds of miles depending upon which of the four main routes were taken, was a trial in itself, and once the people arrived at Fort Sumner, hunger stalked them for all four years. Gladys's father told her

stories of the journey and said that if people were slow, they were killed off. They poked things [bayonets] in the back of the people's leg. This was how they were driven over there. Little children were thrown away. If the people became too tired, they might be killed. It is a long distance from here to there. I do not remember how many days it took to reach it, but once they arrived, they separated the wives from the husbands. It was in this way that the Navajos brought back babies. In some cases, it was by a Black or Mexican father. My father came back from there in a womb and was born ten days after his family arrived in Monument Valley. There was no way of overpowering the captors. This is how he told about it.[11]

Susie's account concerning this time is particularly interesting for three reasons. First, her family was living in the Monument Valley area when the enemy arrived. Their story provides fine-grain detail as to what happened and a sense of immediacy as events unfolded. There is no missing the fear and necessity of flight as families grabbed what they could and headed for hiding places amid the rocks. A second benefit from her account is the specific identification of where the fights took place, where defensive positions were established, and what happened at those sites. One cannot go to Monument Valley and not picture the man-made rock walls and

The Utes, well known for their horsemanship and Plains Indian lifestyle, were traditional enemies of their Navajo neighbors. During the Spanish, Mexican, and early Anglo-American occupation of the Southwest, the Utes generally allied against the Navajo, culminating in the "Fearing Time" of the late 1850s to mid-1860s. Oral history attests to their effectiveness. (Used by permission, Utah State Historical Society)

stone defense work put in place to keep the enemy at a distance. A third point is to realize the effectiveness of the enemy. In southeastern Utah, the Ute and Paiute people often intermarried, intermixed, and were at times indistinguishable by outsiders, even though there were other times that the Utes captured, enslaved, and sold their "cousins."

This was a turbulent era. There is no missing that the traditional animosity between Navajos and Utes was real and that the latter capitalized on this warfare to even old scores. At this time, the San Juan River was a general boundary between the two warring tribes, each of which carried the fight across the river and into their opponents' territory. Monument Valley was well known to the Utes, as witnessed by their effectiveness in ferreting out hiding Navajos. Wolfkiller, a man who lived as a young boy through these events and in this place, mentioned the absolute dread the people felt—not for the U.S. cavalry or Mexican volunteers, but for the Utes. Indeed, even the mention of their presence was enough to get everyone packing and moving to a hiding spot.[12] With the Navajos' release from Fort Sumner, their return to these lands, and reuniting with those who had not surrendered or been captured, they were ready to resume life where they had left off.

Daily Life—Survival as an Art

But that life would not be easy, as Susie's and Ada's accounts attest, even though they were born roughly a half century later. Dependent on sheep and agriculture, the Navajo often had to eke out a bare existence in their high desert environment. Constantly searching for pasture, relying upon the elements for water, and supplementing their diet with wild plants and animals, life had many variables and risks. Although the Navajo are famous for their colorful rugs, sale of wool, photogenic dress, dramatic homeland, and religious philosophy, the people, especially the women, still faced the reality of feeding and clothing their family in a daily life that demanded hard work and situational awareness to survive. As mentioned previously, what these two women encountered in their childhood was entirely representative of a large proportion of women from Monument Valley in similar circumstances. Sloan Haycock summarized her childhood by saying, "I was told to get up before dawn each day and to run or take the sheep out to pasture before the weather became too hot. We were told, 'One should not be lazy, take out the carding boards and card the wool; take out the spindle and spin the yarn; weave the rug . . . learn to do these things so that you can make a living by doing it throughout your life.' There were no jobs available for anyone back then, except agriculture and livestock."[13]

Gladys Bitsinnie echoes what Sloan, Susie, and Ada said, so common to all. She remembered:

My job was only sheep even though I did not have shoes. In the summer the hot sand hurt our feet, and so my five-year-old sister, Jessie, and I sometimes put thin rocks on the soles of our feet and stuck them on with piñon pitch. Our clothes were ragged and made from flour sacks sewn together. When they got torn, we tied knots in the rip that hung at the fringe of our hems. This was how we were raised. We did not have commercially produced clothing, and so everything was hand-sewn. The shoes that were made for us got holes in them all too soon. We had to herd sheep, even if we were crying from a strong reprimand, as we followed the animals out to pasture. We would go back to where we had been the day before even though there sometimes was no water. If we found puddles of water in the rocks, we washed our hair and clothes as we herded. This is how we were raised.

There were seven of us women and three brothers, one older and two younger, in our family. At this time, we were whipped if we were caught playing while herding. Our mother would sometimes come suddenly, so when we saw her, we would start to run. There were many sheep so when it came to maintaining control we were tremendously outnumbered. During the time that the yucca flower blossomed, the sheep ran wild, leaving us crying because we could not keep them together. My older sister was in charge and greatly concerned. If we had a donkey, things would go better. When there were two or three of us, we shared the animal, trying to keep all of the sheep under control and not wandering. We would sometimes herd on foot all the way over to Owl Spring, where we had a camp and a planted field. We listened to our mother and father all the time. He did not even hold a whip upon us; only our mother did. I never talked back to her, and I am still like this today. I still fear her. Now, I just visit and cook for her, but then I am on my way. This makes her feel good, and her food tastes wonderfully, but I do not spend much time there.[14]

Corn was the staff of life. No plant was more important than corn for feeding the family, supplementing as fodder, and observing religious practices. It is not an exaggeration to say that almost every meal had corn in some form, and most prayers used pollen or ground meal. Lorita Adakai recalls:

When I was small, we did not have wheat flour, so we had to process our own corn. I remember learning to babysit my little brother and trying to grind it to make something for him to eat when he got hungry. People used to pick piñon nuts to mix and grind with it to make it last throughout the winter. Sumac (chiiłchin) and other kinds of berries were gathered locally or elsewhere and mixed into a variety of corn foods. We lived in Monument Valley, but my father had a large farm in Dennehotso. He used to haul in the corn from there, and that's what we were raised on. We ground the corn to make a variety of foods like blue cornmeal mush (tóshchíín), dumplings (k'ineeshbizhii), another variety of blue cornmeal mush (tanaashgiizh), white cornmeal mush (taa'niil), and mutton stew with hominy (haníígaii), blue corn bread cooked underground (łeehyizhooh), and tortillas (náneeskaadí) made on a heated rock slab, the only grill we had back then. We used to gather different plant seeds and mix them in our dough to make bread and the cornmeal mushes.[15]

Little wonder that Susie and Ada spent so much time farming alone or with their mothers and aunts to secure sufficient food for the winter. For those interested in the many types of breads, mushes, stews, cakes, and other recipes available in the Navajo diet, see Charlotte J. Frisbie, *Food Sovereignty the Navajo Way: Cooking with Tall Woman*.[16]

To grow gardens filled with corn, pumpkins, squash, melons, and other vegetables required either a digging stick or later a plow. Sloan Haycock dug irrigation ditches by hand with a pick and shovel to get enough water to the crops. After careful watering, weeding, and thinning, the family members harvested the vegetables and prepared them for storage. Men dug large bell-shaped pits with a small opening at the top and a wide base at the bottom and then lined them with juniper bark to absorb moisture. The women prepared the food by cutting and drying it. Sally Manygoats said,

> When the squash was large and ripe and in abundance, its skin and meat would be sliced or placed in the fire. The skin would crack and peel, and then the meat would be cut in a spiral and hung to dry like twisted intestines. Once dried, they could be stored and eaten at any time of the year. If there was meat that needed to be stored, a person would thin-slice and dry it before placing it in a sack in the pit. When it was going to be eaten, the meat was pounded, dipped in melted fat, and served. Cattle, sheep, and horse meat was prepared this way. This is how I have walked in life.[17]

Wild plants supplemented those grown domestically. What may appear to an outsider as a barren desert actually offered a number of plants with nutritious value. This was most apparent in the spring. Jenny Francis described the land as "magnificent. When the warm spring air comes, it was like a cloth covered the ground. Various plants blossomed and sprouted their colorful flowers," a promise of things to come.[18] Sally saw people gathering plants in large quantities once they were ripe. Sour sumac berries, high in Vitamin C, found their way into stews, mushes, and breads, adding a tart flavor. Yucca plants, a member of the lily family, grew large pods at the end of a long stem, which when boiled tasted like celery, while the pods, rich in sugar, were boiled and eaten with corn or made into jelly. Wild onions, wild potatoes, tansy, and bee weed (also known as wild spinach), added variety to the diet and nutritional value as did piñon nuts, rich in fats and vitamins. The Navajos, in tune with the environment of both mountain and desert, were skilled in using the plants, animals, and resources each provided during specific seasons.

There were times, such as during the Long Walk era, that because planting crops became increasingly difficult due to enemy activity, wild plants played an even more important role in survival. Anna Black learned from her mother that "seeds of big tall grasses that grew in sand dunes"

Wild plants provided not only food but also a variety of colors for dyeing wool. Navajo women often knew of specific places where certain vegetation could be harvested and boiled for hours to obtain the desired color. They next immersed the wool in the solution until sufficiently dyed, then removed, dried, spun, and wove it into a blanket or rug. (Courtesy National Archives)

were an important lifeline. "They grew only in certain areas, and so the enemy, who was aware of the places that they grew, would come and attack us. Horses were very helpful and intelligent back then. They used to stand guard high up on hilltops while the people below gathered plants and seeds. If the horses saw the enemy coming, they would become startled and begin moving. That was a signal to escape. This is what my mother told me."[19]

Anna Cly remembers gathering sumac berries (chiiłchin tsétah— Sumac Amidst the Rocks) before bringing them home to be made into various types of food. She bemoaned the fact that "now, even our children would not eat these things. My children used to eat them and now their children will not touch them. They say, 'I don't know what that is' and leave it at that. They will not even eat corn foods. I told them that people survived only on these foods a long time ago. It is like that."[20] Jenny Francis mirrors Anna's feelings about losing the old ways.

> Back then I think we lived in harmony because there were no harsh sicknesses. There were no fevers or coughing sickness, no high blood pressure, cancer, or diabetes. There were no such things like this at that time, when we lived in harmony with everything. Even when we were

bothered by lice, we were told they gave us something to do. This was instituted during the palm of time. I think about this. Maybe the lice sucked out bad blood [chuckle], which prevented high blood pressure.

In the past we ate a lot of corn, and so it was prepared in different ways. Sumac berries, ni'dootł'izhii (green plant on the ground?), tł'ohdeeí (grass whose seeds fall—amaranth, pigweed, or goosefoot), and nídíyílii bináá' (sunflower seeds in center) were all picked and added to however the corn was being prepared. People went out and thrashed the seeds of these different grasses and gathered large amounts in flour sacks, enough to last through the winter. Each seed combined with other seeds to give different flavors and consistency. This was how they made them last. This was what I was aware of. Now, when corn food is prepared, there is an "Ugh, I don't want it." This is what the children say. They no longer eat the corn foods we prepared in the past. They do not even know how to prepare them even though I urge them to fix some. I tell them that we cannot let go of the past like this.[21]

Jenny Francis was also concerned about lost knowledge concerning medicinal plants. She remembered an older man who lived nearby who had extensive knowledge about wild herbs that healed many infirmities. While she does not give his name and points out that he was not a medicine man, he was able, through plants, to help people get over arthritis (agizee), cure problems created by sleeping with a mate after a ceremony before the required four-day celibacy ended, heal someone with sexually transmitted diseases, help those suffering from urinary tract stoppage, and remove pain from a person injured in an automobile accident. Velta Luther believed that the reason she never had any problem with her gallbladder was due to the wild plants she ate that acted like medicine.[22] She thinks that young people today are faced with these kinds of problems because they do not eat these types of wild foods and medicines, as this kind of knowledge disappears.

The same is true of hunting practices. While all animals have their own powers and are killed and butchered according to traditional beliefs, wild animals are generally more potent and so treated with different types of rituals that show an even greater respect than for domestic animals. Take deer, for instance. Hunting was a man's undertaking. Women were forbidden to be involved in the killing, but could butcher and cook the meat in certain circumstances. Men did not hunt for antlers, bring them home, or make things from them. If not taken care of properly, they can be very dangerous, especially if one does not know the songs and prayers. "There is a ceremony called Deerway ceremony (Dine'é K'ehgo) to cure the problem, which will otherwise affect a person's life in the future."[23] Gladys Bitsinnie continued:

> The men used to fix the meat in the proper way, and they never threw the different size stomachs away. They brought them back to the hunting camp and fried them. If a person consumes one, they will be very agile in running over the hills and valleys and never get lost. This was why people ate them. The hunters sang during the nighttime to ask for help in getting the deer and thanking the animals when they received them. If someone had to urinate, they would do it sitting down to show great respect for those being hunted. Food in the camp was shared with nothing hidden. By having everything open, the deer knew there was harmony and the fat, good ones would come out and offer themselves to the hunters.

Anna Black, after insisting that women did not kill these animals, bemoaned the fact that women do today. She remembered the past:

> The deer was brought back with the hide still attached, then skinned right away. Nothing but venison was carried home. The bones were all taken out. None of it was taken near the sheep corral. If bones were brought back, they were cared for with respect. I did not allow the bones to be scattered about, and even the skin was kept away from the home in the place it was killed; it could only be brought back after it had been tanned. Now I see people hanging their deerskin outside of their home. Venison was eaten with respect, but now it isn't like that—there is no respect.[24]

Partial explanation for these beliefs goes back to how the holy people created and taught these creatures. Sally Manygoats, after explaining that different animals are butchered in different ways, says that if these various practices are not maintained, that the livestock will become contaminated. "It will haunt your sheep. The people have songs and prayers for the deer, and they bring them back. Maybe that is how it haunts the sheep. A long time ago it is said, there was a horse, deer, sheep, and various other animals like elk which were made together. Then it was said this sheep's meat will not touch deer meat. If there is a case of mixing the two, it will haunt your sheep."[25]

In those early years, clothing was also an issue, as Ada and Susie attest. Before Euro-Americans came in with cloth and sheep with wool for weaving, nature provided what could be worn. Jenny Francis, referring back to the beginning, told of how buckskin and dried barks were the materials for clothing, and braided fiber from yucca plants was used for shoes. "When it rained, these materials used to leave abrasions on one's skin. It is said that a person could not even lie down on these sore places when this happened. But once sheep were introduced, a woven wool dress called a biil became the standard clothing for women. Nowadays these are worn at squaw dances [Enemyway ceremony] when the lady was prepared to have black soot put on her exposed skin." With the beginning of trading posts, clothing became more readily available, but even then, much of it was makeshift. Kitty Atini remembered, "There was nothing then. We hardly had any clothes and only once in a while would we receive new ones. We used to use flour sacks for clothing, so our clothes were usually striped with the design on the sacks. There was nothing here when I was born. There was just hunger all around."[26]

Sally Ralph Gray, Susie's sister, described what she recalled of the clothing they wore.

> As a child, you tolerated hunger. We even herded sheep without shoes so that the skin under our feet was always chapped. Thorns pricked the soles of our feet, but it could not be prevented, and so we were told to apply piñon pitch, which made it feel better so that we could walk about again. I often think back to my father. After my mother died, he should have placed us in school so that we could have had jobs elsewhere. Our clothes were torn, and our hair was completely filled with lice. Once in a great while they would be combed out, and their eggs would be all over our clothing. While herding sheep, we would build a fire, warm our clothes, and shake off the lice into the fire.[27]

Sally's point about being placed in school raises an interesting issue. Today it is in vogue to talk about the misery of boarding schools as an institution of colonialism that has robbed Native Americans of their culture, oppressed them, and caused severe psychological damage. While there is no doubt that for some this was true, little attention is paid to those who had a good experience and little consideration given as to why the "system" was trying to provide tools for survival in the dominant culture. Certainly, there was abuse, some of it quite similar to what was found in Anglo schools—corporal punishment, strict observance of rules, and an attempt

Susie Yazzie's life, like that of her sisters, (left) Abby Laughter and (right) Sally Ralph Gray, was filled with hard work and constant challenges to provide for her family. Horticulture, raising livestock, weaving, religious responsibilities, and child rearing were just part of it. The traditional dress, gnarled hands, sunburnt faces, and ready smiles summarize her sisters' attitude toward life. (Marilyn Holiday family photo)

to change the student into a person capable of weathering the harsh realities of a turn-of-the-century economy and later Great Depression. The mindset of removing Indian culture and values does not play well today, but there were also skills and discipline that were desired by many and obtained at the boarding schools.

Skills, discipline, and corporal punishment were also part of traditional Navajo life. This is mentioned only to point out that life was not easy, and to prepare for it, certain qualities had to be instilled in youth, readying them for the rigors of adulthood. Velta Luther had many of these qualities ingrained in her through common traditional practices.

Back then children were not allowed to do what they wanted. When it was still dark, our blankets would be taken away and we were told to run or roll in the snow. "If you do not run, someday jealousy will overcome you. You will not be successful. If you run and drink hot water, then vomit (bííłkóóh), the fluid from within the womb that remains inside of you will be pushed out. That is what you need to get rid of by vomiting." They would then chase us into the snow. If you lost one lamb, as soon as you walked in the door, you would be sent back out before you could even eat supper. The whip was being held up for us at all times. That is how we were raised. This was especially true for the older children—the whip was there for us. Our upbringing was very restricted, and we were often humbled. "Card wool and spin it" is what we were told. "Weave a rug and do not weave with crooked edges; learn how to weave stripes first, then learn more." We were forced to do this along with a lot of corn grinding. Even if we herded sheep all day long, we still had to grind corn at night with our mano and metate.[28]

Families often depended heavily on their children to help with all of the work that had to be done. Consequently, a lot of parents did not want their children to attend boarding school to learn things that, at the time, did not seem relevant for the tasks at hand. Others saw it as an investment in the future, as the dominant culture became increasingly prevalent. Susie Yazzie attended for only two years because her father was forced into a proposition. She regretted not being able to go longer. Lucy Laughter, one of Susie's relatives, was sad because she had not been able to attend. "No, I do not read. During that time, we were not permitted to go to school because we had to herd sheep. They would even put us in rock crevices to hide us. If I had gone to school, I would have been somewhere else. I probably would not have made life. That was how it was at that time."[29] Sally Manygoats also wished that she had gone: "No, I do not even know my name. Not even a little bit. I did not go to school. I was told [to herd] sheep and that was why I did not go to school. I do not know anything about paper [reading and writing]. I do not know the Anglo language. I wonder, 'What if I had gone to school . . . could I have been in a Washington office?'"[30] These women felt that their desires and full potential had not been reached because they did not have the opportunity to try.

In spite of all of the shortcomings of boarding schools—and there were many—they did provide opportunity for those who applied the things they learned. But that also could be an issue. How applicable were the things they learned upon returning home? Betty Canyon fell into that quandary after learning how to read. Even though she had minimal schooling, she wanted to hold on to what she had learned. This was not always easy.

We were less fortunate when we were young and going to school because we had to be taken on horseback. When I returned home in the summer, I did not have any books to read or paper to write on. I used to wish I had something to read. The only available material was the labels on the canned food items such as baking powder, salt, sugar, flour, and coffee—which came in a bag back then. I was always happy to get back to school. My parents and everyone else at home were uneducated, so there was nobody to review the alphabet and numbers with us. We had to learn it on our own and at school. I stopped going to school in 1931. I could have gone longer if my parents hadn't told me to marry.

Since marriage was a family decision, including who and when, Betty followed her culture's tradition and stopped her formal education.

Traditional Teachings and Lifestyle

To suggest that there was no learning would be false. There was intense learning, but it was based in the practical world rooted in survival on a difficult land. Parents and grandparents tried to ensure that they were preparing children for the realities of life. Radically different from what today's youth encounter, this training could be harsh and demanding. There were no social safety nets. Anna Lora King recalls:

My grandfather taught me, "This is how you will live. If you are not lazy, you will have life in your hand. If you are lazy, you will go about begging for things. Whatever you are learning, think about how you are learning it. The only way this will happen is if you work on it yourself. If you treat life like you are just running and tagging it but not really studying it, this will not do. Here the sheep stand, and here the horses stand with cattle. These are the main items to make life along with planting your field."

During the time when I came about and my cry was heard, the stores were a long distance away, so corn was mostly used. Only a grinding stone (tsédaashjéé'—metate) was available to process corn. As I grew up, there were no other foods except that. When I became aware of things, that was the only item I knew of as food. We learned to grind corn, so that in the future when one has children, they will not go hungry. If you do not know anything, your children will suffer from hunger and go to their neighbors to beg, only to have their hands hit with sticks. This was what was said at this time. Later, people traveled great distances to a place called Bisdootł'izh Deez'á (Blue Dirt Clod Mesa) and over at Red Lake (Tónehalįįh) to go to trading posts. These were not one-day trips, sometimes taking two to three days to get home. There we bought flour, salt, sugar, beans, and coffee. These were the only things that were brought back.[31]

Men and women have defined roles in Navajo culture that can be per-formed only with gender-specific equipment given to them by the holy people. The tools of the woman are connected to the home and the role she plays as a mother, provider, nurturer, and teacher. The sacred instruments were first created by the holy people, who gave them power to preserve life and provide for the home. These tools, collectively known as habeedí, are paired with each other, such as a woven door covering with the upright en-trance posts, the fire with a fire poker, a cooking pot with stirring sticks, an earthen bowl and a gourd ladle, the metate with a whisk broom.[32] Each has its own prayers and songs and awaits to bless people when shown respect. They are more than just symbols. They hold power as outlined in the origin stories and ceremonial uses as well as in their practical, daily function.

Here the fire poker, discussed at length by Susie, is given as an example of the depth of meaning and variety of roles this simple two-to-three-foot piece of wood has been given. There are two types of fire pokers (honeesh-gish): ceremonial (often made from lightning-struck wood) and those for daily use, both of which can be made out of juniper or piñon. This same tool was also used in the past as a planting stick that tickled Mother Earth when placing corn or other seeds in the ground. Selecting a dried branch from a tree to make one is considered an honor. The old tree is viewed as a grandfather, and so Navajos address the male and female fire poker as a grandmother (used for cooking and tending the coals and so is longer) or grandfather (used to straighten wood and stoke the fire and so is shorter). Offerings are left at the grandfather tree, thanking it for its assistance. The stick is not just involved with food preparation by stoking the fire, but also with protection, and so is kept by the doorway to prevent evil from entering.

Stella Cly had her fire poker made from a green juniper branch. She believed that because it could withstand the extreme heat, that it was an ideal "home sitter," something no family should be without. When a person returns home, one of the first things he or she will ask is, "Where is my fire poker?"[33] If a child gets sick, the fire poker is pressed against him and then blown upon, away from the sick person. When one needs to go outside at night for firewood or water or to drive the sheep into the corral, the poker may be brought for protection. If a sleeping baby needs to be left unattended for a short while, a fire poker may be placed by the infant's side to ensure its safety.[34]

Jenny Francis continues the discussion by saying:

The fire and the fire poker are paired tools and part of the Navajo woman's habeedí. Cooking and heating the home with fire has as much symbolic cultural significance as the practical side of sustaining life, while the fire poker fights evil, protects the home and family, and sets an example of how a woman should be inured to the trials of life.

The fire poker is for protection because it is pushed into the redness of hot coals and comes out unharmed. One prays with it but does not mistreat or disrespect it because, just as with one's fire, water, and other tools, you want it to bless you and your food. This was what I was told when I was growing up. These things are used to pray. I say prayers even for my children who are in school. Everything goes according to the way you pray, so if you say it in a good way, without harsh words, it blesses your children. "By its beauty" (sa'ąh naagháii bik'eh hózhǫ́) is what you say when praying. This is very powerful and most sacred. During war, these words serve as a shield. This is what I was taught way back when I was a child. Now, many parents do not even pray for their children. They should pray for them, starting with the bottom of their feet to the top of their head. This way they will go to school in a good manner. You even pray for the alien teacher who is educating your child that she will accept and love the boy or girl, that they will walk in beauty, learn the alien language, and understand. These prayers are most powerful and help children to live in this manner.[35]

As with many teachings in Navajo culture, when there is a positive side, there is also a negative. What can bless can also harm. This is true of the fire poker, whose sacred name used in ceremonies is Honbąąh nahookǫs tsíłkéí or Ch'ikę́ę́h (literally, "Clockwise Motion Next to the Fire Young Men or Women"). There are prayers and songs related to it.

> If your thoughts are not good, or your life does not come together, the fire poker's prayers and songs are performed for you. This is how a medicine man speaks on your behalf, using these prayers. If a child is struck by a poker, its power may be turned against the offender. Sometimes it will trip you, said the elderly women of times past. You should not hit or even attempt to hit a child with one because it is a healing instrument and not for harming. A person should also not hit a dog with one. If you want a dog to be protective of your home, shove the fire poker into its food. It will also be very protective of sheep.[36]

Other habeedí act in a similar fashion. Take the stirring sticks (ádístsiin), for instance. These are used to mix batter and other foods and are made from peeled greasewood stalks that are about two feet long with varying thickness. If there are nine of them, the traditional number, then they would be thinner than if there were fewer. The main image associated with this implement is that of defeating or killing hunger through cooking. A prayer for rain is said while using them as a wish for more corn.[37] When making cornmeal mush or the batter for the alkaan cake associated with a girl's puberty ceremony (kinaaldá), these stirring sticks assume another significance. Nellie Grandson commented, "After the porridge was finished, there would still be some batter on the sticks. That was the time women said let it rain, let there be a huge crop of corn. They prayed with this. These are the women's weapon to fight against hunger. When it is not washed, it is said there is hunger on them. Hunger says 'Eek' when she is washing her weapon. The brush (bé'ézhóó) that is used for removing leftover particles off of a grinding stone and as a strainer also has prayers and helps fight against hunger."[38]

In Susie's account she mentions, in passing, two significant events in a traditional woman's life—holding her puberty ceremony and thus making her eligible for the second important event of marriage. There is an extensive literature concerning the kinaaldá ceremony. Among the best studies are *Kinaaldá* by Charlotte Frisbie, and *Molded in the Image of Changing Woman* and *Blood and Voice*, both by Maureen Trudelle Schwarz.[39] Each of these works has a particular emphasis—Frisbie on the songs and prayers,

Schwarz in the symbolic meaning of the ceremony, aspects of female physical change, and traditional responsibilities. Steeped in teachings that ensure good health practices for a long and productive life, this ceremony combines spiritual and physical qualities that clearly define what an ideal woman will be like. It prepares her for the many challenges and responsibilities of adulthood.

At the beginning of time, First Man and First Woman found a holy baby and took it to their home on Huerfano Mesa. The baby grew at a rapid, supernatural rate. "A day was the same as a year. The second day the baby sat up, and when two days had passed, she looked around. She was then dressed [in all manner of white shell]."[40] That same day she walked, the third day she danced, fourth ran, and on the tenth received the name White Shell/Changing Woman. On the thirteenth day (actually year) she began menstruating, telling First Woman, "Mother, something is passing from me." This set in motion the activities now associated with the four-day ceremony called kinaaldá held for pubescent girls. Young women who follow in her footsteps become like her. As with Changing Woman, whose first period (kinaasdaah) came as a surprise, it may be the same for young girls who have not been instructed by their mothers, and like "the holy people, though great, become embarrassed at this kind of blood."[41] Once the young woman has her second period and a second ceremony called Kinaaldá Bik'í Dah Nastani, she is able to bear children and is now under what medicine man John Holiday called "The Woman's Ruler"—menstruation (chooyin).[42]

A girl's initial menses launches preparation for the first kinaaldá ceremony. Each of the four days follow much the same pattern, with intensified activity on the last day. Combing hair, running, grinding corn, singing Blessingway songs, and food preparation teach skills and attitudes for her future role as a wife and mother. On the third day, the men dig a large pit in which a fire is built to heat the soil for baking a cake (alkaan) made of ground cornmeal. The last day there is the washing of the kinaaldá's hair and jewelry, a final run, the cutting of the cake, the molding of her body, and the blessing of participants. All of these activities are embedded with teachings and symbolic action, and are done in the presence of the holy people. Both Susie and Ada participated in this four-day rite.

Neither of these women mention their wedding ceremony (iigéh—"Two Come Together"; iiná—marriage), and so only a brief account is provided here. General events include the family of the bride and groom making arrangements as to who will be married, how much property the husband-to-be's family will pay (bride price) for the woman—the two families getting together to lecture the couple about their new undertaking, and the bride and groom feeding each other cornmeal mush from a Navajo wedding basket. Much of this follows a formalized pattern in which the bride's family holds the primary responsibility for the ceremony. Stella Cly mentions one of the cardinal rules that must be recognized before any of this can take place:

> It was forbidden to marry a member of your own clan, because they are your brothers and sisters, your aunts or your uncles. It is also forbidden to marry into your father's clan. One does not marry into the clans that bore them. The parents are responsible for teaching their children about their clans at a very young age so that as they grow older, they will be able to say who they are. I used to drill my children on their clan and kept reminding them how important it is. Now that they have become parents themselves, they do the same with their children. They know their parents' and grandparents' [maternal and paternal] clans.[43]

Details of the marriage arrangements, the gift exchange, ceremony, and traditional teachings can be found in a number of excellent sources that all point to the symbolic meaning and value of establishing such a relationship.[44] A few examples follow. Take for instance, the "bride price," or presents given to the young woman's family. In the past, one of the main items was livestock, horses in particular, the number of which could range from three to twenty. The woman, who could be as young as twelve or thirteen, certainly appreciated the groom's family extending itself through a plentiful gift. Hence the informal name for a wedding—"driving the horses in" (łį́į' neelkaad). The mush that the couple ate was made from white (male) and yellow (female) ground corn, blessed with pollen, signifying not only the union of the two, but also planting the seed for future children in a basket that represented a new life together. When the young man arrived at the wedding hogan, he brought his saddle in and set it beside the doorway, indicating that he was there to stay. If the marriage failed, the wife could place it with his other possessions outside the door, making divorce official. But for many Navajo couples this was unnecessary. Life, just like an arranged marriage, was what husband and wife made of it, staying together their entire time, "until death did them part." Once married, the woman maintained the domestic front of home, garden, and livestock while the husband became involved with his own livestock, conducting ceremonies, political events, and other male activities. Some couples shared and helped with their mate's responsibilities while others maintained more of a distance.

Of Divination, Medicine Men, and Supernatural Power

One thing that becomes immediately apparent with most of the accounts given by the women of Monument Valley, and especially those of Susie and Ada, is their deep religious conviction. If only a single, unifying attribute had to be recognized for these women, religious conviction would rank high on that list. The experiences they share are often far beyond what is encountered in the dominant society. Both Susie and Ada give detailed accounts about using various forms of divination, and so a brief explanation is provided here to orient the reader. Susie's grandfather Atini's interaction with lightning and lightning-struck materials may leave many Anglo readers scratching their heads and wondering if these experiences occurred and powers exist. Both a Navajo and Anglo perspective is offered in this introduction, not with the intent to convince, but to show both sides of a coin, each of which has meaning and is real in its own realm.

Divination is concerned primarily with diagnosing what the needs of an individual may be through spiritual or supernatural means.[45] Techniques used by the Navajo evoke core beliefs of their religious worldview. There are three major types of divination—wind listening (íists'ą́ą́'); star gazing (sǫ'nil'į́) with its subsidiaries sun and moon gazing and their affiliate crystal gazing (déést'į́į'—literally, to see, understand); and hand trembling or motion-in-the hand (ndishniih)—all of which are related in that they are spiritually based and serve similar functions. The origin story of hand trembling is different from star gazing and wind listening, while generally, women may render the former but not as often the latter. Ada was more of an exception. These practices are used to explore the unknown, find lost people or objects, identify a thief or witch, locate water or other desirable resources, prevent danger or evil, and, most important, diagnose the cause of an illness in order to provide a remedy.[46] Unlike medicine men, who heal through chantway ceremonies lasting from one to nine days or nights and who have spent hundreds of hours learning their accompanying prayers, songs, and rituals, the diagnostician may spend only a few hours learning the rite, may compose some of her own songs and prayers, and will require little ceremonial equipment. Chantways are normally performed by men who have a sacred body of lore based on complex mythology, whereas diviners may be either male or female (often after menopause) who received this gift at birth and have had its potential later revealed to them.[47]

The holy people play an important part in identifying future practitioners. For instance, a holder of this power may realize their ability during
a ceremony when its latent force is activated. Apprenticeship follows to
develop the skill. A person may have a dream to help point the way, or
there may be strange supernatural occurrences hinting at the gift's presence. Unlike hand trembling, where supernatural beings make a person
aware that "the ceremony wants you . . . and that you are known," star
gazing is a learned rite that may be acquired in as quickly as a day or two.[48]
Susie's experience is a good example of a person who had the "gift" but
did not want it. Her detailed account provides an inside view of what the
practice meant to her. Often it is older people, who have the maturity to
recognize the signals and answers, that receive the power. Susie was young
when she had this "strange experience" that seemed as if she were going
through a trance. "It's a feeling of anxiety—as if you are in fear of something and you are trying to run from it, but you can't find a safe place. It
feels like you levitate off the ground. It is emotionally tiring and a strain.
It's like remembering something of your childhood and you become very
emotional about it." Many others embrace the power and use it to determine what happened to cause an illness or to explain a situation.

How this can take place requires an extensive explanation, but in its
simplest form the answer goes back to the palm of time as the creation
took place. Everything, without exception, received an inner form that
came about through song and prayer provided by the holy people. Through
sacred language that "connects" with this inner form, the object, animal, or
person, each of which has its own power and personality, can be influenced
to use it. A medicine man, through ritual knowledge, understands how to
reach this inner being to control and utilize its power on a spiritual level to
affect a physical outcome. Unlike Christianity, which views the universe as
a struggle between two cosmic forces—God versus Satan, good versus evil,
light against darkness—power to the Navajo is neutral until one chooses
to use it either for good or bad. The results can be both spiritually intangible and physically visible. For practitioners it is as real as any tangible object. The Navajo name for the ability to summon and use spiritual
forces—"álílee k'ehgo"—means literally "according to supernatural/magi-
cal power." It is the energy by which things are done supernaturally. For
example, a Navajo skinwalker (witch) running at superhuman speeds or a
medicine man performing a miraculous cure are both examples of a divine
ability to control this force through words. The power is not discussed or
flaunted, while its existence is recognized with reverence.[49] This is a difficult concept for those coming from a scientific tradition to accept. Personal

experiences of white traders working on the Navajo Reservation are filled with accounts of things that are totally unexplainable from an Anglo worldview. For example, different forms of divination—hand trembling, crystal gazing, wind listening, star gazing—have been used successfully on behalf of white men, even a few anthropologists, who have confirmed their accurate ability to look at events in the past, present, and future.

Susie and Ada provide examples of the positive use of álílee k'ehgo but mention only in passing its negative application in witchcraft. Navajos, in general, are reluctant to talk much about this because to know too much might indicate that that individual is a practitioner. Older traditional Navajos, however, are very much aware of its presence and potential. Respect, balance, and orderliness become the means by which positive forces are controlled, while evil and witchcraft (iiníziin) have their rituals based on excess, lack of reverence, and chaos. The power is there; what one does with it determines the outcome. Harry Walters, a Navajo teacher and practitioner of traditional religion, explained it this way:

> In the Navajo world everything is organized in terms of female and male, known as Hózhǫ́ǫ́jí (Blessingway) and Naayéé'jí (Protectionway). The two forces do not oppose but complement each other in the same manner that all female and male species interact in nature. Evil is not a separate quality but is viewed as an integral part of Naayéé'jí. When used appropriately, it serves as protection but where it is abused, it becomes witchcraft (evil). Self-protection is a necessity in nature, so all things have an element of evil. Therefore, one must always go about life with great caution and respect.[50]

Clyde Kluckhohn, in his classic study entitled *Navaho Witchcraft*, identifies four types of evil power—witchery, sorcery, wizardry, and frenzy witchcraft.[51] Witchery depends on "corpse poison" or decayed flesh, bones, or sexual fluids ground into powder and used to curse a person. This material serves the reverse function of corn pollen, which blesses with life and happiness. Diagnosis of the illness through hand trembling, crystal gazing, or other means determines which prayers and ceremonies will protect or heal the sick person. Sorcery creates illness and harm by taking hair, nail clippings, clothing, or some other object that has been in close contact with the intended victim. The item is prayed over so that hardship enters that person's life. Wizardry occurs when an individual magically shoots a stone, bone, or other foreign matter into a victim; the cure is achieved by sucking out the object. Frenzy witchcraft utilizes two forms of delivery:

plants, such as datura, or prayers and chants that cause a person to lose self-control and become degraded. Excessive sexual activity or gambling results. While many Navajo people may not think in clinical terms about these four different ways of harming a person, their existence is recognized but not often discussed. The power—álílee k'ehgo— is behind how these forms of witchcraft are delivered.

An experience shared by Gladys Bitsinnie provides a typical example of hundreds of similar stories found throughout the reservation. Gladys began by setting the stage for what happened.

> My grandfather's grandmother was weaving, it is said. She had the fire built up high so that it would give off light for weaving. Two or three of her dogs began barking outside. At first, they were barking loudly but soon began howling. The dogs next retreated behind the blanket, serving as the door, as they ran inside the hogan. Grandmother was very powerful and unafraid, and so she picked up one of her weaving tools, a stick, and ran outside. The full moon lit the surroundings. She saw something sliding down off of the hogan, so placed her weaving stick where the intruder would reach the ground. "Ouch," it cried. Grandmother asked what it was doing and why it was traveling about at night, before proceeding to really beat the skinwalker, cowering in its borrowed skin. Doing this gave her a strange feeling, so she went back inside her home then became very frightened. She built up her fire and remained awake all night. When the light of the next day arrived, the skinwalker had disappeared. She really beat up on it, it was said.[52]

Most of these kinds of encounters happen at night, often begin with dogs barking, and end with the skinwalker trying to avoid contact but sometimes getting shot or tracked to his or her home. The personal confrontation here speaks to the bravery of the woman and her ability to use the protective qualities of her weaving batten stick (bee ník'í'níltłish) to defeat this evil being. As mentioned previously, this is one of the roles of some of the items found in a woman's habeedí. Also, the part played by the dogs is important because they have the ability to detect evil even when humans cannot. Traditional Navajo people usually did not allow a dog in their home—they were to be kept outside and on duty to detect strangers or approaching things that might harm; by their entering the home, it illustrates their fear and the frightening circumstance. Sometimes the identity of the witchcraft practitioner is discovered, but more often it is left to rumor, innuendo, and circumstantial evidence that is gossiped around the community.

Those who become suspect fall into fairly clear categories. While anyone can be accused of practicing witchcraft, there are definite patterns or types of people most frequently identified. Kluckhohn provides a quantifiable basis derived from 222 cases of people blamed for practicing the dark art. Of this number 184 were adult men, 131 of whom were classified as "old" as were all (38) of the women, having reached menopause. One hundred forty of the men and 12 of the women were ceremonial practitioners, while 21 of the men were "headmen" or "chiefs"—a number that Kluckhohn felt was "an exceedingly high figure," given the proportion of leaders found throughout the general population. One hundred fifteen men and women of the total group were considered "rich." All older people wearing medicine pouches at gatherings were feared, and many of the Navajo people surveyed felt that the tendency to practice witchcraft ran steadily through family lines.[53]

Family and Community Figures

This raises a final point. Both Susie, as a granddaughter, and Ada, as a local resident, shared their feelings about a controversial elder named Atini and his father, Hashkéneiniihnii. To Susie, Atini (Át'íní is now often spelled Atine, Atini, or Atene) was a kind, benevolent leader of her family who had strong spiritual powers that he used on behalf of his community. While she recognized his high accomplishments in mastering a significant number of ceremonies, she viewed him as a person who used that power to remove insect plagues, control lightning, miraculously cure people, and assist his family members as a kind old gentleman. Ada, on the other hand, fits him precisely in the category that Kluckhohn described—an old, potent medicine man and leader in the Monument Valley community who, along with his father, used their power to control the elements when stealing cattle and to curse people through witchcraft. Most likely, both views have validity.

Both women share stories that have some historical inaccuracies about Atini. The event that Susie discusses centered around him killing two miners in the Navajo Mountain area in 1884. Known as the (Samuel T.) Walcott and (James) McNally Incident, this episode is well documented through both Navajo and Anglo testimony but will not be discussed here.[54] The same is true of Ada's account of what happened ten years previous when four Navajos, returning from a trading expedition, were caught

Hashkéneiniihnii, pictured here, was noted for his abilities to control spiritual power as well as for influencing events as a leader in the Monument Valley–Navajo Mountain region. He avoided capture during the Long Walk period, knew more than a half dozen lengthy ceremonies, and obtained wealth in livestock, silver, and Paiute slaves. Some Navajos believed he acquired this through witchcraft. (Used by permission, Utah State Historical Society)

in a snowstorm in Grass Valley, Utah. They received permission from a white man to stay in a cabin but were trapped in it by members of the William McCarty family, who killed three of them and seriously wounded the fourth before he escaped.[55] These stories illustrate an important part of Navajo culture and community in that they teach of leaders and personalities who had an impact on local events and who made a difference in its history. Through them, cultural values are perpetuated and personal qualities, (i.e., what is important to the Navajo people), are defined.

Ada shared her understanding of how Atini received his name, illustrating many of the characteristics that made him so important.[56]

The name Atini (The One Who Did It) received that name because he was blamed for killing some white men. While he was being hunted, his pursuers asked, "Where is the one who did this killing?" and the people replied, "He is the man; he is the one who did it." A group of soldiers came out here to arrest him. They asked him why he killed some white men, and he told them because these white men had killed six innocent Navajo people. They had gone to trade and sell with some white traders in a place called Dził Binii' Łigai (Mountain with White Face), somewhere north of Navajo Mountain. These Navajos had taken with them many tanned hides, rugs, saddle blankets, and jewelry to trade for some nice horses. They got what they wanted and started home. It was sundown and very cold, so they decided to camp near Dził Binii' Łigai in some old barns stocked with hay, it being a good place to keep warm. As they were settling down for the night, a couple of white men came by on their horses and told them it would be alright for them to stay there. Next, they opened up the door of a nearby cabin and invited them to move inside for the night. There they found a stove with a pile of wood. "How nice of them. How can we refuse the offer?" they said. Neither side understood the other, but communicated through hand gestures. The Navajos received some drinking water and hay for their newly purchased horses and were grateful for the hospitality.

Before dawn the next day, one Navajo man went out to get his horse then realized that something strange was going on. He became suspicious when he saw that some white men were outside, not too far from the cabin, warming their guns by a fire and loading them. He came back inside to warn the others who were still resting. "Don't be alarmed," one of them answered, "they were very nice to us last evening. Don't worry about them." But the man was afraid, so he went outside, saddled his horse, and rode out a way, pretending to act normal. The moment he took off galloping, he heard gunshots ring out in the house. As he was rounding the corner of the mesa, the cowboys shot him in the arm, but he managed to escape. The white men hunted for him for about a week but failed to find him. He survived for two weeks in the wilderness, treating his wound with natural herbs before crossing the San Juan River and going to see Hastiin Atini to tell him what happened. Atini was furious.

When Atini's captors asked him why he killed the two miners, he replied, "How can I forgive these white men? Our people cannot be replaced! They have murdered my uncle, who was a great medicine man. He used to sing the sacred Male Shootingway (Na'at'oyee Biką'jí), Windway (Nítch'ijí), and the Blessingway (Hózhóójí). He was also teaching me how to become a medicine man. For this very reason, I promised myself that I would have no more mercy for any white man who strayed in our territory from that day on. No matter what condition they were in, I was going to kill them. The white men killed first—two great medicine men and some other people, then took their horses. They are at fault, not me. But, yes, I am the one who did it." He had this meeting with his captors at Tódeezlíínii (Where the Stream Begins). His case was finally settled. That is how he received the name of Atini.

This narrative, like so many others, is replete with cultural values that reinforce the Navajo perspective established in their worldview.

Many of the elements encountered in this chapter will emerge full-blown in Susie's life story. Some will also be found in Ada Black's section. Hopefully, what comes from each is an appreciation of how hard life was in the past and how deeply embedded religious beliefs and cultural practices were that carried these women through difficult times. Nellie Grandson compared life to a saddle that starts out new but eventually gets worn and nicked and begins to fall apart. Things that are good are strong, need to be protected, and are valued, while that which is bad is soft, easy, and can be "easily run into." If it is of worth, it will often be accompanied by struggle. In Nellie's words:

> Where the sheep, horse, and cattle stand and whatever kind of life you have in your hand, it is the same as good. You may be walking around in the harsh cold, but your major thoughts are with your children and what they will have in their future. You might carry a newborn lamb into your home before drying and feeding it some milk. It will grow and grow into the future for your children's survival. As a mother you do this so that they will have something wet to swallow. You drive the herd to

plentiful pasture and water. There are other times when relatives need help. They may come asking for meat, and so this is when you reach out to help them.

Sometimes, for no specific reason, you grow tired because of the sheep and wonder why you do not just sell all of them and live in peace. Occasionally, I am told to do that. My children do not say this to me, but my neighbors' children do to their mother and father, who are very bothered by this. It would be better if they made their parents' feelings lighter, happier, and have a brighter outlook on life. The children should thank them for being there for them. My maternal grandfather said to always put corn pollen where water seeps out of the ground. By doing this, the water will be there, and the sheep and horses will not get tired. This is true for your family, Mother Earth, and livelihood. By saying prayers and giving offerings to the holy people, you, your sheep, and family will not get tired, but have the strength to carry on with life.[57]

CHAPTER TWO

Susie Yazzie

From Creation to Invasion

ray, moisture-laden clouds hung about Mitchell Butte and Gray Whiskers Mesa in the heart of Monument Valley that November day, 2000.[1] The cold wind blew in fitful bursts, sending the fine red sand into the road, out of its depression, and between the sagebrush and yucca plants lining the twisted pathway. Rain or snow—either were a possibility at this point. I drove to Marilyn Holiday's home, not too far off the road, and then proceeded to her mother and father's home—Fred and Susie Yazzie—a short distance away. The layout was typical: a number of outbuildings, a diminished wood pile, some old cars waiting to be worked on, and a gray-plastered rectangular house where the couple lived. Opening the door, the warm air gave a friendly greeting in contrast to the bitter wind outside. The home was comfortable, with pictures on the wall, a couple of beds in adjoining rooms, a living room with a few chairs, and a small wood-burning stove working full-time to send its warmth throughout. Boxes on the floor, dishes draped with a towel in the sink, laundry baskets filled with clothes, and a kitchen table that served as the center of family business spoke of work to be done. But Susie, wheelchair-bound, suffering from diabetes, leg pains, and arthritis, had limited capacity to handle any of it. Her husband was in similar condition—hard of hearing, blind, and often struggling to keep his thoughts organized. Fred stumbled about with his cane, occasionally mumbling to himself, or fitfully dozed in and out of sleep in his favorite chair.

Susie, dressed in a clean, bright pink sweatshirt, a faded green-and-white-checked skirt, and white sneakers with orange stripes, greeted us. The bows of her thick glasses were tucked into her gray hair pulled back and held in place with a hair comb. A few free wisps played about her face. Shaking hands, she offered a slight grasp, her gnarled fingers, twisted from arthritis and poor circulation, signaled a gentle character compromised by age. Her warm eyes sat above a pleasant smile, as they focused primarily on Marilyn, who had taken her place in an overstuffed recliner beside her mother's wheelchair in the living room. The daughter, with a Diet Pepsi by her side, knew how to best get her mother to respond to questions—those that I was asking as well as a long mental list of her own. She knew that this was the time to permanently capture all of those things she had heard in snatches over the years. The interview took on an energy of its own as she questioned her mother about family members and past events that had filled the older woman's life. All of Susie's answers came in a soft voice, one that I feared would be drowned out by the wind whistling and moaning around the corners of her home. Add to that the occasional interruption as Fred searched for something in the boxes or shuffled to his favorite chair by the doorway, the arrival of Marilyn's brother and husband for short visits, and a cousin neighbor dropping by to seek legal advice, and one can see why I had misgivings as to the quality of what would turn out to be a five-hour taped interview.

At noon we took a break, invited Marilyn's husband and parents to eat lunch with us, then went to Goulding's convenience store to purchase Piccadilly fried chicken, mashed potatoes with gravy, corn on the cob, and a six-pack of Diet Pepsi. Clearing the kitchen table, we sat around, devouring chicken and listening to the wind die down, accompanied by sunshine breaking through the clouds. A short clean-up and we were back in the living room to continue the interview. For two more hours we discussed the past, during which time the sun appeared in full force, beating through the two west windows, adding more heat to the house, and making everyone drowsy. We persevered until around four o'clock, when it was time for us to move on to other commitments. The last tape turned off, I gave Marilyn and Susie some money for their time (Susie: "Now I can pay my bills"), shook hands with everyone, stepped out of the warm house, and noticed a skiff of snow extending from top-to-bottom of Mitchell Butte and Gray Whiskers Mesa. An hour and a half later, more snow—two to three inches on the level ground—greeted me when I reached Blanding. It was cold and dark, but I felt a personal warmth for having captured information that could soon be lost. Later, Marilyn translated what we had recorded, appreciative that a part of her mother's life was now preserved.

Each of the interviews performed with the women of Monument Valley had its unique qualities. Most were done in the spring or fall to avoid the heat of summer and cold of winter; some were held in the back of a pickup truck, others in hogans, houses, summer shade houses (cha-ha'oh), or on a front porch; often there were other family members present, interested in hearing and sometimes sharing. Regardless of circumstance, every person enjoyed offering their thoughts while being appreciative of the money or gift given for participating. Each also was happy to receive a copy of the interview once translated from Navajo into English and then transcribed by Marilyn. Susie's interview was longer than most but was also representative of the feelings and attitudes of the women asked to share their thoughts on what the old days in Monument Valley were like. All identified themselves in the traditional way, as did Susie, when she began.

SUSIE'S STORY, PART ONE

My name is Susie Laughter Yazzie. I am seventy-six years old [born December 20, 1924] and belong to the Ute and Red Running into the Water People Clan (Nóóda'í Dine'é—Táchii'nii) and was born for the Many Goats (Tł'ízí Łání) Clan; my maternal grandfather is of the Reed People (Lók'aa' Dine'é), and my paternal grandfather is from the Tobacco People (Nát'oh Dine'é). This is how I am known as a woman. My father, Tom Laughter, had three wives, all of whom were sisters—my mother, Sally, being in the middle. We all lived separately but in one area. Her older and younger sisters are both gone now, the younger one dying a year ago. My father died several years ago. I had paternal grandparents, aunts, and uncles. My paternal uncle, Erected Iron Post (Béésh Íi'áhí), also had two wives. His family was childless, and so I used to help them as well as my paternal grandparents. My great-great-grandmother was Hot Woman (Asdzáán Doh), who was married to Mister Whitehorse (Hastiin Bił́į' Łigai) of the Many Goats Clan. Mister Blackrock (Hastiin Tsé Zhinii) was Whitehorse's son. I do not know Blackrock's English name. He had a brother named Mister No Water (Hastiin Tó Ádinii) with a big brother named Mister Little Whitehorse (Hastiin Bił́į' Yázhí Łigaii). It is through these family ties that the Whitehorses know my side of the family.

My mother's mother died during childbirth. She was married to Mister Atini, whom I will talk about later. He was from the Reed People Clan.

Before I tell about my life, I will go back to the beginning when the land was formed and share a brief history of those who lived here before me.

Teachings of the Land

Long ago, it was said, the earth was covered with water, like the ocean. The holy people wanted to drain it to expose the earth, but they were unsure, once the water was gone, if the land would remain dry. There were many types of fish and animals in these waters, just like in the ocean today. These creatures swam beneath, floated on the surface, and gathered in groups, searching for food and following underwater pathways. Take for instance The One Who Grabs and Holds You to Him (Tééhoołtsódii) with many legs. These creatures were huge, some like giant lizards and fish, others like large cockroaches that ran on top of the water. There was a wide variety of different insects and animals, some as big as boats. Other creatures looked like donkeys, but they lived under the water. Grandfather Atini mentioned another creature he called Yellow Coming Out (Bił Hajo Tsoii) that had a horn and might have been related to our cows or horses. In earlier times, these animals had different names from those used today.

The deep gorges and canyons that you see now were exposed and formed when draining this water. The mesas were on a higher ground level, where trees grew, but as the level dropped, much of the soil washed away, leaving some of the rocks standing up. It was said there was also vegetation under the water where some dinosaurs and reptiles lived. These creatures came from the east and went through these passages toward Navajo Mountain on an underwater trail. This is what my grandfather told me. He cautioned that no one was to make their homes on these trails, but today, we see many dwellings at these sites. Oljato Mesa is called Rock Going Down (Tsé Yanii Áhá) because that land formation descends down to the west but rises up on the eastern end. Where the rock opens near the Seventh Day Adventist (SDA) hospital and mission is called Between the Rocks (Tsé Giizh). This is one of the trails of the huge reptile dinosaurs (tłiish tsoh). The pathway is called "Tłiish Tsoh Bitiin" (Big Dinosaur Trail). They left their tracks along the edges of the boulders close to where the hospital building now stands above the Seventh Day Adventist Church. These rocks were dynamited when construction workers widened the road through the canyon. Some say that people took these tracks with them. Now they are gone.

The large body of water remained until Badger (Nahashch'idí) dug a tunnel to let it out. Everything turned very muddy with animals falling into the slime, leaving tracks behind. The draining mud and water destroyed all of the plants and animals that had been under the water, then solidified into the rocks and mesas we see today. Once the swamp was gone, the land started drying, and the sandstone became mesas shaped by the flowing liquid. The "Holy One" planned it that way. He made the land so that the people could live on it, although it took many, many years for this change to occur; it did not just happen overnight. Grandfather used to say, "You can still see the line of the water level as it went down. It probably stayed at these levels for years before descending to the next visible mark that is still there." Once the water drained, it left the pillars of rock standing, creating the monuments that others come to see. Vegetation began to grow. Some animals that lived before the flood were buried in the mud and became the minerals of today like uranium. Some of these elements are dangerous to human beings.

Stars were placed in the heavens by the holy beings to serve as a guide for the Navajo. It was first believed that the sun rotated around the earth, but now we know differently. The sun goes lower in the sky during the winter and is higher in the summer, while the stars point out directions at night. They have names like Pleiades (Dilyéhé—A Group of Stars), Orion (Átsé'ets'ózí—First Slim One), the Milky Way (Yikáísdáhí—Awaits the Dawn), Evening Star (Sǫ'tsoh—Big Star—Venus), Aldebaran (Sǫ'hots'ihi—Pinching Together Stars), and Corvus (Hastiin Sik'ai'í—Man with Legs Ajar). They tell us what time of year it is, while the sun moves north and south on the horizon, as the seasons change. Medicine men used the stars for crystal gazing by staring at the Evening Star during a ceremony until they saw a beam of light shine down on the sick person. If the ailment was serious or fatal, the star appeared to separate, one part turning red and descending while the other part remained in the sky. That is all I know as far as the stars are concerned. Medicine people know more about them.

I heard these stories from my maternal grandfather, Atini, who was a medicine man. He used to say that many of the sacred ceremonies and rituals derived from past events that took place in the beginning of time. The five-day ceremony, with the "Navajo basket laid upside down" (Holyway—Diyin K'ehgo) is one of them and is a special holy way ceremony. My father-in-law, Little Gambler—a.k.a. Frank Adakai (Hastiin Adika'ii Yázhí) used to identify these formations in Monument Valley as if they were people in a family related to one another. For instance, when discussing them, he would say Eagle Mesa is the father, and next to it is the mother sitting with her children. Then to the east stand the uncles and

Susie's explanation for the creation of some of the rock formations in Monument Valley centers around the subsiding waters that once covered the earth. Other people have different stories derived from the sacred narratives used to teach them. Medicine man John Holiday refers to these rocks as Yé'ii Bicheii dancers performing at dawn and being watched by a group of holy people, all of whom became frozen in time. (Used by permission, Utah State Historical Society)

aunts and grandmothers with the rest of the family. That is how he thought of them. He would ask, "Is it raining on Father Mesa?" or "Is it snowing on Uncle Mesa or Mother Mesa?" He named them this way for his own geographical familiarity with the land. It was his way of knowing what was happening in each area.

The holy people created humans after the flood waters subsided. Birds and all types of animals and insects joined the newly formed First Man and First Woman. These individuals tried to domesticate a cougar, a porcupine, and other small creatures but failed every time. Then First Man tried to do it to sheep, horses, cows, chickens, and other types of animals; he succeeded, they tamed easily and became his pets, and he took care of them. In the meantime, the earth became drier and drier and more habitable as new types of vegetation grew in abundance. The trees and plants that existed before had been replaced.

The holy people gave our great-great-ancestors "holy spirits" or "holy wind" (nítch'i diyinii) to guide and direct them as they learned more and more about their earthly experience. Those ancestors did not wander around in the dark as blind people. These holy spirits, similar to those used in hand trembling, have been present from the beginning of human existence. First Man, First Woman, and all those who came after them were guided by these sacred beings. The messenger from the east was called Talking God (Haashch'ééłti'í), and the one from the west was Calling God (Haasch'éé'ooghaan). The holy person from the east is a male and is the "grandfather," and the one from the west is a female and is thought of as a "grandmother." These two are the first in power and are the rulers.

First Man and First Woman gave life to other holy beings as did Sun Bearer and Changing Woman to Monster Slayer and Born for Water. These twins lived on this earth at the beginning of time and received their spirits from their parents. As holy ones, they were in tune with the sacred prayers of our people and have sacred names. All of them are guided by little holy messengers, like the whirlwind, that come between them and the sun. If the holy beings make any mistakes or perform in the wrong way, these messengers relay this back to the Sun. Each error is corrected by a change, and if it is a serious one, that change might be a major catastrophe like floods or fire. Because of the threat of these disasters, the holy beings are very careful in keeping the sacredness of the earth and their livelihood. They do not want to be destroyed.

Legends say that there is a Great God (Diyiin), who fixed this earth after the flood so that the human race could live here. Not until after the waters had drained did the people start keeping better track of their history and things that happened to them. Some of our people escaped to the west as far as California but eventually came home. It is said that they reunited with other Navajos near the San Francisco Peaks at a place called Tree Loaded with Something (Tsin Bii'łání), where they held a Goodway Ceremony (biijí). They prayed for a happy life and a prosperous future, which is all that the people wanted back then for a good life. They did not want any more suffering, so they continued to pray and perform ceremonies even up to this day. All of these sacred performances go back to those times. The people then moved back to these lands and multiplied in number. The ceremony called Holyway (Diyin K'ehgo), where they set a Navajo basket upside down and sing, as well as the Windway (Nílch'ijí), pertain to the sacred mountains and rock mesas. We shall not forget all the sacred stories and rituals associated with these important landmarks that continue to be shaped even after the flood.

There are many stories pertaining to the teachings about the holy beings. My grandfather used to tell us about them when we were children. I cannot remember them all, only a few. He stressed to us how sacred these stories and prayers were and how they are not to be wasted or joked about, misused, or misnamed. If someone does, the stories and prayers will harm you with their strong powers. These prayers are used to bring rain when performed in the right way. If you want to teach a child about these stories, they have to be old enough to keep them sacred and holy. If the child is not mature enough, they can bring harm to themselves and others through their mistakes or abuse of the words in a prayer or song. This will bring destruction like tornadoes or other disasters. Even wild animals such as wolves, lions, and bears were created in a holy way and released with a "smart" mind. They were told not to make a mistake, so even they can be affected by misusing our songs and prayers. There is so much to tell and teach from these stories; all of them become our "mind." We live and think by them. We learned this way of being when we were children, and so my generation is very careful about handling this sacredness. We were told not to drink alcohol or gamble or be "wild" so that our ceremonies and prayers could be performed sacredly. There were hardly any white men among us at that time.

The teachings say these "first people," who were holy beings in human form, suffered abuse from Big God (Yé'iitsoh) and other giant monsters. The Twins, who were born to Changing Woman, said they wanted to visit their father and get to know him. Their mother told them who their father was because only she knew, and then she allowed them to visit Sun Bearer. The two youths encountered many obstacles and life-threatening incidents on their way, and once they arrived, the Sun "tested" them further to see if they were really his children. The two survived all of the challenges, so he finally accepted them and gave them what they sought—bows and arrows of lightning and destruction to kill the monsters on the earth. The two went home on a bolt of lightning back to the edge of the waters and began to use their weapons to kill the evil beings. From these stories and others come many of our sacred songs and prayers. Although a lot of us grew up with these kinds of teachings and have gotten wisdom, strong minds, and endurance from them, we have failed to teach our children. Instead, we send them to school to learn a different way of life. It is the teachings of our ancestors that have shaped our minds, taught us respect, and kept us from doing wrong. We have lived by these sacred teachings, for they were all that we knew. Some of them are not meant for certain people who will mock or waste them. We do not tell everything that we know because we want to keep it within the immediate family and live by the traditions as it was meant to be from the beginning of time. Others recognize and respect this. The information is almost a secret, as we keep it holy and pray for our children as well as Mother Earth. These stories are very important to our people, and their teachings have no beginning or end. It is an ongoing sacred story. That is how it is.

The Early Years

The Navajo people have a long history, but I will share what I understand about the Fearing Time and the Long Walk period when we were at war with other Indian tribes in this area. My grandfather, Son of Giving Out Anger (Hashkéneiniihnii Biye'), told these to us when we were children. From what I know, four generations have lived since the Long Walk took place. Our great-great-great-great-grandfathers and grandmothers went on that journey. They say the Diné were gathered up from all around this area and other places on today's reservation and taken to Fort Sumner. Some people ran and hid in Tsegi Valley, about ten miles west of Kayenta. They said that long ago, our people fought off their enemies from on top of the mesas to the south of the Navajo Tribal Park, that long mesa [Mitchell Mesa] behind Mitchell and Gray Whiskers Buttes. You can still see some rock walls on top of it. The Navajos had all sorts of enemies back then—some were Indians and others were white men. The plan was to kill off all of the Diné, so those against us banded together to fight and destroy the People. While the Navajos were in hiding on top of the mesas and among the rocks along the valley walls, they never built fires, fearing they would be discovered. They slept in alcoves and crevices, staying hidden from their enemies. Once discovered, they were attacked. The Navajos knocked down walls of boulders on the advancing foe. They had no guns, only bows and arrows, so they killed them with rocks, turning them away and giving the people a chance to find new hiding places.

The Mexicans with their Indian allies searched ahead of the white soldiers. There is a story about a family living in these rocks when Indian and Mexican scouts arrived. Those hiding had small children and infants. One Navajo woman had a baby who would not stop crying, and so she ran farther into the rocky area to keep the enemy from hearing the infant. She went as far as she could, but the baby still cried, and so she put it under her to cover the sound. This did not help; the baby continued crying. In the meantime, the rest of the family, along with others living close by, had also run up into the rocks to hide, leaving their flocks of sheep. The scouts came to their homesteads and set fire to the vacant hogans and shelters. The woman observed all this happening while she continued to quiet her baby. She did not know where her family or the other people had gone.

Everyone was running for their lives as the scouts came on too fast. The fleeing Navajos could not help the little children, so they stuck two of them in a crevice between a couple of boulders, telling the little ones to sit still and be quiet. The woman in hiding did not know that an enemy had made his way to a point above her where he had heard the baby's cry below. He quickly alerted the others, who found the woman and infant. After killing her, they took the child with them, something they often did. The other families went into hiding farther up on the mesa but were able to see the scouts killing the woman. As the enemy descended, the little children in the crevice came running out from cover, thinking that it was the mother bringing her baby home. The enemy grabbed the two little children and took them also. The hidden families saw their home ablaze and watched their children and sheep taken away.

Other families, lower in the valley, had been killed before they had a chance to escape. Some Navajos living closer together in makeshift homes in the rocks were attacked, overcome, or killed in ambush—that was how the people described the conflict. Their children were taken amid the fighting, killing, and screaming that grew so loud that it frightened the goats, causing them to jump over the corral fence and flee to the rocks and mesa. The scouts rounded up only a few to take with the rest of the stolen herds. At another place called Chased by the Mexicans (Naakai Ch'íhoniłkaad), which is the name of a site northeast of the entrance to Narrow Canyon [about eight miles southwest of Oljato], some Navajos escaped up on that mesa, giving that name to the landscape.

The aftermath of all of this was horrendous. The Navajos came out of hiding, calculated their losses, and found their slain people with those who had been hiding among the rocks. All of the dead, who had worn their long hair in traditional buns, had been scalped by the enemy, who put their trophies on their long sharp weapons and guns as they sang and rode away from this scene of carnage. Those who survived remained in hiding for many, many days, going without food and with only a little water, until things quieted down. They returned to the ashes of what had been their homes, now burned to the ground. One homestead on the mesa had remained undetected. A group of survivors stumbled upon it, gathered the nicely tanned sheepskins, and took them to use for bedding and blankets; there was also a piece of burning firewood they used for their future cooking fires. This temporary shelter was made from a couple of posts with a cross beam supporting a bunch of sticks and branches leaning against it; this was a small shelter, about the size of a sweat lodge. Another story tells of the people finding a little dog that had somehow managed to get to a

The Utes, relentless trackers and well-armed warriors, were among the most feared adversaries of the Navajo. Accounts such as the one shared by Susie illustrate why large portions of Navajo land were abandoned, with residents fleeing to more inaccessible terrain and better defensive positions. (Courtesy Denver Public Library)

ledge on the face of a sheer cliff wall. The people heard the animal barking and saw it high above them. They thought that someone might have been hiding on that ledge. This took place in Tsegi Valley west of Kayenta. The aftermath of the massacres was too much for many of the survivors, with bodies and blood strewn about the desert floor and in the rocks everywhere.

Our family experienced much of this. I have mentioned that some people hid on top of Mitchell Mesa behind Mitchell and Gray Whiskers Buttes. You can still see the walls that were built along the edge of Mitchell Mesa and various narrow passageways, so that if the enemy tried to enter, rocks could be pushed down on them. My husband's [Fred Yazzie's] father, Frank Adakai Yazzie, said that his great-great-great-grandmother hid from the enemy up on that mesa. She and her family were never captured; they survived. It was said a handful of people from El Capitan joined them and remained hidden on the mesa. Their defensive wall of rocks is what saved them. My paternal grandmother's great-great-grandmother was captured and killed while she tried to save herself and her baby. These stories came from her great-grandmother, and then she told us. These are the only ones that I have heard about the people who survived without being captured.

It was said that one of our great-great-great-grandmothers escaped from her Paiute and Ute captors and later returned to her people. She was just a little girl when her mother was shot and killed and she was taken away. Different tribes like the Utes, Hopi, Zuni, and some plains Indians from Oklahoma came to our area to kidnap and kill our people, take the children and livestock, and burn our homes. This grandmother, after being captured, grew up among the Paiutes and married one of them. She became pregnant and ran away from her abusive husband. These Paiutes had been hostile to her saying, "You don't have any parents, because they are dead, and we can kill you too. We have taken care of you for no reason." Because of this kind of treatment, even though she was pregnant, she decided to escape. While she had been in captivity, she had occasionally heard news about the Navajos. Fleeing from the Utes and Paiutes, she hid in the bushes, shrubs, and tree roots along the washes as she traveled toward Navajo land. The enemy on horseback tracked her and found where she had been, crawling under objects and over rocks to avoid detection. She stayed ahead of them and one day met a couple of people also heading to Navajo land. They decided to go up on Black Mesa to avoid their enemies, where they survived primarily on cactus bulbs cooked in ashes. Eventually the small group traveled on and found some Navajos camped close to what would later become reservation lands. She became reacquainted with her people and raised her Paiute child, living to an old age. That is why our family has Paiute blood. The Utes and Paiutes are two different tribes. Our great-grandmother was part Paiute and Navajo. After several generations, we outgrew our Paiute bloodline.

My grandfather, Mister Blackrock (Hastiin Tsé Zhinii), used to ride his horse from Douglas Mesa to visit some of these Paiute relatives living near Cortez, Colorado, at the western base of Sleeping Ute Mountain. They would tell each other stories about the past and how he was related to them because of the events of history. The Utes came to Douglas Mesa to visit one time, so he gave them some goats, sheep, and cows to herd back to Cortez. Mr. Blackrock used to associate with them a lot because he felt a close relationship. He often returned home with a load of dried meat, packed in bags attached to his saddle. Atini (The One Who Did It), my paternal grandfather, also used to visit the Paiutes who lived on Douglas Mesa, and they treated each other just like relatives. They had many stories to share, and that is how they linked themselves to us.

There was a Paiute man from Navajo Mountain whose name was Little Black Ant (Wólázhiní). He and his father were both medicine men. My father, the late Tom Laughter, knew them from way back when he and

Little Black Ant lived at Navajo Mountain. Also, Atini used to perform sings and ceremonies on Little Black Ant and other Ute and Paiute people back then when many of them died during the influenza epidemic of 1918. Navajos told stories of how some of these families were found dead in a sitting position, as if they passed away while they were going about their daily chores. Some people even found live babies in their cradleboards that were still propped up against the walls of a home. The Navajos dug a trench and buried the dead in a mass grave a short distance from Owl Spring (Ná'áshjaa Tó'). They call this burial place Paiutes/Utes Lying Down Together (Be'yóodzin Shijéé'). My Aunt Katso, who lives out there, said the bodies were dragged into a pit by mules and buried in a long trench. Many of these people died on top of Douglas Mesa, but for those who survived, they moved to different parts of the country, some migrating to Navajo Mountain, others to Blanding, and others to the Cortez area. These Utes and Paiutes intermarried with the Navajo people and had children.

Atini and his family [parents, siblings, aunts, and uncles] lived along the base of Douglas Mesa all the way down to the San Juan River. The Paiute people lived on top of Douglas Mesa and prohibited the Navajos from living there. My mother, Sally Grey, said that when she was a young girl, her family moved up and down the base of Douglas Mesa. There were hogans sitting here and there all the way down to a place called Turning Back or Dead End (T'ą́ą' Ná'ná'i'ná) by the San Juan River. Navajos used to move around a lot back then going from place to place throughout the seasons. They traveled all the way from the San Juan River to El Capitan near Kayenta and eastward to Cottonwood Rising Out of the Valley (T'iis Haaz Áhá—between today's Mexican Water Trading Post and Dennehotso). The washes or valleys were not as deep then, so people used to have cornfields and homes all along that area. They lived on the banks on both sides with gardens of corn, melons, squash, and fruit trees filled with peaches, apricots, and apples. My mother said they lived there during the summer. She told a story about a boy who used to be very naughty and threw rocks at her and her sisters while herding sheep. Later, when he became a man, he received the Navajo name of Hairy Mexican (Naakai Ditł'oohí) and the English name of Goodman. He became a permanent resident living on the side of the road leading up to Douglas Mesa.

All families moved around a lot, not living in one spot as we do now. They moved up and down along the riverbed or by the washes that extend all the way from Kayenta eastward to T'iis Haaz Áhá and then northward back to the San Juan River. The people constantly searched for good vegetation, pastureland for their livestock, and fine soil for farming. Some planted gardens wherever they lived so one would find corn and melon patches here and there at a site nobody claimed; everyone shared the land and produce at harvest time. Some even planted corn and melons inside their sheep corral due to lack of fencing to keep the animals away. According to my mother, everyone moved about freely. That is how it was.

For those who went on the Long Walk, it was said that they were herded a long way. The soldiers set up tents to camp and rode horses, but the Navajos traveled on foot. Some of these people grew tired and could not go any farther, so the soldiers shot and killed them. This is what my grandfather told us. He said he heard it from his great-great-grandmother. She camped for three days at one location where it was said the enemy tortured, raped, and killed women and young girls. The soldiers hung them upside down, their legs tied to posts, where they remained all night screaming and crying. By dawn the white men stuffed rocks and dirt inside the women's bodies. The Navajo men were very angry at what was happening to their people. There were medicine men in the group who did a special ceremony, causing it to thunder and rain. It turned into a downpour with lightning striking and killing some of these enemies, including horses and soldiers who were surrounding a campfire. This helped a few of the captives to escape during the storm. After the third day, they moved on, leaving the women hanging and scalped. Those prisoners who were able to run escaped, formed small groups, and made their way home. Ceremonies for those who remained and went to the prison camp were important. One day, eventually, all were freed to go home because their pleas through the sacred ceremonies had been answered. My grandfather said, "It is these survivors who became our great-grandparents; if it were not for them, we would not be here today." Our enemies were determined to wipe out the Navajo, but we survived. It was meant for us to live. The "Great One" let us survive.

For those who traveled to Fort Sumner, there was great suffering, their feet turned raw from walking, and they nearly starved. The people suffered while there, and so they turned to their sacred prayers to survive. When they were sick, hungry, or lonely, they performed ceremonies and received help. The medicine men chose their most sacred rituals to overcome these tribulations and used corn pollen for their prayers each day. After they had been there for a while, a couple of medicine men got together and did a special ceremony. They found a cave where a wolf had delivered its babies, and there the men performed a prayer ritual. The next day the people went to the officials to ask for freedom, which was granted, along with a little food to take for the return journey. While they were in captivity, they received food like flour and coffee but did not know how to prepare it, so they drank the flour in liquid form or ate it as a paste and tried to eat the coffee beans whole. Many of them got diarrhea. This is what my grandfather Atini told us. He heard these stories passed down from his great-great-grandmother. Once the people were released, they returned to their homelands, but many of them died from illness and starvation on their way back. Some were still afraid that they might be recaptured, so they went toward the mountains and canyons, where they felt safe. The returning Navajos reunited with those people who had remained in hiding.

Years later, in 1920, the people heard rumors that there was going to be a flood caused by continuous rain. They believed it was true. Some Navajos who lived down in the wash near Cottonwood Rising Out of the Valley were afraid that their wagons might be washed away, so they tied them to cottonwood trees with a bunch of wire. Then they took all of their belongings to the top of the mesa and higher ground, where they waited and waited for the flood, but it never came.

Traditional Childhood

I was born at our family homestead called Where the Cows Grow Up (Béégashii Nit'ání) beyond No Man's Mesa in a canyon about twenty miles from Oljato, Utah. When I was small, I herded sheep with a young aunt. She used to carry me piggy-back after the flock; when I was a little older, she would hold my hand and we would walk after the grazing animals, even during the winter months. This aunt would say, "If a child stays home with nothing to do, they will be irresponsible." We did not have shoes like those available now because there were no stores or trading posts close by. The winter brought a lot of snow—knee-deep on adults—and it lasted a long time. It seemed like winters were longer back then. In the summer, we wore homemade moccasins that my father knew how to make. He also taught his three wives how to sew them after dyeing the leather in boiling water with plants that gave the skin a reddish color. After butchering the cow, they would take the hide and spread it out to dry. Next, they tanned the leather to make it soft, cut it into pieces, and then formed the moccasins. Sometimes the soles were rinsed and reused several times before discarded. We never complained nor asked for store-bought shoes or clothes. No one said anything about buying shoes because it was unheard of back then, and so all the children had homemade moccasins and clothing. Mother made one skirt and blouse for each of us girls, which we wore for almost a year. The hems of our skirts would be tattered and torn,

Children, at a very young age by today's standards, shouldered important tasks within their household. Daily herding of livestock (sometimes for long distances), processing wool, chopping firewood, maintaining a garden, and hauling water were expected. (Used by permission, Utah State Historical Society)

as if someone had beaten them with a stick. There were no coats, so we wore a blanket folded lengthwise and secured with a belt around our waist during the cold winter. That is how we dressed while herding sheep.

We always wore our hair in a knot, and as children, we never had it cut. It is good to keep your hair clean with yucca root shampoo and brushed so that it grows better. My hair got so long that it touched my ankles. Now I occasionally trim the ends, but wearing a knot looks good on women and men, so I still keep that style. There are also a lot of teachings about the care and importance of hair, but I guess they are like everything else in that they teach about discipline, respect, and thoughts. As we get older, even taking care of one's hair becomes a chore. They used to say that if a person believed in traditional ways, they would not cut their hair. If you respect and think in a holy way about the four sacred mountains, you will not do the forbidden. Everything was considered holy. Legend says that sometime during the early part of creation, the mountains went crazy. One mountain, namely Furry/Fuzzy Mountain (Dził Dotł'oi) shaved one side of its head because it became jealous. Some mountains burned; others did not. From these events came the mountain smoke ceremony used to calm and quiet people who do foolish and crazy things. It is said that in the future, when all of our people have cut their hair or shaved their heads, that will begin the end of our era because we will have failed and been overcome by the white men and their ways.

Livestock was a vital part of our existence. We grew up surrounded by sheep, horses, and cattle. Even to have one or two sheep now makes where you live feel like home. It gives one peace of mind, even if a person is unable to take care of them as we used to. To give this way of life up and live without animals—I do not know what I'd do. This is especially true for those who grew up with livestock and have been with them for as long as we can remember. It would be hard to be without them. I was raised in a home where we had sheep and cattle, which consistently provided our livelihood. When we lived above Narrow Canyon at Where the Cows Grow Up and higher on the mesa at Tall Mountain (Dził Nééz), my paternal grandmother, who was homebound, always had sheep and goats. They used to separate the rams and billy goats, sometimes leaving the sheep and their lambs with the goats and kids. When they grew bigger, she butchered them for meat. She used to milk the goats that always seemed to have plenty to share.

I must have started herding sheep with my aunt at age four. Later I was able to go alone. Back then we had good meat. We were constantly in search of plentiful pastureland no matter what the season. Our livestock had lots of natural vegetation and water so they were nice and fat. We herded the sheep all the time to springs with clean water that came down year-round from the mountain. I have heard lately that these springs have stopped flowing in the summer. My aunts sometimes took the sheep past Tall Mountain and toward Shonto, where there were only a few homesteads scattered about. This gave us plenty of grazing land, water, and a good place for lambing in the spring, when the weather was warmer.

Two of my aunts had the responsibility of moving around with the animals, looking for pasture, and so I went with one of them to assist. My aunts taught me many important things, such as how to keep matches dry and how to build a fire under any condition. I would gather the dry limbs from under the trees along with some dry bark to build the fire. During the winter months, we had to care for the newborn lambs. We would clear a dry spot and build a fire for drying and warming them. Sometimes two or more sheep had their babies at the same time, but once the lambs were dry, we would herd all of the animals home together. I remember doing this with my aunt, who took really good care of me. In the winter, I wore goatskin moccasins with rags wrapped around my feet for socks. At that time, most Navajo people did not have socks. I would stay by the fire to keep warm, while maintaining the sheep close by. We lived near a mountain, so the weather was very cold with deep snow and heavy fog. At times, it was easy to get lost, but when you have been out with the sheep a lot, you can find your way around. There were some deep canyons too, where we used to herd the livestock. I remember carrying newborn lambs up those steep canyon slopes. Often, I put a lamb inside my blanket on my back, then carried it home with its mother following me all the way. Once I got the baby home, I'd make sure it was fed and put with its mother. It does not pay to be lazy; if you do not take care of sheep properly, you are liable to end up feeding more lambs that now depend solely on you. Sometimes the mothers would abandon their babies, creating more work. There is a lot to learn when caring for livestock, which also provides excellent lessons for a child. We learned from our experiences.

This was also a time when we had plenty of goat's milk. Grandmother instructed me and my younger sister, Lois, to be at her home first thing in the morning, before the goats started grazing. "Milk will taste good, only before they take a bite, so be here early to milk them," she would say. This forced us to get up and out to make sure we were there on time. We were up early, every morning, even though it was quite a way off and we were barefoot, something we just became used to. If we missed one day, there was less milk at home. On the way, there were snakes and insects, which did not please us at all. We would go around them if we heard one rattle and then continue on our way. These snakes must have been good because we never had problems with them. Even the sheep grazed around and were never bitten. Once we reached the herd, Lois would hold the goat by the hair under its chin and by its horn, while I did the milking in a can. When we brought it home, Grandmother poured some milk into a pot and boiled it on hot ashes. "It's good when you boil it really hard," she said to us. The rest of the milk we took home to my mother, who made milk-and-corn pancakes, then gave us one or two for supper. We boiled the milk and added the cornmeal to make a tasty meal. A twenty-five-pound bag of flour purchased from the trading post lasted a long time because we used mostly corn we had harvested. My paternal grandmother and her daughter supplemented our corn food with other vegetables. These people were very nice and helped us out a lot. This grandmother also taught us how to butcher a sheep as she sat and directed us where to cut and what to do; I was only four or five years old at the time, but I learned how to do it. Since my father had to care for three households, we all ate small portions of a butchered sheep as we rationed our food. We would cut up some meat, dry it, and then mix it with corn and other vegetables. The children learned to eat small amounts, not overeating as some do now.

I also learned many things from working in the cornfields and taking care of the home. We were taught how to keep house and cook. Since there were no grocery stores, we had to learn everything by using basic food supplies. The children were primarily responsible for the livestock and cornfields, while the mothers were busy with rug weaving. They would card, spin, wash, and weave the wool into rugs to be sold in exchange for food. We had no such things as financial assistance programs back then. We could not depend on anybody but ourselves. Money was scarce, and we did not have free food distribution, so weaving rugs was vitally important. When our food was low, the women wove all night by the firelight.

One aunt was always weaving, which was all that she did, while my other aunt and I took care of the livestock. This aunt also cooked, carded, and spun wool for my aunt, who spent so much time at the loom that all she did was weave, weave, weave. The women then took their rugs to the trading post to buy small amounts of flour and potatoes. The store had no meat and hardly any shortening, while the coffee beans were whole, and so we had to grind them ourselves. There were several cornfields with peach trees located in the canyon near where we lived. My father owned two of these cornfields, and so my mother, Sally, and her children were assigned to work there, while father's other two wives were in another location herding sheep. Each household of the three wives and their children was treated the same.

The boys had to look after the horses and other livestock and learned many of the same skills we did. None of us slept for as long as we wanted. We took snow baths in the winter. My parents built a huge fire in the middle of our hogan so we could melt the ice off our bodies once we came inside. My father lectured us a lot. "These baths are for the sake of the children," he would say, "to cure them of their bad habits and attitudes." We rolled in the snow and ran inside to stand by the fire, then went out and rolled in the snow again. This was done every winter. I was the oldest of the children, so I got it the worst. My mother would rub the snow all over my body including my face. It was pure torture, but I believe it has taught me respect for others as well as for myself. I learned unselfishness and not to talk back to people. My father was right about his teachings. To this day, I hate to see others suffer from abuse or mistreatment. Now we have more food because we have stores, and people get financial assistance to help them out. When payday comes, they are on their way to town to buy a bunch of sodas and sweets for their children and family members.

It is no wonder there is more sickness today than ever before. People are crowding into the hospitals with toothaches and diabetes or high blood pressure. Navajos never used to indulge in all this junk food back when we were young; therefore, we hardly heard of any health problems. Our grandparents were raised the same way and so were healthy.

Mother cared for the two large garden plots at Where the Cows Grow Up. I sometimes stayed there to help; we all worked hard. That is how I grew up. Atini gave my mother a couple of very tame horses for us to use. He brought over some sheep too, those that he received as payment for the sings and ceremonies he performed. I remember having this really tame brown mare to plow the fields. We would harness her and then attach a bucket-like plow with a sharp blade to clear the brush and smooth the hills and bumps. If the weeds became overwhelming, I used a harnessed horse with a homemade hoe to clear them. This hoe was used by all the farmers in that area. I led the horse while my mother held the hoe in place as we went down between each row. It took a lot of skill to operate the plow correctly. Whatever weeds were left behind, we hoed by hand every dawn and evening when it was cool. By doing this, we had healthier corn. My mother used to break off the dead leaves from the lower part of the corn to keep it growing. I was very small, so sometimes the horse would step on my foot. That really hurt, but I was always picked to lead her as we cleared, plowed, and then irrigated the cornfield. It was hard work, and there were always weeds to hoe. I led the horse up and down the rows of corn; sometimes I went crooked because I'd be looking elsewhere and not paying attention. My mother or aunts who worked long and hard in the cornfields scolded me, but we eventually got the job done. We also planted a lot of squash and melons and gourds. Gourds were made into ceremonial rattles, but they smell pretty strong if picked when green. I did not like their odor.

When we finished one garden plot, we would move to another cornfield that belonged to my paternal grandmother. Her field had a patch of fruit trees in the middle of it. She was short and large, but she would be out there hoeing the field dressed in a blouse and skirt made from scraps of material that seemed to have been thrown together any old way. Her large sleeves would flap from side to side, back and forth, as she busily hoed the weeds. It was funny watching her. She took really good care of the peach trees that produced a lot of fruit and was very particular about caring for peaches by not letting anyone else pick them.

Once we harvested the corn, it was prepared for storage. We roasted and dried some corn, mixed it with burnt juniper ashes, and made it into dumplings, which the children ate throughout the day. Preserved ripened corn was dried and stored. First, we separated it according to color, type, and whether it was to be used for food or planting. Then we stored it underground in a six-foot hole that was dug narrow at the top and wider at the bottom. In this storage space we put one foot of dried juniper bark on the bottom and then the corn, still on the cob, on top. Corn taken off the cob was bagged and placed with the rest. The hole was carefully covered with logs, a thick layer of bark, and sand to prevent predators from getting at it. This was an excellent storage method. Pumpkins and melons, like cantaloupes, were stored for just a short period of time, kept in horizontal dugouts in the ground after being slightly roasted, pared in strings, and dried. This is called nánees-taz (pared). The dried strings were then wrapped with another strand to create a bundle that was bagged and later cooked. The pumpkins could be boiled with corn while the melons were fixed in a variety of ways. These foods lasted all winter long. I worked all of my childhood years in such jobs, so I know how it was done. I never saw a trading post; store-bought food was unheard of.

With these cornfields, orchards, and livestock, we did well. We dried the corn and separated the blue corn from the white and yellow, then bagged them. All of the corn was ground by hand, after which my mother made many kinds of foods from it. She was an expert cook in creating a wide variety of corn dishes. Mush, pastes, dumplings, and all sorts of breads—even "paper bread"—appeared when she was in charge. All of this food came from finely ground corn and was delicious.

I remember gathering sumac and juniper berries to eat along with other wild plants. These were ground and boiled before consuming them. Sumac berries were dried and stored in sacks for winter use, then later ground and cooked like mush. Peaches also were dried and eaten in the winter. They were very good and nutritious. Today, I don't see anyone out gathering berries, although they still grow in some places. No one makes use of other wild plant foods either. These were our main dishes back then. Today we all depend on grocery stores, especially our young people who only look for ready-made foods. They don't know the slightest thing about how to prepare, cook, and flavor corn recipes, but only eat junk food. Many adults do the same thing. I blame my ailments on the food we eat nowadays, having had health problems for almost forty years.

We grew up in that vast canyon country and hardly went out in public. We rarely saw other people, staying primarily in our area until I was eight years old, when we moved only a few miles to the northeast to a place called White Spotted Hills (Dah Nidadziłgaai). My mother continued to work in the fields with me assisting her. It seemed that whenever we

These women preparing squash and melons will slice them into segments, expose them to sunshine and dry desert air, and then place them in a specially prepared hole in the ground for storage. By the end of winter and early spring, supplies were sometimes exhausted, and so wild plants, such as Indian rice grass and other early bloomers, supplemented the diet.

finished hoeing weeds, the rains would come and the weeds would spring right back again, forcing us to start all over again. If it did not rain, we watered the plants using buckets. My father never built a decent hogan for us, only a circle of tree stumps in a row that he covered with branches before hanging a tent on the inside walls. We lived in this summer shade home, but when it rained, my mother had to cover the overhead branches to keep our belongings dry. These homes were a simple circle of cut trees, so we were very cold during the winter, especially since we slept on the ground. Father had two other wives with families besides my mother, so he was rarely home.

As I grew older, more chores were added to my daily work. After I herded the sheep home in the late afternoon, I had to gather firewood. There was no automobile or wagon to use for this, and so I took a rope and ax and carried the chopped wood home on my back. I also had to fetch water with buckets. All of these necessities were quite a distance from where we lived. People had to move around a lot, in search of water, pasture, and wood. Those fortunate enough to have horses used them for locating resources and carrying things home. I learned to cook and take care of feeding the children while my mother wove her rug. I also ground corn with the sacred stones [mano and metate]. I was not good at it at first but improved by doing it often. I was about five years old then. We had very little flour, coffee, or sugar. Corn was our main source of food, plus the goats and sheep.

As children, we were constantly busy with little time to play. When I joined the other children for an activity, my mother would bring out her whip and tell me to get some firewood, haul water, grind corn, cook food, or clean our home. Cutting hair was forbidden by traditional teachings, so all of us had long hair. My mother told me to brush the children's hair and rid them of lice. There was always something to do and never a free moment. Today it is different. We have automobiles, barrels of running water, yet our children are too lazy to step outside and carry in a bucket. If there are two or three youngsters, they ask each other to do it. The same is true for gathering and preparing firewood. They don't want to help. When I compare my childhood with theirs, it is so very different. We were not allowed to stray or go where we pleased or play or eat to our satisfaction. We were kept busy all day. In the evenings, I'd come home with my skirt wet up to my knees from walking in the snow after the sheep. We slept on sheepskin and used goatskins sewn together for a blanket. That was my childhood life. We were not comfortably wrapped in fancy quilts or the like, but slept under goatskins that barely covered our bodies.

I was very active when I was young. I rode horses and drove wagons to haul wood and water. I feel confident in myself to talk about these things because I have lived long enough to know them. I have the willpower to take on the challenges of life. I used to run and jog all the time while I was growing up. I also had a kinaaldá ceremony performed for me by my grandfather Atini. I made underground corn cake and ran to meet the dawn. I have since participated in kinaaldá ceremonies for other young women, and I believe I can still outrun every girl if I wanted to because I was fast. I began distance running at age eight when I ran several miles a day, increasing the distance each time. I used to jog in rough terrain, over sand dunes, and through canyons, everywhere, and it became easy. I alternated between running and sprinting, remembering to always turn clockwise when I was ready to return home. I believe this kind of exercise has helped me to deal with many health problems and to have lived this long, while the snow baths gave me a strong mind. A person has to have this kind of self-motivation to accomplish the work and goals we have before us. I feel that I had a good, full life, and that gives me a feeling of accomplishment. I have taken part in everything, such as childcare and other important practices, while fostering respect and love for all people and animals. I enjoy my life.

When we lived with my maternal grandfather, Blackrock, he lectured us all of the time. He was a great teacher and used to make us work hard. He cautioned, "Don't depend on others or live off of others. What you learn will be for your own benefit, not for other people. They work for themselves; likewise, you should work for yourself. You have your own feet, hands, eyes, and brains. You cannot go to other people's homes looking for something to eat or taking your children with you. You have to do everything for yourself and work at it, even if you have nothing. Care for your own children and do not leave them with someone else." Some of his children and grandchildren did not listen to him and went their own way, but I hated to see grandfather's teachings go to waste, so I stayed and listened. His lectures were meant for all of us. Since his death, I have never heard another person teach like he used to.

What he taught proved to be true. When my husband and I got married, we had nothing, but I wasn't about to live with either of my in-laws or my mother. I knew better. We made our own homestead and lived according to what I had learned. I had the knowledge for making a living, and now was the time to try it out. My husband worked away from home, while I stayed there and cared for the children and our sheep. I have never depended on anyone, nor placed my children in someone else's home. My children have all taken advantage of their education and finished high school. They have learned the important meaning of life, which makes me very proud and thankful. I am grateful to my grandparents for their teachings by which I have been rewarded. I am not as strong anymore because of my health problems, which is also true for my husband. We stay home a lot as our children experience their own lives. Still, our grandparents were right about everything, and my life and that of our nine children would have been very different if I had not lived by what the elders taught. My children learned and now live by the same things that I knew at their age.

Exposure to the White World

The first white men that I saw surprised me. I had been told that they were like the holy beings and that our people were doomed to become like them. Because of their "holiness," they did not hesitate to invent things or to try to achieve the impossible. They were given the talent to succeed and accomplish everything. In the beginning, our people received the same ability, but it was taken away because the Holy One feared we would destroy each other if we kept it. Legend says the Anasazi people were allowed this gift and used it only to eventually be destroyed. They planted gardens and kept inventing new things and making replicas of holy signs and symbols. Their religion gave them extensive power and abilities to prosper, and so there grew an overpopulation. They dug up the earth because they were curious, climbed the rocks to unbelievable heights, invented a way to fly, discovered fire, and reached the point where they duplicated the tornado and whirl-wind. Their new inventions concerning air made it possible for them to travel by flight and reach difficult places where no normal human being could go. At this point, they were suddenly destroyed by their own inventions. The air vanished along with every living thing on earth. The holy beings have warned our people that if we do not keep our beliefs sacred, we will be destroyed just like the Anasazi. That's what my grandfather used to say. White men are following in the steps of those people.

I saw my first automobile when I was six years old. There was a sheep dipping immunization program in Shonto. Everyone was asked to reduce their sheep, but my father did not want to do it, so we left the lambs and baby goats behind. My parents took the rest of the herd to Shonto while my older brother Herbert Laughter and I remained behind at Tall Mountain to take care of the remaining livestock. Late one afternoon, a couple of policemen came out of the woods on horseback. They took the herd away from us and said they were bringing the animals to Shonto to be with the rest of the herd. We did not know how they found out about this part of our flock. Someone might have reported us, but these officers were also going from camp to camp, checking out everything. A few of these policemen were Navajos. They told us to go home, which we did, while they arrested my father for telling a lie about not leaving part of his herd at home. He was given the alternative of giving up all the hidden goats and sheep and spending time in jail or else sending some of his children to school, which is what he agreed to. They told him to bring them to school in Tuba City within ten days. If he sent us there, he could keep all his sheep, which is what he did. My brother Fred Laughter and I had never been away from home, so it was our first time to see what was out there. A medicine man, Short Man Who Can Hear (Hastiin Adiits'a'í Yázhí), sang prayers on us before we left. Four days later, we traveled on horseback to school in Tuba City. That was where I encountered my first automobile. It was a truck coming in from Kayenta, bringing in other children for school. It appeared suddenly and scared me.

When my older brother and I arrived at the boarding school, we had problems with some mistreatment by other students. They would trample all over me and sometimes hit me or pull my hair. This aggressive behavior was bad, and I dreaded it. For two years I attended, remaining there for the full school year before returning home. We spent the whole winter there until classes ended, and we rode home on horseback. It usually took a couple of days for the trip, camping along the way. I remember some children being shipped to other schools at Fort Wingate and Albuquerque, New Mexico, as well as Phoenix and Fort Apache, Arizona. They left in trucks. I found out later that my future husband at this same time was taken to Fort Apache. Once I arrived home, my parents told me to remain there to take care of the household and livestock. My younger sister would take my place and go to school. I have always regretted not going back.

While I was attending, I usually enrolled in my traditional clothes and moccasins, but later received clothing provided by the school. Our parents never bought us school clothes like they do today. This experience made me realize how it feels to be without any decent shoes or clothing. It was also from this experience that I told my children, "Get a good education. The first year is always the hardest, but you will find some friends. Be nice to everyone and obey your teachers. Help those who need you, especially the little ones. Clean their noses and tie their shoes, for it is hard to be a 'victim.'" I lived according to how I had been taught. My husband and I have raised our children and taught them these things. He has helped me a great deal. They are now all grown up, and I am happy to have accomplished this.

In those early days, as I recall, there were not many people living in Monument Valley and Oljato. My in-laws lived in a place called Dark Woods (Tsin Dithitii) near the monuments, where they raised their family, including my husband. I do not remember how these other people reacted to this new thing called an automobile; it all happened so fast. I had my first ride in one going to the clinic in Kayenta. It felt good to ride in a truck, but its smoke was quite irritating. This vehicle had to be cranked up in front to start it. I remember going to the Shonto Trading Post in a truck. The roads were steep and rugged; it had rained that day, and some parts were washed out. For some odd reason, our driver took a wrong turn, and we ended in a gully upside down. We had to crawl through the windows to get out. At this time, most of the people only owned wagons and horses. There were hardly any roads in Monument Valley, which is probably the reason that the trader, Harry Goulding, had a jeep. The only road out of here was through the mission canyon, then to Promise Rock, and on to Kayenta. The road north went straight across the desert by Guy Holiday's camp and past Eagle Mesa where Billy Yellow lives. It was more like a wagon trail. Only Harry Goulding's jeep could make it through these trails. The only other vehicle around was the one that the Oljato trader used. I started to see more automobiles make their way around here in 1940. Gradually, a few of our local people started owning cars. Frank Bradley from Kayenta was the first Navajo that I knew of to own one. Most of our people went to Kayenta to find a ride because hardly anyone in Monument Valley had a vehicle.

Surprisingly, I saw an airplane before I did an automobile. They occasionally flew above our home at Where the Cows Grow Up. We were at first afraid of them because we were told that they were looking for children, so we hid when we heard one. Some of the adults were afraid of them too. I've flown a few times, for example when my broken bones had turned to cancer and I had tuberculosis. I flew from here to Fort Defiance, then Socorro to the hospital, where I spent two years in a sanatorium. Planes ride like a car, rocking and dipping above the canyons, but the bigger they are, the calmer it is. I flew in a huge plane from Loma Linda, California, to Phoenix, and it was very calm. I have also ridden the bus many times and traveled on a train, going from California to Flagstaff.

CHAPTER THREE

Susie Yazzie

Spiritual Life in a Physical World

S usie took a deep breath and continued. All through her account she
mixed what Anglo people would call spiritual or religious things with
the more mundane elements of daily life. There was no separation.
While each individual is unique, she was not known as a medicine woman
or one with special experiences that set her apart from others. Yet the intangible world was intertwined in everything that she said and did. This is
an important point to consider when looking at the lives of Navajo women
in Monument Valley. The entire world and every object in it has an inner
form, songs, prayers, and a relationship with mankind, as previously discussed. While Susie did not give a doctrinal explanation of her views, it
becomes apparent that she thought of her experiences as special but not
out of the acceptable bounds of belief. To an Anglo person, some of her
thoughts range between mystical, supernatural, and "impossible because
unexplainable." For Susie, they were everyday examples where the sacred
met the profane.

In the following narrative, it is important for the reader to understand
that the events and practices that Susie shares were given in a matter-of-
fact rendering that was no more questionable than the sun coming up in
the east each day. Her husband, Fred, spoke of his own experiences that
were just as dynamic. Later in life, they felt that the old medicine people
who understood fully the laws and practices given by the holy people
were then disappearing. The couple switched to Christianity in the form
of the Seventh Day Adventist religion, which had established a church

and hospital close to where they lived. Fred and Susie invested their faith in this religion but still had strong beliefs and a deep respect for the old ways. Where Christianity is often exclusive, insisting on "one Lord, one faith, one baptism," Navajo and Native American belief systems are often inclusive, open to many religious possibilities. The couple remained full of faith and spirituality to the end, Fred passing on February 15, 2002, and Susie on February 6, 2009.

SUSIE'S STORY, PART TWO

Hand Trembling

I had some strange experiences as a child, seeing or imagining things like a vision. I used to see lights at night. Traditionally, if this happens to a person, they have to have a sing or ceremony performed for them. I did. It was during one of these episodes that I experienced "hand trembling" (ndishniih) for the first time at the age of thirteen. I was asked, "How can you use this special gift to the best of your ability?" Then a medicine man did a prayer for me, and sure enough my hand began trembling. I had a vision and was told to interpret the meaning of what I saw. When I started to hand tremble, I first felt a huge stream of air which narrowed down to a thin line as it entered my arm. This scared me. I felt it raise my body. My hand started trembling. I could hear the others telling me I had received the sacred power and urging me to concentrate on the vision I had received, to think about what I had seen. In this vision I saw my mother and me herding sheep, when out of nowhere a man appeared riding his horse past us and on to the top of a hill, where he vanished. He had left no tracks when we went to look for them. In the meantime, this strange force in me had driven my body toward where my mother sat. It literally threw me around all over the place, dragging me from the wall to the center of the hogan to the door, where she was watching. If I had been working with this gift correctly, I would have "thought for it" and controlled my thinking by seeking answers through it. The force was very strong and rough on my body, nearly making me sick—both emotionally and physically. According to what I thought, it was clear that someone was trying to kill her through a horse she was riding. At this point, my mother had been divorced from my father for some time. Feelings told me that the man in my vision was someone from my father's relative's side. I knew that as long as I guessed or got the answers to my vision, it would not happen. I continued to have these hand trembling experiences. They affected my heart in a strange way and made my mind whirl as if I was dizzy. I was too young to really understand what was happening, so it frightened me. Sometimes you will end up uncontrollably striking yourself as this stream of power passes through your body, making you feel like you are going up and down, with your heart racing, seeming to enlarge it, and moving the body about to a point where it weakens you.

Everyone encouraged me to build on these sensations and increase this strange power, but I did not want to. Sometimes when I began hand trembling, I slapped myself, or the power dragged me around. It weakened my heart, and I felt numb and hollow on one side of my body. This happened off and on for two years. My mother wanted me to have a special ceremony so that I could keep the power and use it like medicine people do, but I did not want to. It made my heart hurt and scared me, especially when I was alone. Although I do not do hand trembling anymore, I still have the mental or psychic power. I seem to be able to foretell future events or figure out problems. My mind is capable of answering complicated questions. I have changed my religious beliefs to Christianity, but I still have it. Voices tell me to do this and that, to pray or act according to what I think. It still works the same way. I found out these things through my hand trembling experiences. That is how it is.

We used to hold different sings and ceremonies for our family's sicknesses. I met my husband, Fred, when I had a "crystal gazing" done for my sick son. Fred was helping another medicine man, Jack Gillis, with the ceremony. While they were doing the crystal gazing, they went outside the hogan to perform part of the ritual while I stayed inside and held my son on my lap. The men saw a bright light surround us and a black shadow in the form of a porcupine, which kept coming close to us. Still, they could not figure out what it was. They also saw lights that indicated that we should stay south of them, since all of the north side of this vision was dark. Mr. Gillis pictured a great white object sitting in the distance, which he felt meant something good awaits us in the near future. Just five months later my husband and I were involved with a movie outfit from Hollywood that really helped us. We lived on that site for six years, taking care of their equipment and things. It seemed impossible that such wonderful things would happen, but they did. These crystal gazing ceremonies helped us to see what lay ahead, and that is why people use them and hand trembling a lot.

It is said that tiny whirlwinds come down from the sun and carry "messages" to the earth, just like radio signals do. These messengers are still about on the earth and are called nítch'i diyinii (holy wind), and they are the ones who guide the people. This same holiness is used in the hand trembling ceremony. It works for some, but not for others. The nítch'i are here on this earth with us now. They are often given to those who are mature in their beliefs and who may be naturally gifted. It is a strange experience, one of anxiety, as if you are in fear of something and trying to run from it but cannot find a safe place. It feels like you levitate off the ground, becoming emotionally tired and strained. It is like remembering something of your childhood that you become very emotional about. Perhaps it is a song or place.

Because I was afraid of this power, I told the medicine man, Mister Rock Ridge (Hastiin Tsé Dahsitání), to take the special gift away from me for good. He tapped corn pollen on the soles of my feet and the palms of my hands, the top of my head, then all over my body. That was the end of it. Hand trembling never happened to me again. Before that though, I used to get ill from it, even when I tried to throw a stick at the sheep. It automatically started, and I would get scared because I just did not want to use it. The actual hand trembling stopped, but the "questioning" or the thoughts remained with me for quite some time afterward. It did not leave right away. The meditation was still present and questioned me, or I would question things; it seemed to tell me what was good to do and what was not. The mental state of mind persisted. If I were to dwell on that feeling, it would be possible to regain my hand trembling power, but I kept myself from it, so it never came back. I sometimes think to myself, "It is probably because I gave up that special gift that I am suffering from so many health problems today."

Medicine Men

When Fred and I were first married, we believed in the Navajo religion. Whenever one of us or the children became sick, we called upon a medicine man. The medicine people back then were very good and kept everything sacred. The peyote religion had not really been introduced to the Navajo people in Monument Valley at that time. There were only small Presbyterian churches in Oljato, Kayenta, and Tuba City, with an Episcopalian Church in Bluff. Monument Valley had primarily medicine men. People would pick the one they preferred and pay a small fee. These healers' prayers and songs were good. They would name the holy ones such as Dawn Man (Hayoołkááł Hastiin) and White Shell Woman (Yoołgai Asdzáá) and Changing Woman (Asdzáá Nádleehé) in the evenings. The

Susie (right) and her sister Joanne sit in the traditional posture for females as taught by Changing Woman. Susie, at one point, had the opportunity to hold the power of hand trembling, but declined to develop it, fearing its domination. (Marilyn Holiday family photo)

holy person in the east was called Talking God (Haashch'ééłti'í) and in the west, Calling God (Haasch'éé'ooghaan). These were the holy ones who took care of the earth and its people. That is how we were taught and how we kept the traditional religion sacred.

It was nothing to joke about, and we were forbidden to discuss things like suicide, for if we did, it would affect us and our loved ones. If we ask for the unknown, we will eventually fall victim to it. We had to keep the holy rituals sacred and obey the words of the medicine men. Our minds were oriented to the east with our back to the west. We were told not to take off our shoes without untying them because we have hands to undo the laces. We are to untie our shoes and set them side by side facing east so our minds will remain straight. Do not be messy, for you have eyes to guide you. If you are unorganized, you are asking to be blind or have misfortune, so take care of yourself wherever you go.

People prayed for many things in their sings and ceremonies. They asked for both male and female rain to help the vegetation grow. Rain can harm you if you do something wrong, or if you do not sit still while it is watering the land. If you curse, it will bring you bad luck sooner or later. This is what my grandfather told us. We are like a seed. The lightning activates the earth, but it is also inside our bodies, which makes us alive. That's why we are to keep all things sacred at all times. "Tsin ąhnaaghai bik'eh hózhóón" means the lightning and the thunder. Likewise, our bodies move and we can talk because we are made with lightning. It is because of this that we need to take care of ourselves.

Navajo medicine men control many spiritual powers and are important people in our community. My great-grandfather Hastiin Atini was raised by his parents with his brothers and sisters around Eagle Mesa and the monuments in the winter, then moved in the summer to El Capitan. They were able to have homes in a number of different places because there were hardly any people living around here back then. My mother said there were a lot of cattle out here, too, that belonged to Mormon ranchers. These cows and bulls were mean. There was plenty of vegetation with more juniper trees on the hills, and the grass was so thick that the animals tunneled trails through it as the Navajos herded sheep and goats over this very different landscape. There were not that many gullies, so the water formed pools all over the flat land. Mother said that it would be years later before the washes appeared.

Grandfather Atini received his name through an incident with two white men who were exploring for minerals around the Navajo Mountain–Kayenta region. These white men came in pairs or small groups, riding horses and traveling through here. [In 1884] the Navajos complained that these particular miners were mean and had mistreated some of the local people, so some of the Navajos told my grandfather to do something about it. He went to Kayenta and killed them, but many years later, the military came looking for the person who had murdered the individuals. They asked, "Who killed the two white men? Who did it?" or in Navajo "Atini," The One Who Did It. My grandfather, at that time, was living where the Oljato Trading Post is now. He had a garden where he planted corn and melons at the base of the rocks. This was when he received the name Atini. Prior to this he was known as Giving Out Anger's Son (Hashkéneiniihnii Biye').

Navajos say that a whole army of soldiers camped out at the place they call "Moonlight Water" (Oljato—Ooljéé'Tó; Wetherill Trading Post). They had come to kill the man who had murdered the two white men. This army of at least one hundred men came on horses with pack mules. The army men were searching for "The One Who Did It," and so when my grandfather received the information late one evening that he was being sought, he left immediately on his horse, went to the San Juan River, and made a special offering with sacred prayers before returning to Oljato. The soldiers sent word that he and his wife were to appear at the army camp the next morning. That night, as the white men slept, their big army mules wandered down to Oljato and into my grandfather's cornfield. These soldiers were tired and overslept, so they did not hear the mules leave. Grandfather had prayed, and I believe this is why it happened. Mother told us about it. Grandfather and Grandmother saw the mules, but they just looked and left to meet the army men searching for them. Grandfather was not afraid because he had faith in his prayers and beliefs. He and his wife rode their horses to Oljato and the military camp. Upon arrival, a group of soldiers happily came to greet them. Some came up and hugged them and cried. "We are glad you came." My grandparents stood there holding the reins of their horses as others joined in.

The army had cooked a big breakfast which they spread out on a blanket. The soldiers brought all kinds of food, so they invited the Navajos to sit down and eat with them. Since there had been such a friendly exchange in greetings, Giving Out Anger's Son told them about their mules in his cornfield. The army gave him and others an assortment of gifts including a horse with a saddle and blankets as well as a pack mule loaded with merchandise. They received all kinds of presents as they sat surrounded by the soldiers. These army men had forgotten what they came to do; Grandfather saw many of their guns laid in a row propped against a wall, but instead of fighting, the Navajos were treated with respect. Grandfather and his wife returned home with their packed mule and horses. My mother, Sally, described how the mule had a crisscross saddle that had large canvas bags attached to it, filled with food and blankets. My grandparents' horses were just as overloaded. The army did not harm them; they just got to know them and let them go. That is how it happened, and that's where his name came from. Now, his children and grandchildren go by that name, for instance, Kitty Atini, Tom Atine, et cetera. Some of them translate "Atini" as being "The Rich One," but my side of the family does not say anything. They can choose whatever they want. For those who understand the origin of the name, there is a different meaning.

Grandfather Atini was our great teacher of sacred stories and prayers as well as a medicine man who had a heart of kindness. He performed sings and ceremonies for the sick, accepting only what they could afford. He would say, "I have done and will do sacred ceremonies for a loaf of bread, fresh from the underground oven with ashes still on it. That is how we medicine men are supposed to do it. We are not supposed to perform ceremonies to become wealthy; the gift of healing comes from the holy ones, not us medicine men. We should not ask for a lot of money or riches; we are not to put ourselves higher than the holy ones; it is not right, for they go above everything. That is how we medicine people should be." Today, this is not the case. The bread he mentioned is called nanoyeeshi ("into the ground flowing"). One stirs the cornmeal into a pancake-like batter, then pours it into the hot sand and covers it with more hot sand. It stays in there until the dough is cooked. When it is taken out, it is brushed off, then eaten. A real medicine man will take this as payment without cleaning it. This is all he needed because the healing power came from the holy ones. He never used his ceremonies to become rich, but gave his services to the people to help them. His siblings, however, accumulated a lot of sheep and other livestock. Not Grandfather, who might have had a few sheep but was always generous to the needy. I remember him bringing back clothes and blankets used in a ceremony and giving them to family members. My mother got a blanket, and us little girls received cloth material. If he got a horse for payment, he would bring it home and give it to his children.

Giving Out Anger taught his son, Atini, many things because both were medicine men who avoided going on the "Long Walk." The father used to do ceremonies and sings on behalf of the Navajo captives staying at Fort Sumner. He and several other medicine men performed a ritual where they made the sacred stone offerings as part of a prayer requesting the people's release. Before too long, the soldiers let the Navajos go. I do not know how far back Atini learned his ways as a medicine man, but he was very knowledgeable. He would not allow anyone to circle around the hogan when he was performing the Nightway, Hailway, Mountainway, Enemyway, Blessingway, Evilway, and other ceremonies; he was recognized for his extensive ceremonial knowledge and ability by many people. He would tell others to keep away from where he was performing because the holy beings were present and working through him, making it very sacred. Also, he made sure that the Navajo basket he used had an "opening" or "doorway" woven into it, and he would not use one that was woven closed. Yet many people accused him of using witchcraft because his medicine powers were strong. We attended many of his ceremonies, moving after him whenever he changed locations.

Even though there were fewer Navajos back then, he got together with many other medicine men to learn the trade. They usually learn from one another, sharing their knowledge and practice with others. Those performing today argue about the correct way to say the names of certain animals such as a horse or sheep as these titles are used in ceremonies. They call the horse The One Who Put Its Foot Through the Earth (Nahasdzáán Yighá Deeł'eezii) and a stallion The One Who Picked Up the Earth) (Nahasdzáán Nédiiláhii) or Ground Blower (Ni'néinisołii). Some call a mare The One Who Picked Up the Earth. In spite of the differences, medicine men know these holy ceremonial names and do not want to share them with others; they keep them to themselves.

Grandfather taught whoever was willing and mature enough to listen and learn about traditional ways. These people were usually very careful and critical about teaching others. They did not want to make a mistake by providing sacred information that someone could "mess up" because those mistakes and problems go back to the teacher, who was blamed for the student's mistakes. The medicine man usually made sure his pupil was mature and would keep his information sacred. When he gathered us in his hogan and lectured us, he talked of how we were sent to this earth by an unknown holy one and that there was a God, so we should watch what we do and say, not curse others, and keep it sacred if we had a sing performed for us. We should never tell someone to die. If he saw that a student was living a good life, he was willing to share the most sacred knowledge; otherwise he did not. Atini's sons probably learned from their father, too. Their families moved around to wherever he lived.

Grandfather was a very respectful and kind person, greeting everyone by their clan and family relationship. My mother, her sisters, and my father,

Tom Laughter, really honored and deeply respected him, saying, "Here comes our father. Lay down nice blankets for him to sit on, and cook a special meal." They treated him extra special, and he did the same for them. He often greeted his family with, "My children, my grandchildren, my little granddaughter, my little grandson." When he asked for help, he would say, "My little granddaughter, please do this or that for me." He never spoke without his special greeting first. That is how he interacted with all of us, and that is how we knew him. I remember him saying, "My little granddaughter, put on some hot grease, stir in some flour and cook it until it's brown, then pour in some water and boil it. Add some salt and we'll eat it with the bread." This was when all we had to eat was bread. He used to sing the Windway (Nílch'ijí) ceremony on me and my oldest daughter, Arlene [born in 1942], when she was barely starting to walk.

Grandfather knew a lot about controlling the elements and working with the weather, including rain, hail, and lightning. There was a time when it did not rain for at least six years, causing a drought over the land. All of the plants, trees, and grass turned brownish red (hodiichii'), and much of the vegetation died and disappeared. Several people such as Hastiin Doo Lá Dó ("Mr. Oh No" or "How Great It Is") and his niece, as teenagers, along with my mother and her older brother, went down to the San Juan River with Grandfather. The water was hardly running with only a slow trickle. He said a prayer and sprinkled corn pollen as Doo Lá Dó walked on one side of the bank with his niece on the other. They, too, sprinkled corn pollen, prayed for rain, and placed stone offerings as they ascended the dry riverbed. Soon the wash filled with water from a rain so intense that it washed away much of the dirt covering the hogans and soaked the people's belongings as it rushed everywhere. The downpour was so hard that a few Navajos began to panic and felt that Atini had done something wrong, perhaps had even used witchcraft to affect the weather and drown them. Shortly after the rain stopped, the vegetation began to grow back in abundance, and the San Juan River flowed again. My mother told us about this incident. She said many animals had died from this drought. That is what happened. White men explain it in a different way, saying the world is off course, so that is why we experience all of these changes in weather.

Grandfather also performed ceremonies that could even bring back people to life when struck by lightning. Many have witnessed this. I understand that he even went to California when some Navajos requested his assistance. That was his job, to help others in need. One time a family called him to Black Mesa to perform a sing on a man who had been struck by lightning while riding his horse. The bolt killed the horse and threw the

Atini, even as an old man, was a controversial character who played an important role in the history of southeastern Utah. He followed in the tradition of his father, Hashkéneiniihnii, as an accomplished medicine man and leader. (Used by permission, Utah State Historical Society)

man several feet away. Grandfather told the people not to touch or disturb the body, which barely showed signs of life. Atini arrived, dressed in his Yé'ii Bicheii clothing, and began a Shootingway or Lightningway ceremony. He prayed and sang as he stepped back and forth over the person from his feet to his head. Once finished, he drew lightning going from the body outward. Soon it began raining, and as the people stood at a distance, lightning suddenly struck again, engulfing the victim in a ball of blue light, causing him to sit upright then get up. Grandfather gathered the surrounding plants at that spot, chopped them up, and put them in some water for the person to drink, singing and praying while he did this. The person walked away healed as if nothing had happened. Many people witnessed this incident.

Another time, lightning struck a woman, putting a hole in the top of her head. Atini did a special ceremony for her, and she revived, living long enough to have more children. Once one of my aunts was bitten by a snake. After they found it, Atini grabbed it by the neck and ripped it down the middle into two strips. He knew the sacred ways of the lightning and snake, so he was not afraid of them. He used to say that the harmful acts of these two beings were sent by people who had bad thoughts and used witchcraft against the injured person. It is better for one to keep their mind away from these kinds of things so that they can have a better and more pleasant life.

Many years ago, there was a plague of grasshoppers that invaded the Dennehotso area. The cornfields and vegetation had become infested with millions of these insects as the community struggled to know how to destroy them. They called upon grandfather for help, but there were those who said that his powers would not work. Still, many people who already knew him gathered to observe. He used hand trembling and crystal gazing to determine what to do and performed a prayer with an offering of "little sacred stones" (ntł'iz) to a small spring in that area. He did this for a couple of days before departing one morning. The people kept asking, "Is that all he is going to do?" By noon, dark clouds formed above Black Mesa, and it began to rain heavily before turning into a powerful hailstorm. Community members were frightened, lightning covered the skies, and hailstones piled up four inches deep on the ground before melting and washing over the land. Streams of water, heavy with foam, flowed in every direction, flushing away heaps of battered, dead grasshoppers. They had fallen from the trees, bushes, and other plants and died from the cold, pelting hailstones. The people were amazed. They praised grandfather's work and talked about it for many years, astonished to see that all the grasshoppers had been

Prayer is the principal foundation of Navajo religion. Medicine men like Atini, Hashkéneiniihnii, and Hastiin Tso of Monument Valley controlled the elements, healed the sick, and foretold the future through prayer. This woman is using her life feather (hyiná biltsós) to protect her family and bring good blessings to their home. (Drawing by Charles Yanito)

destroyed. Many of those witnessing this were other medicine men, including my husband Fred's father, Frank Adakai (Adika'ii Yázhí—Little Gambler), and his wife, whom I have also heard tell this story as well as other great things Atini had performed.

Another incident took place far up the canyon of Mystery Valley (Tséyáaniichii'—Red-Streaked Rock Valley) near Where Sheep Were Killed by Water (Dibé Tó Bííghą́ą́gi), northeast of El Capitan. Grandfather said that lightning had repeatedly struck a large oak brush–covered hill for three consecutive days until a small round object (a ball of lightning) remained trapped under a mound of dirt and roots. He described what the object looked like, saying it was very shiny and covered with tiny lightning currents, like electricity. It made a sound each time it lifted the mound. Some people observed all this from a distance, questioning what would happen to it and what they should do. They went to grandfather for advice, but there was no doubt about what had to be done. Many people gathered to watch what happened. He prayed and prayed as he dressed in his Yé'ii Bicheii clothing, walked to the mound, and spread a deer hide on the ground. The skin he used was from a deer killed ceremonially without using a weapon. It was a special hide that medicine men get by catching or trapping a deer and then suffocating it. He sprinkled sacred corn pollen, ground white, blue, and yellow, and mixed corn powder all over the deer hide. Next, he prayed and talked to the lightning object, which eventually came out of the mound of roots and fell on the deerskin. Grandfather scrambled over and quickly wrapped it in the hide, when in seconds, lightning struck the bundle and took the object away. People wanted some of the "powders" or "shake off" from the lightning left on the deer hide, but before this could be done, it was gathered up and taken to a place where medicine men held a sacred prayer ceremony (bijí) for a day. Not until it had been completed were they able to distribute small amounts of the lightning shake off (ii'ni' baa nahoogháád) to everyone who wanted some. It was considered very holy.

My other grandfather, Blackrock, received some of that shake off, which he kept for many years. He gave me some, but I do not know what happened to it. I had it for quite some time, as well as some "rainbow shake off" made by leaving sacred pollen and powder at the base of a rainbow. When it leaves a "blue" colored substance, it is mixed thoroughly with pollen and powders, then prayed over for a day before it can be distributed. Blackrock had mixed the two shake offs together and given me some, which I kept for a long time. Many people kept asking for a portion of the special mixture. For those who had some of this, they would take it to ceremonies and include it in the blessing and prayers performed for them to replenish sacredness.

The only person who knew I had it was my mother. I think she might have taken it. When I became very sick and had to be hospitalized for a year, I left my belongings in her care and never saw my sacred bundle of mixed shake offs again. I've lost many of my sacred arrowheads too. These were used during the ceremonies and sings. One was propped up inside of the hogan door posts, and one was placed in each of the four directions and in the center. All of this was around the inside of the hogan where the sing was performed. These arrowheads were packed with the sacred shake offs, but they all disappeared.

Grandfather Atini used to go hunting with a group of men each year. They rode their horses across the San Juan River near Mexican Hat when there was no road or bridge. He knew the hunting ceremony with its accompanying songs that helped the group harvest a lot of deer. He taught everyone how to hunt the sacred way, singing the songs before, during, and after the hunt. Some women went with them just to prepare the meat by cutting it into really thin slices, cleaning it off the bones, drying it, then sorting it into small packages. If they had to cut or break the bone, the women marked it with ashes before carving it in half. The bones were dried and kept separate as the men packed the meat on their horses and crossed back over the river. It was sacred.

They told me that my grandmother was very happy when one of these expeditions returned with so much meat to their home on the north side of Eagle Mesa. She took a large pot and boiled the fat deer meat and, with the men, had a big feast. That evening she started hemorrhaging, which continued for two days until she died from loss of blood, while her newborn baby died from hunger because there was no one to feed the infant. People say that one should not eat meat if they have a baby or if the woman had surgery or is sick. It is dangerous to eat meat. When this happened, her brother-in-law, Tom Laughter, took the young girls back to Where Cattle Grow, close to my father's place. Tom ended up claiming my mother and her sisters as his wives. By this time Grandfather had become widowed, and so Tom arranged a marriage for him to Kitty Atini's mother, who was young and was Tom's niece. My mother had more stepbrothers and stepsisters through this union. She had a large family and knew all the happenings within it, but she hardly ever told us about them. It is very sacred, and Navajos are critical about sharing these stories because not everyone will understand them. Some people do not care about their importance, but I believe that my mother has had a full life because she dwelled on these sacred beliefs. She was here until a few years ago, when she died close to the age of one hundred years old. Mr. Atini also died when he was very old. His hair was pure white, but he still could see and hear very well. People say he died peacefully in his sleep after having a cold for only two days. No one knew that he was dead until the next morning. My oldest son, George, was only one year old when Mr. Atini passed away in 1944.

Traditional Teachings

When discussing traditional teachings, there is so much information that is considered holy and too sacred to mention or talk about. This makes it difficult for anyone to complete a story in detail because many of the missing parts make up the whole narrative and provide clarity. Omitting important parts lessens the significance. The holy beings created this earth and its teachings with the People in mind. We were put on this earth to participate in and benefit from what is here. Like this pile of wood sitting in front of us. We burn it to keep warm, but where did it come from, and who put it here for our use? We discovered and learned how to build homes from this wood while using the dried roots of cottonwood trees to make spindles that create friction for making fires. This was already thought of from the beginning of creation, knowing that man would use it.

Weather is different now. It used to rain a lot back then. Our winters were filled with snow, and the spring always brought rain, especially during the summer and into the fall. People did not catch colds or sickness as they often do today. There is too much illness, heart disease, appendicitis, and colds. Now we have many hospitals and pharmacies with plenty of medications to treat sickness, but too much medicine is also dangerous for one's health. We often compare our body to a house that is run on electricity that produces lighting and powers appliances such as the refrigerator, water heater, and water pumps. Without it, nothing works. Likewise, our body parts work—limbs move, internal organs function, blood flows, and brains think—all because of electricity. When we are thirsty or hungry, we automatically reach with our hands to get a cup of water or something to eat. People are alive with that electrical power that runs throughout their body because that is how they are made. We were put on this earth with this "power" so that we could have life and the ability to function.

Our bodies are sensitive to a lot of things. We tend to "jump" when we hear thunder because it scares us. In our traditional ways, we have prayers for that so that we can talk to the lightning and thunder to calm it down, while at the same time encouraging rain to continue.

There is life in lightning and thunder just as there is in both female and male rain. Quiet, gentle rain is female; the quick thunderous, rugged storm is male. Lightning produces moisture and causes it to fall on the earth, nourishing plants to give them life and keep them green. The same is true for humans, who are kept alive by this power. Each time we want to go somewhere, we take a step without thinking. All parts of our bodies "work for us" together with our eyes, mouth, and ears as everything functions together. We were given this gift of life for temporary use; we can keep it into our old age if we live correctly. It is as if we "borrowed" this life for a while and are given the opportunity to use it as we live from day to day, going about our tasks from sunrise to sunset.

There is a saying that captures an important principle of life: "Our minds are to the east and our backs to the west." This refers to our prayers. In the morning Navajos use white corn pollen for their prayers as they face the east before dawn and ground yellow cornmeal for the evening prayers as the sun sets in the west. I would go out away from my home to say these prayers. They are given in the morning to go with you from the east to noon, when the sun reaches the middle of the sky. The evening prayers come from the west and unite with those from dawn in the middle. They are said for children, grandchildren, all of the immediate relatives, daily activities, the earth, air, and environment. We ask for protection from "grandfather of darkness" (chahałheeł bicheii) and "grandmother of darkness" (chahałheeł bichó); we ask for many more years of prosperity and good health; to enjoy our life and overcome our weaknesses. That is what I mean when I say "shitsii' jį́ hózhǫ́ dooleeł" (beauty is ahead of me to my head/mind); "shi-kéédéé' hózhǫ́" (beauty is behind me); "shizah hahóózhǫǫd" (beauty is well below me and beauty is all around me; let the sounds of beauty come from within me and be heard). We were given the gift of speech so that every-one can hear us. That is what is in our prayers. We pray for the people, we pray for the rain and snow that makes beautiful flowers grow, we pray for vegetation that brings us life. We pray, "Let there be beauty to me from the east, let there be beauty to me from the south; let there be beauty to me from the west, let there be beauty to me from the north; let there be beauty to me from the midst of the heavens; let there be beauty to me from the depths of the earth, let there be beauty all around me and from within me, let there be beauty to me from the mountains, the canyons, the desert; let all the holy spirits be around me. Let them have respect and love for me. We enjoy the life we were given through all these things. We pray to our father, the sky/heavens, and Mother Earth, the sun is our protector. The air of black, blue, yellow, and white are just right for us to breathe and live on. Everything was made for our comfort; the weather was made just right. We don't hunger or thirst. The holy ones made all these things so we, the Diné, could live happily with our people. We pray for all the blessings. We are humble and have hope and faith in the holy spirit. Let there be beauty all around me. Let the female rain fall on me, let the male rain fall on me, let its harmless and joyful rain fall on me. Let it make my earth beautiful; from this rain let there be life and beautiful plants and flowers that bring forth seedlings to replenish the earth with a harvest of food. May these plants bring forth my sheep, my horse, my cattle, which bring forth the young ones to increase my livestock; may I live abundantly and happily for the rest of my life."

This is how we pray. The prayer seems to follow a sequence and ties to each element. Even the medicine men pray this way, but they use different kinds of arrowheads and "nayéé" (a weapon the Holy One uses against things that harm). An individual prays to have such strength too, to fend off evil. With the "nayéé" you ward off the feared ones, and with "nayéé" there will be beauty around me. I will live in harmony with my people; they will think of me and treat me like they want to be treated and thought of. We will think well of each other. We are not to say we hate someone because that means you hate yourself. What comes out of your mouth is sacred, so speak well of others.

Our home reflects these same teachings and a person's life. Whenever someone builds one, it should be planned to last for a lifetime. The builder should pick the best logs, about three hundred of them, before starting to make it. These are cut and grooved so that they will be forced together for strength. Once the outside is built with all of these logs, any holes and cracks in between are filled with bark so that water will not soak through. Then the entire exterior is covered evenly with dirt. The compacted bark and dirt help hold the logs together. When a hogan is well built, the occupants do not have to worry about it caving in. Once completed, the owner has a blessing ceremony in it even before making a fire inside. The door always faces east because it is the path of beauty that keeps the Navajo in good order for the things of life. During a ceremony the men's area inside a hogan is on the south side and the children and women's is on the north. After the ceremony, these use areas are switched. This is because all sacred songs and prayers, ceremonies, and rituals, are done that way too. After the blessing ceremony, the family moves in and lives there for however long they desire. When it is time to move, the logs may be taken apart and used again at the new location, in the same pattern as before.

The hogan, traditional home of the Navajo, has a variety of teachings that represent it as everything from the universe to the womb. There are two types; pictured here is a male hogan with its slanted walls that come to a peak, while the female structure is rounded and larger. The summer shade house (chaha'oh) to the left keeps the rays of sun at bay and allows desert breezes to blow through. (Used by permission, Utah State Historical Society)

The hogan has its own sacred songs, as do many other things in the Navajo world. The whole earth is like a hogan. The east is always first, then the west, south, and north. Our minds are fixed to that. The east is a good, positive direction, a good way of life, in all ways. If we had no sense of direction, we would have scattered thinking. A good home is wonderful, and we are responsible to keep it that way. A hogan is where we think and teach our children. A home is the basis of our teachings, so we tell our children, "Here, this is your home, don't stray from it." Once a person has a home, they plan for additional things such as livestock and a cornfield. This was especially true in earlier days when life could be hard and tenuous. There is much to teach children while living in their home, making the hogan very important.

The home is the domain of the woman, and so many of its tools and teachings revolve around female things, while male activities and concerns go along the line of politics, war, hunting, and protection outside of the home. One of the central features inside, and of primary importance, is a burning fireplace. Even in death, the expression of the elders is "carry on the firestick" (kǫ dootį́į́l). The aunt, uncle, mother, father, and other relatives shall pass the burning firestick on to younger and future family members. The fire symbolizes this household, continuing to "burn" or exist among family members. We are not to lose ourselves in the dark and so need the fire or family influence to continue, going from one generation to the next. Prayer is an important part of this, and without it our lives become impoverished. We cannot do without prayer as part of our daily lives. Thus, a home is a place of refuge and stability where one gets rejuvenated and prepared to complete the tasks of life.

The fire poker that is used in the fireplace is an important tool of one's household. It is used to fix or make things, as is an ax to chop wood, a knife to cut, a shovel to dig, and a bucket to carry water. They are all important tools for use around the home. Imagine life without them. You would be sitting in the desert with all your belongings out in the open because you did not have what was necessary to build a home or fetch water. When a woman builds a fire, she should look for a long stick to poke it with to keep it burning. Some people are known to reverse the good powers of this poker to "bewitch" another person, which is bad and the opposite of what it should be used for, but this has been done. One should not be that way and should use the fire poker for what it is intended. Some people put it beside a sleeping child or baby who will be unattended for a period of time. They also utilize the tall grass brush used for combing hair or cleaning the grinding stones the same way. A mother uses the fire poker and the hairbrush all the time, so when she leaves the child, she will leave one of these items "to sit" with the infant while she tends to her duties outside the hogan. Maybe the mother thinks the poker or the brush represents her so that a feeling of closeness is passed on to the child while she is away. Whenever a woman sits down to cook, the first thing she looks for is her fire poker, an essential tool. Sometimes when a person is sick, they will take out of the stove or fire a red-hot coal with their fire poker. This is done four times with the embers placed in a cup of water and then mixed before drinking the contents. This cures colds and any other sickness a person may have. I do not know if this actually helps or if it is a psychological cure.

Stirring sticks are an eating and cooking utensil. They were one of the first tools our people used before modern spoons, forks, and knives became available. They are considered an important household item with different values that go along with them. Some use them to share in-depth beliefs, but I feel there are better ways to teach without using these household items. All of the beliefs behind them are about discipline and respect. Rug weaving, on the other hand, is a trade that helps fight poverty. When an individual develops this skill and becomes very good at it, they will know everything there is to learn about how to prepare wool including carding, spinning, and weaving. It becomes a way of life for them, just as a farmer knows how to grow vegetables and work with the land. They know what it takes to produce a good crop. Likewise, a rug weaver looks forward to making a high-quality product so that it will sell for a good price, bring in food, and meet other needs. It is all in the mind. We do our best at everything, seek improvement, and want to be better than others. Our hard work produces good things. As a rug weaver, one prepares the loom in a special way. The wool is carded and spun for strength so that it will last a long time. The strands are even and without crimps. Some use a little bit of moisture to make it smoother. The posts for the loom are tied together very tightly so that they will not shift and loosen. The frame has to keep in balance and be stable for a good rug. The loom yarn is bound around the loom posts without looseness, with even tension as it is set in place. This is the base of a good quality rug. The design is all in the mind. You have to plan ahead and begin the design according to how you want it to look. The comb for pounding the yarn in place has to be used with even strokes all the way across. This is for the texture of the weave, determining whether it will be hard or soft. Before welfare assistance, we grew up having to weave rugs for a living. Before we had food to eat or new clothes to wear, we had to weave.

I never tried making a Navajo basket, but watched others make them. One thing that a rug weaver and basket maker need to do is put in a trail to the center from the outer edge in their creation. They say if this is not done, the weaver will become blind and have a closed mind. This is why a colored thread on the rug or a colored strand of white sumac in the basket has to lead out to the edge to act as a doorway. I do not know if it really causes blindness or has an effect on someone, but that is the belief. Making all of these crafts takes physical strength and skill. Once a person gets older, they do not have the ability anymore.

Just as the home and its tools are blessed, so is a person's horse, and now, their car. People always blessed their horses by putting corn pollen on key spots. On a female horse, they placed pollen from the end of the tail to the mouth and back to the tail. Then from one leg to the other in both the front and back, praying as they did, asking that the horse remain healthy, strong, and safe, bear good colts, and bring wealth to its owner. People say the tail and mane symbolize rain. Today automobiles are blessed, as was the horse, both inside and out, following much the same pattern.

Life Stages

When a pregnant woman is about to deliver her baby, her hogan is prepared for the event. A piñon tree pole, which has been nicely smoothed with a rope tied to the top, is used by the woman in labor, who pulls on the rope during contractions to help push out the newborn. Beneath the mother and baby is a sheepskin or blanket. Once the child is born, it is cleaned off and wrapped in a different blanket. The baby is welcomed and prepared for life. One of the first tasks is to wash the infant and quickly clean the airways. If a child breathes or swallows much of the blood associated with birthing, they might have birth defects or problems that affect them later in life, such as a hunched back or swollen joints with arthritis. The blood that comes with childbirth and a woman's monthly menses are the same thing; it should not be touched or it will cause damage to joints. Some mothers have ceremonies performed by a medicine man when they experience difficulty in delivery. Now modern hospitals have taken over most of the birthing process, but in the past, Navajo women had their babies at home without any medical facilities or medications. Some of them died during the event or after delivery from loss of blood. That is how it was back then.

Life for children was filled with teachings and learning skills. Once a young girl reaches puberty, responsibilities intensify and shift toward being a woman and a mother. Her first menses is the sign that she is now able to reproduce and have a family. Her period indicates she is like a flower that blooms and ripens, whose seeds will dry and be swept away to the ground to have more of its kind. To acknowledge this new gift, the young woman participates in a puberty ceremony called the kinaaldá that blesses her with the best things of life. As parents, we want good things for our children, which are obtained by providing this four-day sacred blessing ceremony for our daughters. The family and relatives sponsor the event to show appreciation for having a young daughter, granddaughter, niece, or cousin who has become a woman. Out of love and respect, they will make sure she has this ritual that has been carried down since creation. The first woman, White Shell Woman, also known as Changing Woman, had this performed on her, and so we practice it just as it occurred the first time. There has to be a changeover before reproduction can occur, just as vegetation goes through the same cycle to ripen and reproduce. The young woman should have the ceremony done twice, to recognize her first and second menses, the first one initiating the ceremonial process.

Bonds of motherhood extend through each generation. This grandmother, holding her grandchild in a cradleboard, has responsibilities to teach her sacred stories and customs, while the mother often instructs in daily activities. (Used by permission, Utah State Historical Society)

As young girls, we were unfamiliar with such things, but when our mother took us to attend a kinaaldá at someone else's home, we started questioning everything. I think our mother did this on purpose as a way to give courage to face what was coming for each of us. We realized we had to follow these beliefs and perform our part when that time came. It was nothing to be ashamed about but rather to be proud of, to hold sacred, and to build self-identity. After the two menses, the girl can definitely have children. Our mother would tell us, "You girls will all be going through this someday. It is part of a life cycle, and there is no way around it, so take extra care of yourself and have self-respect. As we observe all living things around us, they go through the same process. Fruits and vegetables produce seeds to reproduce. Even corn has stalks with pollen that gives it the ability to create. This all works the same and does not change. Each one reproduces its own kind. That is how it is." Long ago, when a woman resumed her monthly cycle, she had to stay away from her family homestead until it was over. A small hogan built like a sweat lodge or a dugout became her home during that time. For men to be anywhere close to a woman who was having her period was unclean because the waste was dangerous. People were afraid of becoming contaminated, and so she was not allowed home until it was over. Even inhaling the odor could cause illness.

Young boys go through some changes too, but without the problems and restrictions associated with females. As girls we were taught to take care of ourselves and refrain from sexual encounters: "Take care of your body, be selfish, and don't share it with anyone, not even during your menses when you're married. If you have self-respect, you will not indulge in sex during that time. Keep yourself pure until you meet and marry your husband. If you don't take care of yourself, you'll have children before you are ready, and that's not right. There are a lot of crazy men out there, and they can ruin your life if you let them, so keep away from them." My paternal grandmother used to tell us about these things. She would say not to stare at any man, especially a stranger who is not a relative; if you do, he will get the idea that you want him. "You need to take care of your eyes; don't let them stare so much; it will get you in trouble if you're careless. The man that you stared at might catch you when you're alone," she would say. It seems that men always want to be in charge and test their wife's love for them by asking too much. For instance, they might say, "If you love me, you'll do this, or if you don't love me, then stop." They treat you like they own every part of you, which is probably alright, but it can also be a problem.

Couples were lectured if they had a child every year or a few months apart. "Why are you working yourself to death; you are at fault for being careless and having one baby after another. You should know better! Why are you having another baby while the other one hasn't started walking yet; you are just piling them up, one on top of the other, and not giving the babies or yourself a chance. Who is going to help you? This situation is all your fault." Concerns about this led to the advice that a woman should practice abstinence on the thirteen-day principle so that she would not immediately become pregnant again. If a woman is married, she should not have sex during the period of twelve to fourteen days after the end of her menses. Those days should be kept sacred, but they also serve as a type of birth control, so that a woman does not bother with sex. If this practice is not followed, she will have another child right away, but if this is done correctly, then the children will be spaced three years apart, which is healthier. That is what my paternal grandmother taught us. What seemed strange was that she had several daughters who did not have children, while others had only one or two. Men, I suppose, were taught the same, and for those who respected the teachings, they respected their wives. Men are a part of the team in making a good marriage. If they practice the teachings, they will do well, but for those who are careless, both he and his wife will suffer the consequences that could have been avoided if they had listened. I knew of a woman who had babies every year. She had some stillbirths too, all of which affected her health. She blamed having all of these children on eating sheep that had been treated with a fertility herb ceremony. Some people treat their sheep with a fertility herb so that they might have multiple births during a year. In reality, I think this woman was too careless with herself.

Taking care of one's body within correct practices was, and still is, essential for all girls, but now it is more difficult. A young woman might say, "Why is she telling me this? It's none of her business." Children today are unfamiliar with a lot of things and do not seem to care or listen. I am sure many of us elderly ladies were brought up with these strict teachings and lived up to them. They were quite clear what they meant. Navajo young people now get married but have no home of their own and do not know how to care for a cornfield or own livestock. Many do not seem to have a future. I was fortunate enough to be able to apply what I had learned, which makes me happy. I still have future hopes, even though I am getting old. I am glad to see my children progress in life, although one might occasionally take a wrong step. I encourage them to stay straight because they know the consequences. I talk to them because I love and care for them. This is how I am.

Another thing that is different now is the number of Navajos interested in the same sex. In the past, there were only a few, but today there are a lot of them. People used to say that some had both sex organs, while others only had one, which made them act like the opposite sex. Animals may have homosexual tendencies too. A female goat or sheep will look and act like a billy goat or ram and will not have babies. I do not know why homosexuals were highly regarded in traditional Navajo culture. All I know is that a homosexual man is treated like a female because he does a woman's job. He cards, spins, and weaves wool; grinds corn with the sacred stones; and cooks and cleans. I think we have more homosexuals now because we are overpopulated. It was not supposed to be this way, but our moral standards are deteriorating. It does not look right. All human beings were created with definite roles as females and males, but some have failed to live by them. It is an uncomfortable situation and a problem. Now it is difficult to tell who is and is not a homosexual because they hide under a disguise, are confused, and live first as a male, then a female. Thank goodness most of us are normal. One must be strong and think straight to make it in this troubled world. We cannot marry our relatives or have sexual relations with them, nor with animals.

Human beings are made for one another, just as the earth and heavens were made for each other. It will cost us our life if we do not obey, so we have to be careful in everything we do and keep our minds clear. If a person has troubled thoughts, he should have a sing and prayer done for him. We were encouraged to have one done on us every now and then. When one participates in a ritual, they should wear turquoise jewelry, moccasins, and have their hair tied in a knot. This is how it was done back then. My husband and I took turns having these ceremonies performed at our home, which also blessed our children, home, and livestock with peace and safety. Our children and grandchildren are not familiar with these teachings from our traditional religion because we failed to instruct them.

Old age and the inability to do things that used to be so easy can lead to depression and sadness. If one does not have strength of character, he or she will suffer both mentally and physically. We have to keep a strong mind and think ahead. Many of our ancestors lived long enough to die of old age because they had the willpower. I witnessed a couple of women die of old age. One family built a separate hogan for their elder, so she lived alone. At the time we were living up on Hoskininni Mesa at a place called White Plain Hills (Dah Ndaasgai) above Narrow Canyon, ten to fifteen miles southwest of Oljato. This woman had a great-grandson by the name of The Deaf One (Jaakáł) who took care of her. She used to crawl around pretty fast at first, but later became very slow. She would crawl to the doorway and yell, "My children, I am hungry!" We lived not too far away and so could hear her. My mother used to make cornmeal mush and then send me and my sister, Lois, to bring her some. I remember seeing her long, long nails; when she grabbed me on the hand, I could feel their sharpness. We were afraid of her. One of Billy Yellow's little sisters, who was older than us, used to brush her hair. We would watch and see a lot of lice all over her body, especially in the folds of her skin. It did not seem to help to get rid of them, even after all the brushing and cleaning. Miss Yellow had to tie the woman's hands together in order to comb her hair. Sometimes the young woman would tear off the elder's blouse, wash it in boiling water, dry it, sew it back up, and redress her, but that did not help get rid of the lice. She never scratched herself because her aged skin was probably too insensitive. On the other hand, she could really see. When we went to give her cornmeal, we would barely push aside the door blanket before she saw us coming. I would walk in very softly, cautiously, and put the bowl of cornmeal in front of her. She grasped for whatever she saw, grabbing and spilling the food, then picking it off the ground and eating it. The woman crawled around and ate the sand and stones, feeling her way on the floor and eating what she found. She never left the hogan, not even to use the bathroom; the family just let her be. If she caught hold of you, she refused to let go. That is why Lois and I kept our distance. The other woman that died of old age was the same way. The words that describe this condition are "yínih" (worries) or "chánah" (mourn). They carry the feelings of hopelessness and loneliness with no place of refuge. This way of thinking can become permanent and incurable to the point that a person becomes ill and dies from it. Some people do not come out of it, but for those who have faith in a higher power that can heal, we pray for wellness and curing and depend on the holy ones to help us. This is the only way out.

We all experience this feeling to some degree in one way or another. Sometimes the situation is too extreme, leading to death and destruction. One of the worst times is at the loss of a loved one. When my mother died, I felt these feelings come over me. I did not realize just how important my own husband and children were. Close family members helped me pull through my pain and sorrow. We were taught not to mourn a lost one for long periods of time because we only made it more difficult on ourselves and even harder for the dead. We should let go of their spirit and allow them to rest in peace. I know it is easier said than done, but that is a fact.

Navajo people do not talk a lot about death, but Grandfather Atini said that long ago, there was a woman named The First to Die (Áłtsé Daaztsáanii) who was the first to have that experience. He said that after she passed, her family kept her at home covered with a blanket, patiently waiting four days for her to arise, but she never did. Finally, the family lifted the blanket only to find that she was gone. They did not know what happened to her, but later in the day, they saw her sitting a short distance from their hogan brushing her hair. Family members moved toward her, but she motioned them away, then indicated that she would be leaving. After this fourth day, they never saw her again. That is why when Navajo people die, the beliefs and accompanying practices follow the same pattern. People feel that even when the physical body is gone, the spirit may be around to harm them. I believe that harm is self-induced by becoming afraid, thinking that the dead person might come after you. Problems and psychological worries affect the mind and body through illness. On the day that a person is born, their length of life is already planned; when the appointed time comes, they die. The breath one is given is taken away and goes back to where it came from. My grandfather used to tell us, "Live every day in a sacred way; pray each day and keep sacredness around you as you dwell on this earth; be respectful of all things. Live a good life, full of good things, until your day comes. Everything will have been done in good faith, and you will be at peace." One cannot go beyond the designated day of death. At the time of birth, we were given a spirit and a body. That spirit is taken back, and the body returns to dust. He used to tell us not to be afraid of the dead, for they are no longer physically alive and can only hurt us through fear. To him, death was natural and peaceful. We should not ponder a person's life activities, because they no longer exist. We are not to scare ourselves, since death is a normal process, but only respect it.

Religion

Ten years ago [1981], my husband and I joined the Christian religion. We noticed that the real medicine men were vanishing and the rituals were not being kept sacred. True medicine people do not charge large fees like they do today. There are only a few good traditionalists left, and even some of them now mix peyote and the Native American Church into the old ways. It seems to me that the Christian religion and traditional beliefs share similarities. Each teaches that there is a God and we need to pray to him, but one cannot have two faiths at the same time. As Christians, we are taught that there is one church and one true belief. It is up to us as to how we observe it. Teachings about its sacredness are the same. Our prayers are the most important thing; everything else is temporary. They are answered by the same God as we pray from our hearts and keep it holy. As Navajos sing and pray their sacred songs and prayers, they are definitely answered. My husband and I grew up with our traditional beliefs and ways—that was all we used throughout childhood and into adulthood. When we joined the Christian church and were baptized, we continue to pray in earnest.

Sometimes prayers are answered long after the individual has forgotten about them. Either side of religious beliefs, as long as it is kept holy and sincere, will work. Some Christians criticize Navajo beliefs and say

Susie mentions frequently the importance of the teachings that her grandfather Atini shared and the impact they had on her life. His grandson, here, was also the beneficiary of his many years of experience and tradition. (Used by permission, Utah State Historical Society)

they are the devil's way of worship, for he too can work wonders. This can become confusing. To avoid this problem, we pray and sing Christian songs every day, always praising the holy one. It is a good way to live. Our children have their own beliefs, and since we know both ways, we continue to pray for them every day. To have a belief is like following a path. It is a roadway to a good and happy life if those ways are practiced. God lives in all things—here on earth and in the heavens, everywhere. Everything is alive through Him. I hear people talk about how our world is in commotion and that is why so many things are happening with the weather, shifting seasons, and destruction of all kinds. One religious belief that has become popular with the Navajo people is the use of peyote. When it started, it was easy to notice, because it was a "new thing" going on in our community. Like a fad, everyone wanted to be a part of it, but my husband and I never partook because it seemed unreal. Many people joined this faith when we lived at the mining site at VCA (Vanadium Corporation of America). That is when peyotism was first introduced to some of our people. A man named Jackson came to my sister and her husband's home located close to us there. One day she told us that they had joined the peyote religion and wanted to know if we were interested. She asked us many times, but we refused and continued to practice our traditional beliefs before we became Christians. She tried to convert us, but we told her we would rather not. She said peyote was good, allowed one to "see everything," and that "even those who tried witchcraft against you will be discovered because you are able to see them clearly." We never joined but stayed with the Navajo religion until joining the Seventh Day Adventist Church. Our children had attended their school while others remained in public schools. All of us chose to either be a Christian or traditionalist. By this time, we were experiencing a lot of health problems, so we went to the hospital often. That was when we decided to join the church. Occasionally some of our children would ask us about traditional religion, and we would tell them about it. Some still follow those beliefs and use them. We all experience difficulties in one form or another in our lifetime and so become desperate, seeking ways to cure our physical and mental illnesses. We turn to a source of higher strength, higher power. It is their choice as to what they believe.

Some families who were raised with traditional beliefs had parents who were medicine men or medicine women and so passed on their teachings to their children. For instance, we know of one medicine man in Kayenta whose father was also one. The father's name was Heavy Set Medicine Man (Hataałii Ditání), and now his son follows in his footsteps.

My father's father was a real medicine man, too. He taught some of his sons what he knew. The only problem was that the traditional beliefs became mixed in with those of peyote. This should not have happened. A person can never be true to their beliefs when they keep adding newer teachings, especially with something that was not our religion to begin with. How can someone have a "substance" [peyote] similar to wine or beer and use it as part of a religion? Why "alter your state of mind" to worship? Why say that this false state of mind is a true thing? I don't think so. A true Navajo medicine man does not use any substance to practice his religion. They are in their right state of mind when they do their ceremonies. That is how I feel and what I believe.

We first heard about peyote when it came to the Dennehotso area before it slowly spread to Monument Valley, VCA, and the Oljato areas. Many people joined in the beliefs and practices. We also heard that the Utes in Blanding were using it but that many people died from peyote's effects. Some of the Paiutes who remained at Navajo Mountain used to be a part of it, too, because they did a lot of socializing with their people in the Blanding area. These Paiutes are now more like the Navajos since they intermarried with the local people. Many, many from our tribe now practice the peyote religion. They say that "peyote is good," but we do not believe it, so we never use it. It is just a fake or false state of mind, but that is not our business. People have their own choice of religion. We can only wait to see what the future will be like for them and their health. It is better to be in your right mind and to worship what is real. If you were a believer of our old traditional religion, then it is easy to transfer your beliefs into Christian beliefs because they are the same.

As time moves on, we are approaching what my maternal grandfather, Blackrock, used to teach about. He said there were only "twelve sacred songs" in the songs that were performed at a ceremony. These are sung from the beginning to the end, then repeated all the way back. According to the story, the people believe there will be twelve generations that will pass. In 1940, Grandfather said eight generations were already completed and that there were four more left. After the four have finished, everything will change, and a new or different beginning will occur. In the first few generations, our people lived freely, without a ruler. It is different now. It was said that if there were going to be a ruler, it had to be a male, the one who would wear a hat. If a female became the leader, there would be chaos and confusion. When women changed their skirts for pants and cut their hair, they began living the white man's way. They became a bonus to that society, not to the Navajo. That woman became a prize to them but

a failure in the eyes of her people. She was considered "captured" (yisnah).
If this continues, we will outgrow our religion, lose our beliefs and respect,
and have conditions worsen. When a woman starts wearing men's hats,
living a man's lifestyle, and assuming male characteristics, we will lose all
respect for our clans and not know who we are. Then "the end" is near as
our crops fail to grow and our youth become lost. This will happen when
women take charge of this world. People will not die from old age alone,
but there will be new ways introduced. Our minds will be small because
we will not think like we used to, then lose all our senses. This is what my
grandfather used to tell us, and I believe it is true because it is happening
now. When I compare these old teachings with the Christian teachings,
they are similar in many ways. The medicine men in the old days sang and
prayed in earnest about these things.

Today our children live by what they learn outside of the home. In
earlier times, parents were fully responsible for teaching their children and
making them work around their family. The youth were forced to listen,
respect, and abide by what they were taught, so it was good. Today is different. A child might be well educated, yet dwell in inappropriate behavior.
The younger ones follow their example and fail, too. Our young people
want to be independent and live the way they want. They do not think
about their parents until they are in deep trouble and do not want to believe traditional religion, in fact do not believe in anything. I think this is a
universal problem for all races. We are at the end of our era, and that is why
we have chaos everywhere, and it is getting worse. The hope for reviving
the old medicine ways or relearning our traditions seems impossible and
hopeless as the situation deteriorates. Our true Navajo religion is dying
because it has been mixed with other beliefs, like peyote or Christianity.
People used to have respect for each other, for their clans, and loved one
another. It is all gone. We have lost our love, understanding, and communication. Everyone speaks with hatred to each other. Individuals think they
are better and greater than everyone else and are selfish. Some of our young
children leave their parents and live on their own, which is what they want.
This causes them to lose their identity and potentially carry on sexually
with their own relatives. Babies who are born out of such relationships will
not have a chance to live a decent life. Say a person was of the Reed People
Clan and was born for the Reed People, making both sets of parents from
the same clan. It would be a difficult situation for that individual because it
is not right in our society and brings shame. Their peers would look upon
them as worthless, while older adults would view the parents as stupid

or crazy to have allowed such a thing. That couple's teachings will not be respected because they have made a big mistake.

Children in this situation develop attitudes of guilt, revenge, envy, and jealousy, causing some to kill. Their minds are destroyed, they have lost all respect for their clans, and they live worthless, meaningless lives. When people are disrupted this way, it is hard to teach them. When we were young, we were taught how to identify ourselves according to our parents' clans and our maternal and paternal grandparents' clans. If all is well and correct, a person can proudly say who he or she is and people will respect them.

All of these practices and events today reduce the quality of life for the living. Whether it is through war or atrocities or natural death, it takes place throughout the years and reduces our people. When I think about it, I often wonder why it happens that way. We have fallen short of doing our jobs and all that we once did with farming, herding sheep, and traditional life. Because of our illnesses and health problems, Navajo elders cannot do much anymore; our jobs are left undone. There is less of what we once had among all living things, including vegetation and water. Our world is growing old, and the life it once offered has greatly diminished. Drought has shrunk our cornfields and withered our corn; in the last four to five years many of our local people died of cancer so that now only their children are here. I wonder why everything has changed and think that as one grows old, so does everything else. Grandfather Blackrock used to say, "We will clearly notice only the first people up to the twelfth generation, but after that everything will be out of order, unclear, and confused." He said the first sign would be that our cornfields would no longer grow due to lack of rain; humans will be born with white hair signifying old age; sheep and goats will speak and say, "Have mercy on us, have mercy on us," and dogs will warn, "The end has come, the end has come."

Old teachings tell stories about how four kinds of walking metal (béésh naa ashii) vanished into the mountains in the four directions. These were the metal people (béésh dine'é) who dressed up in arrowheads. These four metal people said they would return when the world was about to end. When they initially separated, one, Dark Metal Walking (Béésh Diłhił Naa Ashii) went to the east; Blue Metal Walking (Béésh Dootł'izh Béésh Naa Ashii) went to the south; Yellow Metal Walking (Béésh Łitsoi Naa Ashii) traveled to the west; and Shiny or Crystal Metal Walking (Béésh Disxǫs Naa Ashii) moved to the north, all going into the mountains. I think about this sometimes and wonder if this should be interpreted to mean uranium minerals and similar types of rocks with properties that help produce an atomic bomb capable of destroying the entire world. These "metal people" will come back by way of uranium and other forms to destroy our earth. That is what I think it means.

All these thoughts, feelings, and experiences are part of our life process. It was meant to be, and we need to learn how to deal with them. We should not take to heart our ill feelings. If someone "talks us down," we should not dwell on it, but rather plan ahead and think positively. We have to forgive others in order to feel good about ourselves and to be happy. We need one another for support and love and can find it if we look. We should remain in good spirits and live our lives to the fullest in deep faith.

Even toward the end of her life, Susie remained loyal to her livestock and many aspects of traditional culture. Her daughter, Marilyn, also feels like no place is home unless there are sheep and to this day keeps a small flock to maintain balance in an ever-changing world. (Marilyn Holiday family photo)

CHAPTER FOUR

Culture and History

Patterns in Time

During the months of October and December 1991, I was able to visit seventy-four-year-old Ada Black three times at her home near Promise Rock, Monument Valley. She was a friend of Marilyn Holiday and was eager to share her teachings with concern that they may be lost once she was gone. For hours we sat in her home, her husband, Harvey, sometimes present, asking questions but allowing her to direct our discussions to topics she wished to discuss—and there were a number of them. Very much like Susie, she started with the holy people and their activities in the worlds beneath, adding details to the emergence story previously outlined. Her depth of religious belief, comparable to Susie's, was an unshakable foundation. She knew there was a divine plan sculpted by the holy people and that success and peace were the outcome. Deviation led to eventual disillusionment and destruction. Her answers to our questions were as much a plea to follow what the holy people had laid out for the Navajos' benefit as it was a recounting of the past.

In this chapter, some of the topics addressed in the previous two chapters will surface. Both women talk of their daily life, divination, landscape, habeedí, the Long Walk, and other subjects. Even within those topics, however, there is not much repetition and some real variety. For instance, Susie's main thoughts about the time of emergence focused on what took place after the holy people had arrived in this world, while Ada discusses events beneath this world; each teaches of the meaning behind different topographical sites, but Susie dealt more with those in close proximity to her home; she also quickly rejected performing any kind of divination, while Ada embraced a number of different types; and Susie had a taste of boarding school, but Ada had none. On a broader scale, Susie spoke primarily of Navajo culture, various life stages, and the role of medicine men and religion in her life. The beginning of Ada's teachings will pick up some of these same threads in her own experience, but she focuses more on historic events that affected the people of Monument Valley. The Navajo reaction to prehistoric Anasazi remains, the devastating influence of the influenza epidemic of 1918, the introduction of trading posts, uranium mining in the 1950s and 60s, and the role of tourism today give the reader an understanding of how Navajo women viewed these important phenomena experienced in their culture. To Ada falls the task of providing her personal witness of both the change and stability the People have experienced living amid the red rocks of this desert valley.

Before moving into the history of this area, Ada's cultural contributions are recognized. Previously, I made brief mention of The Inner Form that Stands Within (bii'gistíín). This is a fundamental concept that explains Susie's and Ada's close connection to the landscape and everything within it. Soon after the emergence from the worlds beneath, the holy people took an active part in physically and spiritually forming the new world they now inhabited. They started to plan and prepare their environment by first creating everything spiritually. Thinking and then speaking it into reality were at the center of the process. Through words and by meshing mists and other physical elements, the first spirit/soul/inner form developed, as the holy people created all things animate and inanimate. As these spiritual entities that initially had a human form came into existence, they needed a physical body and location to inhabit. Some of these beings were placed in the mountains, others in animals and insects, still others in clouds, water, rocks, and even the cardinal directions. There was no place and nothing that did not receive an inner form; regardless of its outer shape, there was inside of each a human-like spirit that could respond and interact.

Each of these spiritual beings has a personality that can be either good or bad, helpful or harmful, easily approached or difficult to access. They have their likes and dislikes, and since each was created through songs and prayers, these became the way to ask for their assistance in using the special or unique powers each holds. While they are all part of this earth under the control of White Shell/Changing Woman and were created through an extended Blessingway (Hózhǫ́ǫ́jí) ceremony by the holy people, many of the teachings about them are found in the chantways and tied to specific rituals. When one analyzes the prayers and songs used in healing, protecting, or seeking assistance, it becomes apparent that it is the inner form of a particular place or object that is being addressed. Whatever it is, it can think in human terms even though it may appear as a mountain or a fire poker. Thus, rocks, rivers, and other inanimate objects, as well as those things classified by Anglos as living, comprehend communication when the right words, prayers, and songs are used. Rivers can either help or hinder when being crossed, they have specific sites where information is delivered through shifting sand patterns, and they can provide protective power when entering hostile territory. If a certain stone or rock slab falls from a cliff, it can be a sign that something foretold is about to happen; the flight patterns of birds may provide an answer to a troubling question; and the wind or stars may have something important to make known. Those who are trained and practiced in receiving these messages can do so for the benefit of others. This is possible for those who understand the language, form a proper relationship, and maintain respectful procedures, bringing harmony through the peaceful order of words.

Ada discusses at length mountains, rivers, rocks, piñon trees, specific sites where power or medicine can be obtained, and objects like the stirring sticks or the weaving loom, each of which can give assistance and render something desirable. In her words, "Our relationship to all living things should be harmonious and follow the instructions given by the holy people to show respect and concern according to their abilities and power," including those things that an Anglo person would not consider "living." Mountains, rivers, and stars also have the potential of helping or hindering, depending on the respect, prayers, songs, and offerings given by the petitioner. This is true when dealing with wild and domestic animals as well as people. Foundational to all of this is establishing a reverent working relationship (k'é). The same is true in fostering positive interaction within the family, clan, and with outsiders as one interacts. Indeed, if there is a single word that describes the most important concept in Navajo social and religious beliefs, it is that of relationships. All else is secondary.

Ada's account of her childhood circumstances, like Susie's, underscores not only the difficult times and harsh environment, but how hard she worked to escape poverty by building her capability. Ada was particularly determined to learn food production and processing, weaving, silversmithing, moccasin-making, and other forms of livelihood to escape dependence and impoverishment. All of the running, rolling in the snow, hard labor, and strict discipline—culminating in the teachings of the kinaaldá ceremony and her launch into adulthood—were to prepare her to be skilled

"Making a living" entailed many skills that are now fading from the knowledge of younger Navajo people. How many today know how to butcher and clean a sheep, harness horses to a wagon, build a fire, make moccasin footwear, and cook different types of traditional corn breads? Elders often mention their concern at this loss. (Used by permission, Utah State Historical Society)

and independent. While every Navajo woman is different, this core goal of self-sufficiency was the direction that caring parents and grandparents wanted their sons and daughters to pursue.

In 1954 anthropologist Richard Hobson published an important study called *Navajo Acquisitive Values.*[1] In it, the author identifies eight qualities of action that explain how a good Navajo person should be. They are a summation of 335 statements given by seventy-seven men and women over a fifteen-year period. Their responses led Hobson to conclude, "The desire to accumulate wealth is perhaps stronger among the Navajos than among most other similar groups."[2] While not all had the same goals and concerns, making it necessary to qualify this statement, many people followed the general pattern laid out in Hobson's findings encapsulated in the phrases shared here.

"Make a good living" is a cardinal rule. Ada's work, previously mentioned, can be added to her reaction to the loss of her family's herds during the livestock reduction era, what she did to support her husband in uranium mining, and her own efforts nearby when the mine was closed. Gaining the necessary skills to make a living is an important quest in life. Knowledge—whether caring for livestock, weaving a rug, growing a garden, healing with herbs, or conducting a hand trembling ceremony—provides a living that both economically and socially raises an individual and family out of poverty into a more comfortable existence. Ada started young. "Making a living became increasingly important to me. I held fast to the sheep, cattle, and horses, but I also learned how to weave when I was eight years old, and by ten, I was really good." She points out with pride that she was well known and that people from far and wide came to see her because of her skills.

"Work hard and don't be lazy." Hobson is quick to point out that Navajos faced challenging personal and familial tasks necessary for survival. Consequently, there is often a deep sense of responsibility for taking care of themselves and their family members. "Look after your family." Laziness is unacceptable. Women were just as industrious as men, sitting at their looms for hours at a time, growing and preparing food, and wrangling livestock. Living on the edge left little time for play. Tall Woman, a Navajo matron whose long life and thoughts illustrate the importance of diligent work and family efforts, told of her mother counseling her to keep working hard preparing meals and keeping all of the family's property in good condition. Her mother said:

> I've taught all of you [Tall Woman's sisters] to weave, and all of you are good weavers. You will find you can support yourselves with that. You can feed your children with it, even if there is no other way to acquire food." She then reminded me when I was small, and growing up with all of my brothers and sisters, lots of times the only way she and my father could trade for things to eat before he started farming was with the rugs she and my older sisters were always making.[3]

Three of Hobson's formulas seem to be at odds with each other: "Have lots of property," "Don't be too rich," and "Never get poor." All of these need to be qualified. Navajos often pray for wealth to come their way. This is especially true in ceremonies where frequent mention of "hard goods" and "soft goods," which include both tangible items such as jewelry and blankets as well as intangible such as ceremonial knowledge, is found in the prayers, explained in the teachings, symbolized in the door structures of the hogan, replicated in the gateposts of a corral, and assigned to specific mountain ranges on the reservation. A family's reputation is often determined by the size of their herds and flocks, how well they are cared for, how they dress, the jewelry they own, their knowledge of ceremonial practices, and the horses or cars they use for travel. Nedra Tódích'íi'nii remembers her grandmother cautioning, after stressing how hard life can be:

"Someday when you have good things, save each one. Build them up and think about them. Then you will be comfortable. Nobody will laugh about you. Nobody will make decisions for you."[4]

Public opinion was a powerful force in determining status. That is why Ada mentions praying to the sheep to receive more wealth, viewing a car as "an important tool for our livelihood," and seeing her children and grandchildren working in the tourist trade or some related employment as a "great joy to see such a sight." On the other end of the social spectrum, "getting poor," which is rewarded by ostracism and loss of respect, is counterbalanced by "don't be too rich." Avoiding poverty is easy to understand. Wasting resources, entering into foolish ventures, gambling, drinking alcohol, and other unproductive activities will not take a person where they should go. In Ada's words, "There are many things that are just nonsense and useless that will not bring money or other forms of wealth." Yet becoming too rich could indicate a person is either stingy and does not care about helping others or they may be involved in some form of witchcraft by which this wealth was obtained. Ada's mention of Hashkéneiniihnii and Atini, who became rich from stealing Mormon cattle among other activities, illustrates how they used their powers to obtain livestock. Those who did not align themselves with this powerful medicine man might find themselves in trouble. Anthropologists discussing Navajo behavior often mention "leveling mechanisms" within the culture that try to maintain everyone on an even economic plain. To be too rich or too poor could lead to jealousy, accusations of witchcraft, and unfair practices, on one hand, as well as the belief that the underdog is angry and seeking revenge against that wealthy person on the other. This is true not only of material wealth, but also those serving in public office, ceremonial practitioners, and families that just seem to be "ahead" or more fortunate than others in the community. Thus, being too rich or too poor had their own social consequences.

Turning now to historical events, Ada lived through many of them and provides firsthand knowledge. Here, a brief contextual summary of each, which she and Susie encountered, will broaden their personal perspective. For those interested in more information in the prehistoric or deep history of the Anasazi, see my *Viewing the Ancestors: Perceptions of the Anaasází, Mokwič, and Hisatsinom,* and for historic events, *Navajo Land, Navajo Culture: The Utah Experience in the Twentieth Century.*[5] The latter has chapters on deer hunting, trading posts, livestock reduction, film industry, and uranium mining, all from a Navajo perspective.

Anasazi and Death

The Four Corners region is covered with thousands of prehistoric sites belonging to an ancient people who inhabited the region roughly from 1000 BC to 1300 AD. Although their culture has been studied extensively by archaeologists, researchers have paid less attention to views held by Native American inhabitants of this locale. The Navajo have a particularly rich body of lore that explains, from their perspective, the history, culture, and ultimate destruction of these prehistoric people. Their perception of the Anasazi tells more about the Navajos' worldview than archaeologists are willing to accept based solely on the physical remains. They view the sites and objects through religious, spiritual eyes as places filled with power that can harm and have permanent effect upon those who transgress culturally established bounds.

Briefly, these prehistoric people are viewed by archaeologists as passing through a series of developmental phases that led to a cultural climax by 1150 AD and an abandonment of the San Juan drainage area by 1300. Navajos are not concerned with this type of evolutionary and classificatory thinking, but look at it from a more humanistic perspective. The Anasazi, to them, were a highly spiritual people who had been with them in the worlds beneath, separated from them upon the emergence, lived throughout what are now Navajo lands, and were blessed by the holy people with sacred knowledge that allowed them to manipulate both the physical and spiritual world they lived in. Endowed with power far greater than what the Navajo hold, these people were able to control natural elements like lightning, the winds, and water; ascend heights through magical means and fly using supernatural power; and interact freely with the holy people. There were, however, problems which led to their eventual destruction. Much of what they had they began to take for granted, turning the sacred into the profane. Holy symbols became commonplace, enslavement of people was a norm, and addiction to certain types of hallucinogenic plants, excessive and incestuous relationships, and other activities deemed inappropriate according to Navajo beliefs became so pervasive that the holy people decided to act.

Pride goes before a fall. The Anasazi, convinced that they were more intelligent and powerful than the holy people, had lost their humility. With all of their inventiveness, competition, and greed, they pushed to the edges of acceptability and doomed themselves. Their destruction took a variety of forms according to different Navajo teachings, but whether it was the loss of air to breathe, strong whirlwinds, stones flung about by

Anasazi ruins like this are found throughout the reservation, left by a people who the Navajos believe were skilled yet fallen. These are sites to be avoided since those who died there may still be present. Medicine men who understand how to control their powers may use these places and associated objects for healing. (Photo by Kay Shumway)

powerful winds, fire that engulfed their homes, or drought, the result was the same. Most were killed, but a few escaped and left the area. Skeletal remains; tools like pottery, blankets, and arrowheads; pictographs and petroglyphs upon canyon walls; and their homes were all that were left behind. These sites and objects became a mnemonic device to remind the Navajo that they were subservient to the holy people and should never turn away from the sacred. Parents taught and followed strict rules of behavior that called for avoiding the sites and everything associated with these people because their power and presence could affect anyone who transgressed and became involved. Only medicine people who understood how to control these powers could go to the sites and use them for healing purposes. Sloan Haycock from Oljato tells of her experience as a little girl:

> When we were children, we used to explore these ruins and find many storage places containing corn cobs and other things like their pottery. There are many other ruins located in this area with artifacts strewn about them. All that I ever heard about these "ancient ones" is that they once lived here and became extinct. Their death is a mystery. Some say they died from being smashed by rocks. We were forbidden to go near

these places, but we would sneak a look to satisfy our curiosity and saw braided sandals that were woven and tied together as well as grass quilts bunched up in the ruins. There were also many assorted sizes and colors of decorated pottery lying around. We never touched them because it was forbidden for us to do so, and besides, we were afraid of it. Later, I went back to see these things again, but they had all disappeared—someone had taken them away. People were afraid to go near or handle the Anasazi's belongings because it would bring them death.[6]

Death is a seldom discussed topic among the Navajo. Ada and Susie rarely broached the subject, since to think and talk about it too often might just cause it to happen. That is another reason why things Anasazi were avoided. Yet Ada's fear of the Anasazi is tied directly into this concern, which was real, and so a quick foray into this topic is relevant to both these prehistoric Puebloans and the influenza epidemic of 1918. Father Berard Haile, a Franciscan missionary stationed at Saint Michaels, Arizona, provided the most extensive study concerning Navajo beliefs of the afterlife. While there are differences in what occurs following death, depending on age and circumstances, Haile provides a general understanding of how the dead are treated by the living.

The dread of the dead is universal. Preferably a person is permitted to die outside of the hogan. But if death occurs inside the hogan, some cover the corpse with sticks or brushwork, securely bar the entrance, vacate the hogan, and allow it to decay and collapse in time. Others appoint two or four men to put the corpse away. They strip to the breechcloth, untie their hair bundles, bathe the corpse in silence, dress it in new or best clothes, beads and silver jewelry, then make an opening in the north wall of the hogan, through which the corpse is passed, as it is considered improper to carry it out through the regular entrance. It is then carried to the place of burial, which is either in the ground, or it is placed under a stone ledge, and then securely covered with sticks and stones to protect it from scavengers. After interment shovels and other tools are broken and left on the grave, and the men skip and hop over brush and stones lest they disturb the soul on its return journey. After bathing themselves they join the mourning family, and remain in mourning for four days. Meanwhile, vessels and pots used in bathing the corpse are broken while the hogan is set afire and burned to the ground. The spot is avoided and called "nobody's home." The purpose of dressing the corpse in good clothes and ornaments, of shooting the owner's best saddle horse fully rigged, of removing sharp edged tools and arrowheads from the corpse is to insure the person a peaceful entry into "ghostland" (ch'įįdii-tah), and to avoid cause for fear to the inhabitants of that region.[7]

Haile's account is very much in keeping with Anna Lora King's description of what she witnessed.

> There was no talk of the person once he or she died. The body was washed after the family left for a shelter of circular branches made behind a hill. "Hurry cook, so that the children will not cry. If they ask for water and do not get it, they will cry." Food was prepared in a hurry and after eating, only two men went back to where the person had died. They prepared the body and buried it, then returned. From here they went to the burial site with their hair down, body covered with gray ashes, and wearing hats made from yucca. They attended to the burial and did not come back until all was finished. As they returned, the men talked to the dead person's spirit saying, "You have come alone into this world and so you feel like someone has to follow you, but you will have to go by yourself." This is where corn pollen was used. Once the men reached the shelter, family members built a fire for them and they washed. The relatives remained there for four days and prayed with corn pollen again. Following this period, the family moved a short distance from the brush shelter and built another home. They had to travel only as far as where the sound stops [out of hearing range from the grave and deserted home]. The family slowly moved away from there.[8]

In general, death is looked upon as a disrupting and fearful occurrence for those who survived.

The Influenza Epidemic of 1918

Elderly Navajos who lived through the influenza epidemic of 1918 viewed it as a cataclysmic event in which they encountered death on a large scale. The Spanish Influenza (Dikos ntsaa—Big Cough—pneumonia; or Sickness That Goes Around but Is Unknown; naałniih—general term for a virus) raged across the United States and much of the world primarily during the fall of 1918 through the spring of 1919. Just in the last week of October alone, it killed over 21,000 Americans.[9] According to the statistics of the Office of Indian Affairs, 24 percent of reservation Indians caught the flu between October 1, 1918, to March 31, 1919, with a mortality rate of 9 percent, about four times as high as that in the nation's big cities.[10] For the Navajos, recently revised figures suggest that within a population of 28,802 there were 3,377 deaths or a 12 percent mortality rate, while in the United States, in general, 548,452 people died with a mortality rate of roughly 2.5 percent.[11] The disease, with an incubation period of between twenty-four and seventy-two hours, attacked the respiratory system and acted as a gateway to other forms of illness, primarily pneumonia, by lowering an individual's resistance. Symptoms included severe headaches, chills, fever, leg and back pains, intense sore throat, labored breathing, and total lassitude. Once infected, a person had little desire to do anything but rest and avoid exertion. Almost half of its victims were healthy young people.

In understanding the higher mortality rates among the Navajo, one has to consider the physical and cultural circumstances found on the reservation at the time. Oral tradition has kept alive the trauma that accompanied the "Great Sickness," and though much of what was done to prevent it may appear to an outsider as ineffective, the main issue for the Navajo was a religious one. Events do not just happen, as indicated by omens appearing beforehand. On June 8, 1918, a solar eclipse occurred, presaging misfortune. Sun Bearer, an important Navajo deity, hid his light from his people because of anger, warning that a catastrophe would soon take place.[12] During the summer and fall, dawns and sunsets had pronounced reddish hues that bathed the landscape in an eerie color.[13] The tips of piñon and juniper trees started to die, a sign indicating that sickness was in the area and would be visiting humans, while some Navajos had bad dreams portending disaster. Informants indicate that the holy people sent the disease in order to make room for a growing population of the younger generation; still others suggested that poison gas or the smoke and fumes from artillery rounds fired in World War I somehow infected the Navajo.[14]

Once it struck, the disease was devastating. A few examples illustrate how quickly people died. Some Navajos tell of a Yé'ii Bicheii ceremony held in late October at Blue Canyon, approximately eighteen miles east of Tuba City. Large numbers of people congregated for the performance and contracted the disease, but showed no symptoms until suddenly they were dead. Navajos in the Monument Valley region claimed to have received the sickness from Paiutes and Utes as they moved through their area.[15] Gilmore Graymountain, a local resident, encountered a man, four women, and some children who asked him for assistance in building a fire and constructing a shelter. "They were just under a tree and it was very cold, with the wind breezing through the spot."[16] By the time Graymountain returned with a wagonload of wood, two of the women were dead. To Tallis Holiday from Oljato, the high mortality rate among Utes and Paiutes he attributed to not having the prayers, songs, and ceremonies that protected the Navajos.

Food was scarce, cold intense, with sleet and snowstorms frequent. Whole families died, while the living barricaded the doors and blocked the smoke holes from the outside to keep wild animals from entering and eating the corpses. Later, Indian agents sent teams around to burn the hogans and bury the deceased, but in the meantime, those who survived fled to other people's homes for refuge, thus spreading the disease.[17] Even those who remained at home were often deprived of their warm winter hogans, abandoning them once a person had died inside, keeping with Navajo tradition. In other instances, those who were about to die might be placed outside, hastening death but allowing the other occupants to have shelter.

Response to the illness came in two forms—spiritual and physical. Since the roots of the epidemic were thought to lie in religious beliefs, it was on this level that the most emphatic acts of prevention and treatment were found. There were two types of ceremonies to cure or prevent this illness, the Blessingway and Evilway (Hóchxǫ́ijí). From an Anglo perspective, some of these cures created more problems. While sweat baths provided both an external cleansing and a spiritual preparation for prayer, the cramped space and intense heat put those infected in extremely close quarters. Since influenza was primarily a respiratory disease, the sweat bath, like healing ceremonies held in a hogan, encouraged its spread by those infected. To the Navajos, they were divinely inspired means for countering the illness as were the bitter plant remedies made from boiled sagebrush or juniper trees to wash the body and cleanse internally. Sagebrush tea soothed sore throats while juniper pitch mixed with a red ochre was plastered on the outside of the neck.[18] Well-known protective symbols such as arrowheads and fire pokers also embodied defensive values to fend off the disease as it worked against the people. Pearl Phillips, living in Monument Valley at the time, recalled, "At night my father would lean a wood fire poker against the north wall of the hogan. He would sit up and tell us, 'Sleep my children, but do not go on the north side; if you want to go outside, go only on the south side.' He would pray all through the night. No illness came over us, not even a headache."[19]

In summarizing the response to the influenza epidemic, it is clear that the Navajos at this point were totally responding to the pandemic in traditional terms. From divining its origin, classifying it as a new illness—one not covered by traditional medicine—to praying for and testing new remedies, to reacting to circumstances for both the dead and the living, and to accepting the traumatic consequences, the People defined the experience according to their time-tested teachings. Except in a few isolated incidents, such as Navajo children in boarding schools, Anglo medicine was not a factor. Gathering together for ceremonies and sweat baths, inhabiting isolated camps, living in difficult conditions, hauling water and firewood, obtaining food, and surviving winter weather all worked against those needing help. This time was particularly hard on medicine men, who were sought after for cures against this invisible unknown enemy killing the people.

Trading Posts, Technology, and Tradition

Not everything the white men brought to the Navajo was bad, an example being the trading post. These all-purpose stores on the reservation were granted approval by both the federal government and the people living in the surrounding community. As an all-purpose focal point for Navajos living in a certain area, these posts provided basic food necessities such as flour, sugar, coffee, and canned goods, as well as cloth, clothing, tools, and household equipment. In return, the trader received wool, lambs, woven rugs and blankets, and other products such as baskets, piñon nuts, and handicrafts. There is an abundant literature including personal accounts from many of the men and women who staffed these posts, detailed economic and cultural studies, and individual store histories. For those interested in additional information about the posts in Monument Valley, see Frances Gillmor and Louisa Wade Wetherill's Traders to the Navajos: The Story of the Wetherills of Kayenta, which has a number of chapters on the first Oljato trading post (1906–10); Samuel Moon's Tall Sheep: Harry Goulding, Monument Valley Trader; and for the stores of southeastern Utah as a cultural scene, Both Sides of the Bullpen: Navajo Trade and Posts, which I wrote.[20]

The golden era of trading posts in the upper Four Corners reached its height during the 1920s, and so it was with Monument Valley. With a reservation whose boundaries continued to expand (ten land additions between 1900 and 1933); the economy and investment practices of the "Roaring Twenties"; the government infusion of assistance in the form of agents, livestock, and agricultural programs; and a tribal council to approve business transactions, trading posts on and off the reservation mushroomed. Using Klara Kelley and Harris Francis's Navajoland Trading Posts

Encyclopedia as the most current baseline of information concerning the location and number of Navajo posts, between 1900 and 1940, there were twenty-four new stores in or near southeastern Utah and southwestern Colorado. Although there may be some discrepancies in terms of official starting dates due to the transient nature of beginning establishments, what follows paints a general outline of what was taking place. Between 1900 and 1909, four new posts started; 1910–1919, five; 1920s, fourteen; 1930s, during the Depression, zero; and 1940, one.[21]

The Oljato Trading Post, founded in 1921 by Joseph Heffernan, has a long history as a focal point of the community. Navajos depended on posts like this for basic supplies that could not be grown or manufactured at home. The traders, for the most part, were eager to assist and sensitive to their customers' needs. (Photo by Kay Shumway)

John and Louisa Wetherill introduced the first store in Monument Valley approximately a mile south of the present Oljato post. This trading venture lasted only four years before the owners abandoned it for greener pastures in Kayenta. A second Oljato post, the one referred to by Ada and Susie, was started by Joseph Heffernan in 1921, and he operated it until 1925, when he died. His wife, Ann, stayed for a short time after with her daughter, Ana, but eventually departed, and they were followed by a string of owners including John Taylor, Jim Pierson, O. J. "Stokes" Carson, and others who kept business functioning until the 1990s.[22] Around 2010, this post closed. In 1925 Harry Goulding and his wife, "Mike" (Leone), began selling goods from a tent in Monument Valley proper, but eventually built a two-story stone structure with the store beneath and living quarters above. They lived there until they died—Harry in 1981 and Mike in 1992—and were an integral part of all of the events and activities of the Valley, from movie production to mining, and from trade to tourism.

At the turn of the twentieth century Monument Valley was still very isolated and insulated from white encroachment. The establishment of trading posts offered the first glimpse of a white man for children and others who had not ventured far from home. Before that, these strange creatures were a terrifying group of people to be avoided, as their Navajo names testified. Nedra Tódích'íi'nii gives great detail as to how she understood who Anglos were and her first encounter.[23] They had several names, one of which was "The One Who Wins You" (Nóhóíbįįhįį). This is in reference to the fearful Anasazi leader from Chaco Canyon who had this title and is often referred to as The Great Gambler, a name he obtained by enslaving the people he met who were willing to wager all that they had, including their freedom and their children. Only through the assistance of the holy people were they able to regain what they had lost. Anglos gambling with cards was an extension of this. "The cards were each colored white on one side and black on the other, the light side being the white man's side, and the dark side being the Navajo's." Everyone would bring their possessions, put them up for stakes, shuffle the cards then throw them into the air. Whoever had the dominant color won everything, and according to Nedra, it was always the white man. Another name was "The One Who Lives in Feathers" (Ats'os Bii' Bighanii) perhaps referring to the feather mattresses or quilts Anglos slept with. Today they are referred to as "bilagáana," the derivation of which is unclear, ranging from "Those We Fight With" to "The Ones with White Hands (gloves?)" to a poor pronunciation of the Spanish term "Americana." Regardless of the name, Nedra's grandmother taught her that they were "crafty," "never satisfied," and to be avoided.

Nedra was twelve years old and alone herding sheep when it happened.

> Suddenly I saw this creature, whatever it was, carrying a bundle slung on his back. I just started running. As I frantically ran, I thought to myself, "What was that thing!" It is said that at that time there were a lot of tramps around. I ran really hard, dashed behind another red rock, and stopped. I was sitting with my dog when it started barking. I was wondering what it was so I ran out to see. Then I saw him as he came closer with his pack. That's when I really started running![24]

She hid in an outcrop of rocks until evening, and in spite of her family's efforts to find her, she did not return home until after dark. Later, with coaxing and additional exposure, she became accustomed to these strange people. For others, it would take two or three trips to trading posts with their parents before these scary white men became more approachable. Lula Stanley's first encounter with a white man was the trader at Oljato. "One time I went there with my grandmother and I saw one. Then some of them just wandered around here in wagons. Another time there was one sitting by the road, and I sure got scared. I was really scared of them. We went over to him and he gave us some food. At that time, many white people were very kind. I was very little when I first saw a white man."[25] Sarah Begay also grew to know them through the trading post. The dark black beards growing all around their faces were intimidating, but as she traveled with her parents or white men visited the family, she stopped hiding behind her mother and became used to them. Sarah noted some good things coming from these strangers.

> When a rug was finished, my parents would roll it up and took it to the store by horse. In about two days, the horse galloped back with flour, coffee, and other things. When somebody returned, there would be a crowd waiting for him, and the goods would be distributed among everybody, which did not leave too much. They would run home with what they got. The people would eat just a little. The coffee grounds would not be boiled once then thrown out, but they had to re-boil them meal after meal. They would use the same coffee grounds again. This is how some people lived.[26]

In reality, the trading post was a friendly environment where the proprietor did whatever he could to ensure his customers were happy and would return. Most posts, including Oljato, had a guest hogan where a visiting family could spend the night; provided wood, water, and a few necessities for their stay; gave a can of peaches or tomatoes, tobacco, and sweets to customers and their children; and kept prices competitive with neighboring posts. Gladys Bitsinnie remembers that the Oljato trader, perhaps Stokes Carson, was a friendly person.

> He really understood the people's language very well and helped them, too. He used to give my father flour, shortening, and coffee and bought sheep and goat hides. At the time, candy cost a nickel and we became aware of sugar at fifty cents for a large size bag. Flour was only one dollar. Women wove rugs and the price was high for them, providing a lot of food when it was purchased but we never paid in money because no

one had it. The trader had only the kind of food that would last awhile. If you arrived at his post and you were hungry, he would give you tomatoes and crackers for free. This was what both of the traders [Oljato and Goulding] did. Traders now won't even give you something of little value. Nothing. It is like that now, but at that time the traders had hearts. When a person is going to have a ceremony, the traders helped with food and bought fabric. If the person needed help, they could get it on credit. We were sad when the one called Tall Sheep (Harry Goulding) was no longer there. When an Anglo is helpful, he or she is like a grandmother. In those days I used to make rugs, which I made to raise my children. They were large but this led to hurting my arm. I do not weave anymore.[27]

Personal relations were a big part of the success or failure of the posts. Traders who worked in Monument Valley became increasingly integrated with the activities and ceremonies held locally. Sloan Haycock remembers,

I do not know how these traders got here or where they came from, but they were childless before adopting two Anglo children, a boy, "Ashkii Yázhí" (Little Boy), and a girl, "At'ééd Yázhi" (Little Girl). They were raised with great love and care and used to help around the trading post with the chores. The traders were very helpful toward everyone and extra kind. They used to bring food out to the people's homes and sometimes ready-made yeast dough. We had Dutch oven pots with which to bake it by putting red-hot ashes around and under the pot and on top of the lid. It was good. These traders later moved and I don't know why. Their two children were like our children, going to different Navajo homes to play and ride horses. I remember how they used to stay out late in the evening to play while their parents waited for them at home. These two children never turned up their noses toward anything and were never picky—they were just like the rest of the kids. The Navajo children liked them very much.[28]

Together, the traders and the Navajos experienced many changes that brought them into the Anglo world of the twentieth century. One of the biggest transformative items of technology that came to the Valley was the automobile, the first ones arriving between 1910 and 1920. They came from two directions—those from Bluff around 1917 when a rough road appeared snaking its way down Comb Ridge, while John and Louisa Wetherill encouraged some daredevil adventurers, a collection of uncles and brothers of the Zahn family, to make their way from Kayenta to the

San Juan River in 1915. Roads followed—first sand then eventually macadam—helping to melt the isolation of the Valley.[29]

But when these "creatures" first appeared, it was anyone's guess as to what they were and how they worked. Anna King's first impression, when she was eight years old, was that "they were out of the ordinary and strong looking. We were piñon nut picking on the hills when it came our way. I was told that it was called chidí. To me it looked like a spider moving forward, swaying back and forth. The exhaust fumes smelled terrible even though we were quite a distance away from it. It even stank after it was gone for a while."[30] Jenny Francis had a car drive up in front of her, too. The elders, who probably knew what it was, used it to scare her, saying that it would chase after her. She sat as close as she could to her father, but then Mister No Hat (Ch'ah Adinii) said there was fire coming out of its rear (taillights), which was even more mystifying.[31] Gladys Bitsinnie wondered what it looked like and if she could ever own one. "There was no knowledge about flat tires or mechanical failures and what could go wrong. What did it run on? I was told the 'car's water' [chidí bitó' or gasoline] and that it had a heart [battery], and that whatever we were told not to bother, it was made from that. Things are taken out of the earth to make it."[32] Today, trucks and cars are the workhorse of the Navajo, who historically have been a mobile people, traveling long distances for the things they need.

Livestock Reduction

Eventually, however, as circumstances changed, sometimes gradually, other times precipitously, the tenor of daily life shifted. In the world of traders, posts, and Navajos, the era of livestock reduction presented one of the greatest challenges. The topic is multifaceted and complex, and has been discussed extensively.[33] Here, it is approached in terms of its effect on the Navajos; however, without a basic understanding of events, one cannot fully assess its impact. Briefly, the U.S. government determined, as a result of the economic and environmental disasters of the Great Depression years, that there were too many animals on the Navajo Reservation and that they had to be eliminated to save the grass, topsoil, and surrounding area from the effects of erosion and overgrazing. The Bureau of Indian Affairs in the late 1920s and early 1930s attempted to have the Navajo voluntarily reduce their herds, but when this did not happen, the Soil Conservation Service, precursor to today's Bureau of Land Management (BLM), enforced the eradication of large numbers of sheep, goats, cattle, and horses.

By the end of 1938, the mass slaughter of livestock drew to a close, with smaller numbers being removed into the 1940s. The trauma for the Navajo people created through this action was intense, compared by some to the Long Walk period of the 1860s.[34] A few facts and figures from south-eastern Utah illustrate what happened. During 1930 in the Montezuma Creek and Aneth area, 19,514 sheep and goats passed through dip vats filled with medicine to prevent scabies. The Oljato and Shonto areas pro-duced 43,623 more animals, while some Utah Navajos undoubtedly went to vats at Kayenta, Shiprock, Dennehotso, and Teec Nos Pos. Still others probably skipped the process entirely, but if the known totals from Aneth and Oljato areas are combined, at least 63,137 sheep and goats ranged over reservation lands of southeastern Utah.[35]

By 1934 the entire Northern Navajo Agency reported that govern-ment officials had killed or sold 70,000 animals and that the Utah Navajos' herds were down to an estimated 36,000.[36] Because the nation was experi-encing the depths of the Great Depression, the agent could price a sheep at only two dollars and a goat at one dollar. The annual report went on to say, "[A]n excessive number of goats and sheep were slaughtered for food. There is every reason to believe that the next dipping record will show even a greater reduction than indicated by the number sold."[37] Horses and cattle suffered a similar fate. Garrick and Roberta Bailey note in their economic history of the Navajo that "by the late 1930s, [Commissioner of Indian Affairs John] Collier had been successful in implementing most of his policies. . . . Along with the inability of Navajos to secure off-res-ervation employment, livestock reduction had considerably mined Navajo economic self-sufficiency."[38]

What this meant in actual loss of animals, monetary sums, and sense of well-being will never be fully understood. Tribal figures indicate that dependence on agriculture and livestock had decreased to 57 percent in a little more than a decade, although this figure varied by region, by outfit, and by individual, depending on the extent of the losses.[39] In terms of slaughtering the animals, mostly round estimates exist. For an individ-ual such as medicine man John Holiday from Monument Valley, however, there was a clear, numbing reality. He drove thirty-seven horses into the stock corrals and came out with only thirteen. Of his six-hundred-plus sheep, he kept 354.[40] In New Mexico, one study noted that between 1930 and 1935, 61 percent of the goats—the poor Navajos' food staple—were eliminated.[41] Thus a round estimate of 50 percent seems conservative con-cerning stock loss.

Corrals like this doubled to contain the sheep for dipping to remove scabies and other diseases and to serve as holding pens for slaughter during livestock reduction. Within a ten-year period, the government removed over half of the Navajos' sheep and goats. (Courtesy National Archives)

To maintain this number of animals grazing on reservation lands, the government in 1936 introduced the Taylor Grazing Act to the Navajos, which divided the land into grazing sections evaluated by how well each one could support a cow, a horse, or five sheep as a unit of measure. The tribal government then allotted a family a permit to range a certain number of animals on a specific piece of land. This limited Navajo herders to such an extent that very few remained economically self-sufficient. Men left home to earn money; women herded the sheep and goats that were left, wove rugs, and hoped their husbands would return to help keep the family intact. The end result—dependence on the wage economy and a new way of life.

This is a somewhat clinical, academic evaluation of the sheer trauma that Ada and other Navajo women and men encountered at the killing pens, in ravines, and on desert lands of Monument Valley and elsewhere. A few eyewitness accounts confirm what Ada said and what most Navajos felt at the time. Sloan Haycock remembered "seeing the animals killed by the hundreds in Oljato. They were shot to death with a gun. Our people did not understand the real reason behind this cruel action. Many of our horses, mules, and donkeys were destroyed too, because they had 'bad blood.' The people's main source of livelihood was brutally wiped out as the sheep and goats were destroyed without any good reason. It was a horrible

experience." Imagine being a young child like Stella Cly, who described
the ordeal as "scary," "being worried and confused," and "seeing our food
wasted."

> I brought the sheep home that evening with my little brother. We were
> told to bring them closer together so they [range riders] could catch
> them. Then we watched in horror as they slit the animals' throats; the
> outfit doing it belonged to John Collier. It was strange to stand among
> the blood-soaked dead sheep, with the few that were left. The people did
> not like it but were forced to do it or else they would go to jail. I remem-
> ber my father was there to watch it, too. It was a violent crime against
> our people. Later, when I was fourteen years old, our horses were marked
> and taken away to be slaughtered and were never paid for. Many of our
> people suffered the consequences.[42]

Lucy Laughter, Susie's sister recalled,

> I was a small child at the time, when my mother and grandmother herded
> the goats to the local sheep dip and were told to put some of the goats
> in a separate corral with a lot of other livestock that kept being added to.
> Then the person directing this took the animals to Tuba City and Gap.
> Next the people were told to butcher the sheep and goats; there were
> many of them. They were driven into a box canyon and into the rock
> crevices and were killed, leaving the place white with bones. Later, it was
> the horses that were rounded up, marked, and driven out of here, but I
> do not know where. Maybe all of this happened in two summers. People
> who did not want to part with their livestock went to jail and lost their
> animals anyway. After that there were no more horses. It was through
> this that many laws came about and we started being controlled through
> grazing permits.[43]

Little wonder that the Navajos refer to this time as "when the goats vanished" and "when the horses were being chased away." Sites such as Tsé
Giizh (Between the Rocks near Goulding's Trading Post), "on this side
of Tséyáaniichii' (Red Rock) behind Tse'zhinłeezh (Black Rock Earth),
and Halgai (White Earth)"—where some of the slaughtering took place—
became memory joggers upon the land for years to come.[44] Kitty Atini,
when talking of the white men supervising these operations, said, "I wish
I would have banged something on his head for what he did . . . he did a
very dirty thing to us."[45]

As destructive as the killing of these animals was to the Navajo economy dependent on livestock, there was also a heavy emotional toll on the people. The personal relationship between animal and man may be hard to understand for those not invested in this kind of daily interaction, but the Navajo herder knew her animals, their personality, and intrinsic value. They were not just a herd or flock, but sentient beings that one interacted with and that would work for a person if they took care of them. That is why Betty Canyon, as an eight-year-old home from school for the summer, still felt the emotional trauma of what she witnessed.

> I remember the people herding their goats inside a wire fence a couple miles northwest of Goulding's Trading Post—at the old dump site—where they shot and burned them all. The people cried. The same thing happened with the horses. My father cried when they took them because they were very special to him. One of them was a female that used to wear a cowbell around her neck and led the other horses everywhere. Another one was a sheep-herding horse with a white face. We saw them being shot. This ordeal was a traumatic experience for all the people, young and old. Just imagine taking the animals away from the children—animals they loved—then killing them before their eyes. Many of our people suffered mentally and some died from these feelings.[46]

Lucy Laughter concurred. "The people really went through a tragic feeling over this. There was great depression from the loss being felt. Many women said this happened to them. My great-aunts and grandmother did not like this because they used to ride horses to herd sheep all of the time, but now they were taken away. Now, the elder women sobbed as they herded the sheep and traveled on foot after them. There were only a few goats and horses left to the people."[47]

There is a final point to this tragedy, one that few Anglo people understood or connected to livestock reduction. There was less rain. In Navajo thought, when nature, man, and the holy beings are functioning together in harmony, each is empowered to bless and call upon the others for assistance. In the case of sheep, they knew the songs and prayers necessary to bring rain from the skies and water to the land so that vegetation would grow, fatten them, and make their life happy and productive, thus helping the Navajo with their food supply and wool. Blessings for all resulted. Killing the sheep destroyed an important part of the equation, leading to a shift from grass to noxious weeds, rain to drought, and abundance to scarcity and starvation. The entire function on the landscape started to shift.

Sally Manygoats captured the intimate relationship in this important cycle.

> When I was a child, there was grass two feet high that curled up on its red tips. Now, there is nothing like it. During the time before stock reduction, it would rain constantly, bringing plenty of vegetation. When people began talking against the sheep, many things no longer followed the same order. The water was dammed up and all of the rain stopped. Even some of the Anglos were killed by the water when they rode in boats upon it. A long time ago, water was treated with great respect and given corn pollen. It was viewed as sacred, as were the mountains when elders offered ntl'iz to them. In this way, life was in harmony and it rained often. Now there is not that much rain, the earth dries out, gets hard, and very little grass grows. I think what is happening now is a real consequence of this. Also, where water seeps out of the earth, corn pollen is offered by someone who knows the sacred names in order to do this. The men who know these things and put corn pollen there bring the rains.[48]

Search for Stability—Uranium Mining

The world of the past, as the Navajos knew it, had increasingly turned against them. They had to start adapting to other ways and a new wage economy, most of which was off the reservation—whether working for the Civilian Conservation Corps, building railroads, seasonal harvesting, construction work, manufacturing during World War II, shipping freight, or enlisting in the armed forces.[49] This often meant that the women stayed home to tend the crops, manage what livestock they had, weave rugs, take care of children, and hope that their husband would return with a paycheck to pay bills at the trading post or in town. Many Navajo women saw this as a low point in their history, now tied to the reservation by limited transportation, few employable skills for off-reservation work, diminished livestock, and family responsibilities that kept them working from dawn to dusk without an end in sight. The assistance that the government had provided through the CCC program of the Depression and government pay in war-related industries evaporated in the 1950s, when financial help was really needed. Both Ada and Susie mention how limited they felt, not having obtained an education and being resigned to the day-to-day routine of life.

Navajo miners worked hard under dangerous conditions without much compensation. For roughly twenty years, starting around 1950, a major source of employment for men in Monument Valley was mining. Many small "dog hole" mines were operated entirely by Navajos, while the larger Monument Two mine was at 90 percent Navajo employment. (Special Collections, Marriott Library, University of Utah)

There was, however, a partial reprieve, although some might see it as a curse, lying in the rocks and desert sands of Monument Valley. Vanadium (used to strengthen steel) and its companion uranium (used for nuclear fission) became highly sought after for national defense and steelmaking. As early as World War I (1914–18), John Wetherill mined small amounts of vanadium in Monument Valley, but it was not until 1944 that the Office of Indian Affairs leased its first claim for a mine located on the eastern end of Oljato Mesa. The tribe received a 10 percent royalty. Soon after, the Vanadium Corporation of America (VCA) opened its first operation called Monument One on the desert floor. In 1950, with the urging of Harry Goulding who provided rock samples, nineteen-year-old Luke Yazzie found a vein of ore that became the second largest mine, Monument Two, on the Navajo Reservation. Eventually it employed 140 Navajos in three mining shifts that worked twenty-four hours a day, seven days a week. For over the next twenty years, Monument Valley and the surrounding area was busily involved in extracting and processing uranium from mines big and small.[50] Navajo men flocked to mine sites on the reservation, sometimes bringing their families, but more often they were alone or with other men.

Mining was a male-dominated business with women working on the periphery as support staff. Ada's account makes it abundantly clear that female family members maintained the home front while the men worked with pick, shovel, and dynamite. It was a dangerous undertaking at the time. Jenny Francis said that her husband received less than one hundred dollars a pay period, but that was enough to encourage them to go "into the mouth of death."[51] Cave-ins (especially in the small impromptu "dog hole" mines), working around heavy equipment, handling explosives, processing ore at a mill in Mexican Hat, and dozens of other issues led women like Ada Black to encourage their loved ones not to take on this dangerous employment, but many men needed the money, enjoyed the camaraderie, and found satisfaction in the hard labor leading to a paycheck. The women submitted and hoped for the best.

Ada's account speaks to these issues in a day when people were much less aware of the invisible problem of radiation, something that most miners at the time knew little about. As time progressed, more and more became aware of its danger; the government, sole purchaser of the uranium, made feeble attempts to warn about it; and medical science was starting to get a firm grasp on its consequences. Today one shudders at drinking radioactive water from a mine, eating its clay as a food extender, and building homes from mine residue. Even in the 1990s there was not a clear understanding of how radioactivity affected people. Bessie Katso, perhaps confusing cancer with tuberculosis, said, "There was no discussion about cancer at that time, but only recently. The workers probably inhaled this into their bodies, which infected them. The yellow powder probably hardened, then turned into stones in their body so that when it becomes rock, infection sets in. They probably were not aware of this happening to them. If an infected person spits and someone gets into it, that individual will also get sick from this disease. They used to eat by themselves during that time."[52] Gladys Bitsinnie washed her family's clothes and cooked their food from water seeping out of the ground from a mine, while Anna Black later blamed the prevalence of cancer among people associated with mining on consuming greasewood. "I believe that the mines caused it. Sometimes I say that what they have eaten is what is eating up their insides. Homes are made out of uranium, too. Gravel was brought in and used to build them. My neighbor's house is like that. Many ladies have died in this area."[53] For more information on the impact of this industry during this era, see Doug Brugge's *The Navajo People and Uranium Mining*.[54]

Tourism and Today

The final part of this chapter looks at two connected threads—the ever-expanding role of tourism in the lives of the people living in Monument Valley and the concerns this brings to the elders. When I conducted my interviews in the early 1990s, tourism was well advanced from the sandy roads and relative isolation of the 1930s. It and uranium mining were the prime movers that got roads paved and minimal services into the Valley in the 1950s. In May 1960 the Navajo Nation solidified its investment in the tourist industry by dedicating the Navajo Tribal Park with its iconic rock formations, dramatic vistas, and historic culture. Development of the 94,000-acre park cost an initial $275,000, which included a visitor center, campground, and network of roads that wind between and around some of the most-photographed monoliths and mesas in the world. The growing number of visitors attests to the park's popularity: in 1960 there were approximately 22,000 fee-paying tourists; in 1983, 100,000; in 1993, 292,721; in 1999, 380,575; and 2019, an estimated 600,000.[55]

The older people living in the area have mixed feelings about what is happening today, as reflected in Susie's, Ada's, and other's comments. Some appreciate that their children and grandchildren are employed as tour guides; as workers in local restaurants, motels, and stores; and as business people selling crafts in a new visitors' center. Others feel like most of the money that comes into the Valley flows back out to the Navajo Tribal Government. Just the sheer volume of people who spread over the land can be daunting. As Guy Cly noted, "The Anglos just flock and stream into the area. I do not know how to slow this down. Now they are crawling all over behind our back. There is no hope."[56] The older women of Monument Valley expressed similar sentiments.

Ada and Susie touch upon three related issues concerning the land, culture loss, and the future. Starting with what was known by the elders as the Ranger Station, but is now called the Navajo Tribal Park, there were a number of older women who did not want it from the beginning. Jenny Francis said that initially, those who lived in that area opposed it but to no avail.

> My husband put up a fence so that the Anglos would not get into that land, but they paid no attention to it. Harry Goulding was in favor of

opening Monument Valley to movie companies, and there were some huge disagreements with the Navajos, and the company would leave. After some sort of settlement, it would return and make the movie. Some of the sacred places were ruined and are not used anymore because of all of the people visiting them. In the early morning there used to be a great strength in the sunrise. As it rose, the strong rays would grow dimmer until the strength was gone. From the sun one could see the redness of the rocks and the green trees with its rich vegetation. Corn grew just over the hill from where the Ranger Station is. Now, there is nothing like that.[57]

Gladys Bitsinnie agrees.

We were not told everything, and we have no power to do anything about it. We have leaders, but they are not given information, so the Anglos just do as they wish. There is no such thing as the people having a say in this matter. It seems like the white man just came for a visit to eat out of our home. To this day we are of no value to them. We don't like it. There were elderly men there once who were like guardians, protectors of that place. Now that they are gone, only their children are left, and most of them have moved out. The people who own that land do not bother with it now.[58]

Bessie Katso expressed fear that the road down through the monuments might be paved, even though the Navajo people opposed it. Underlying part of the resentment was that with the improvement, the Anglos would take away the land. Plus, their presence was "ugly" as those with "bushy hair crowd into the stores" and bring "bad tobacco through here," and sacred places were being desecrated. "A long time ago, we were told there were certain things that should not be done in these holy sites and not to harm Mother Earth. Now we cannot chop trees for firewood. There never used to be words against this, and there was not a lot of sickness going around. I think that is the reason we have problems now."[59]

An Anglo listener might look askance at these ideas, but in the Navajo worldview, it makes perfect sense. Everything in the environment shares relationships in a sentient universe. To run roughshod over the land and its "beings" defies the type of interaction that brings peace and harmony. Nellie Grandson believes,

We should have not abused Mother Earth, but the Anglos are doing it. They have also gone to the heavenly bodies like the moon. We are abusing the element of harmony in every direction up, down, and in the sacred places. That is why sickness comes to us without hesitation. In this day and age, things have changed and are not like they should be. The earth attacks us without hesitation. Some of us say no to this outrage of destruction, but it is becoming clear that the earth is of no value to many. We are at a stage where we say our prayers but feel like there is little response to our pleas. White men are designing things so quickly that we will come to a point where there will be no way of avoiding what they have done.[60]

Sloan Haycock adds: "We no longer have large planted fields. We do not see the younger generations out there planting, hoeing, or irrigating, much less herding livestock. Only the sheep dogs look after the animals these days. In the past, we had to herd the sheep out to the grazing pastures, not the dogs! Our younger people are now employed at all kinds of odd jobs."[61]

Yet not all of the problems the Navajo face are solely the doing of the dominant culture. Elders recognized that their children and grandchildren have been raised in a very different environment than the one they knew and that it has shaped the younger generations in different ways. It is a two-edged sword. Being caught between the high value placed on learning and earning a living while following traditional teachings can sometimes cloud the path to embracing what lies in the future. For instance, Sloan Haycock had strong feelings about education but bemoaned some of the accompanying discordant notes that went with it.

I believe education is extremely important. Any uneducated person will tell you how much they wish they had gone to school because it opens many good opportunities for an individual, and helps one to find a good job and make a decent living. A good education will help a person to go far in life and be competitive. He or she will have the ability to make it in this world. I have seen many women working in business offices or teaching, and that is good. One has to know how to read in order to learn and know how things work. I can't read my Bible because I don't know how. To be illiterate is to struggle. Unfortunately, some of our young people are taking their schooling for granted. They would rather waste their time and get into trouble with drugs and other harmful things. Many of our young people have gone crazy and do not respect others, much less themselves and their clans. They do not want to listen to their parents

There is no more iconic rock formation in Monument Valley than the Mittens, sitting at the doorstep of the Tribal Park's Visitors' Center. Betsy Yellow reported that in the early days, when the Gouldings were just starting, they rode into her camp and kept pointing at the rock formations, repeating "money, money." Betsy could not make sense of it at the time, but now, the meaning is clear. (Photo by Stan Byrd)

and teachers. I think this is happening because of all the social activities that go on in the schools, like dances, movies, and so forth. In some cases, they have become hostile.[62]

Stella Cly sees similar problems.

Our children seem to be more respectful, but the youngest generation is not and likes to argue and raise trouble. They get mad because they don't want anybody else moving into the valley, while the older generation is not like that and is kinder. People used to live in harmony when they lived in the Tribal Park valley. This land was made for everyone. We cannot say it is ours. For those that were born and lived here the longest, they have seniority. The land was always here; it has not changed, but the people have. I do not know why everyone is fighting over it because that is wrong. It already belongs to the unborn, who have their right to live on this land, too. Some people in the valley claim the famous rock formations saying, 'This mesa is mine,' but that is not so. These mesas were there long before their time and our land sculpted itself—not us humans—so we should not argue over it. When I visited the valley, that was all I heard among our people. I was fortunate to have lived there, all alone, before this commotion. It would be nice if the people would quiet down.[63]

In comparing the past to the present, Betty Canyon felt that a tremendous amount had been lost and that the Navajo culture, as she knew it, was in great jeopardy.

We no longer have or live by our elderlies' teachings, they are gone. Our people live as if they were small children, tending a household, while their parents are away. As far as our environmental conditions, we have more devastating windstorms and less rain, and when it does rain, there is more lightning and thunder, which is scary and dangerous. Our vegetation and water supply for our livestock has become depleted, the land exhausted and barren, and ceremonies diminished. I believe this is due to our people no longer practicing or believing in the sacredness of our traditional faith. All we hear nowadays is "Ch'įįdii-bí." (It's the devils). The sacred corn pollen, arrowheads, and "hadahoniye" (sacred mirage stone) belong to the devil, therefore, I do not want any part of it. I only want Christian religion. That is what some of our people are saying. I remember, when I went to school in Fort Wingate, we had many people and preachers come to speak to us. They preached saying, "You don't steal, use foul language, or tell lies, etc., because the end will come in five years." I never understood what they meant by that. It has been many years since then, and nothing has happened. They must have meant the end of their own lives, for they are no longer alive. When I hear people say, "It belongs to the devil," I think to myself, "Of course, he is the owner of this world. The devil has been here since creation, along with everything else." I believe it depends on our prayers, and that is all we can do—pray.

Some of my people have asked, "Why are you praying with corn pollen? You don't need it," but I don't think there is much difference between our traditional beliefs and the Christian ones because we all pray to the same God. My grandmother prayed with white ground corn in the morning, corn pollen at noon, and yellow corn in the evening, and we have survived this long. Furthermore, our population has grown to what it is today, so I don't believe that sacred corn pollen is worthless. I know it is powerful and works. Still, many of our young people do not like to perform the rituals involved in a ceremony, especially when they have to undress for the "sacred wash" or "sacred charcoal application." They are too embarrassed and have a difficult time repeating prayers after the medicine man because they do not know their own language. I have witnessed many of them. In one instance, I saw a young boy have a "sacred smoke sing" at John Holiday's place. The boy did not want to cooperate and kept running off. His family had to hold him down and help him say the necessary words to the prayers. I heard he returned later and asked Mr. Holiday to perform a second sing which went pretty smoothly; his mind had healed and he was able to say the sacred prayers so that today he leads a normal life.[64]

Many other elders are also concerned about young people turning away from their language and culture by accepting that of the white man. Not only did the holy people give this language to the Navajo, but it is also the unique core of understanding and thinking about elements within the culture. Movies and social media reinforce these losses. Traditional Navajo beliefs teach that what one talks about, acts out, or thinks will become a reality in that person's life. Early Westerns often portrayed the Indian as the villain, who at the end of a movie gets killed attacking a wagon train, fighting the cavalry, or getting shot by a white hero. Even though the movie industry extended a financial lifeline to those seeking employment, it also challenged traditional beliefs at odds with Anglo culture. Betty Canyon points this out when referring to Indian extras who died prematurely because they had "practiced" it when filming.

> Movie outfits sometimes do "outlandish" things; it's no wonder most of our Navajo actors are dead today. Our people were forbidden to take part in such things, but the money made them blind. Another wrongdoing occurred when Mr. Hite Chee, a medicine man, was asked to make a sandpainting inside a hogan, while a coyote stood atop watching him through the smoke hole. The coyote was taking part in the movie. This was absolutely forbidden in our beliefs. It caused Hite Chee's death. Many of our people complained about this, but it still happened. The white men took our sacred sandpaintings and did what they wished.

Alcohol is another concern. Although the reservation has historically been "dry," there have still been far too many drunk-driving accidents, broken homes wrecked by booze, and lives captured by the bottle. Nellie

Grandson testifies that "our children" are seduced by drink and "go crazy" with beer and wine. They fail to listen to the voice of reason.

> Beer has no relatives. We plead to the people not to drink, but the Anglos keep selling it to our children because of money, and there is no power to remove it from our land because they have papers claiming they can sell these items. When our children consume it and something happens, we are blamed by the police officers who say "This is what your child did," how much the bail is, how many days in jail, and that our children cannot be visited. Yet it is the white man who is selling it, but it is our children who step off the road. This is what I say.[65]

Many of the comments shared by these women in the early 1990s were a representative expression of how they viewed the world. The elders did not mince words. Ada's comments are perhaps more hopeful and reflect a more forgiving attitude toward members of the dominant culture. The adoption of and adaptation to elements of twenty-first century America has decreased knowledge and practices of traditional teachings and has become the environment of choice for those who know relatively little about the old days and ways. For those who lived and loved those things of the past, there is a sense of real loss; for those who never experienced and do not understand them, there is a superficial appreciation without a strong desire to return to what, for many, seems almost foreign. There are, of course, those who hold in high esteem their elders, practice traditional values that are often segregated from the work-a-day world, and attend ceremonies. But even many of these need to have help with ritual etiquette and word translation. Cultural change has become a constant.

Sally Manygoats speaks to Navajo beliefs concerning the end of the world. In a sense, she described much of what is going on today. Most elders who have been taught about this would agree that we are close to that time. The signs are upon us. Sally taught that:

> There will be an end to how we know our life. When we approach this time, the songs will be forgotten. The people will start asking each other about the songs of the mountains and which order they go in. Now we are close to that. No one is relearning the songs or knows the ways. None. There are some elderly women who know many of the stories because they probably asked their maternal grandfather, grandmother, and father. It is said there would be prophesied events that will happen in the blink of an eye, and it will end just like it did for the Anasazi. All that will

remain are the broken-down homes in clusters. This is what is called the coming-to-an-end when all of the people will be withdrawn off the earth. When this happened in the past, water forced the holy beings to come to this world. When it is going to happen this time, there are predictions of what will take place. The sky will grow to the ground from this side, then this side, then this side, then this side, and when it comes to the middle, that will be the end. There will be no people, none. One of the elements, such as fire, will be used to destroy us, but life will go on. It will be like this.[66]

Thus it ends and a new beginning starts.

CHAPTER FIVE

Ada Black

Engaging the Navajo Worldview

Marilyn and I arrived at Ada Black's home near Promise Rock in Monument Valley around 10 a.m. on October 11, 1991. A handful of chickens and a few dogs greeted us as the car doors swung open and we started toward the house. The sun, heating up the day after a chilly night, was welcomed; a short rap on the door, rustling and footsteps inside, soon brought forth a short gray-haired woman peeking through a small crack between door and frame. Marilyn knew Ada but was not related and had only slight interaction with her over the years. Addressing the elder through kinship terms, Marilyn explained that we were there to talk to her about life in Monument Valley and how she viewed the changes taking place. As a seventy-four-year-old, she had weathered many of the storms that had blown across Navajo country over the years—livestock reduction, uranium mining, the expansion of tourism, and other historic events. She had survived them all. Would she be willing to share her thoughts?

The door opened, and she invited us to sit by the stove on a chair and couch, while she banked the coals of her morning fire. Breakfast had been over for some time, and her husband, Harvey, rested on a section of couch, while Ada pushed and prodded the larger pieces of burning wood into the center of the fire with her poker. Adjusting her dress and smoothing her hair, she sat down before us and introduced herself.

My name is Ada Black of the Tł'ízí Łání (Many Goats) clan, born for the Tódich'íinii (Bitter Water) Clan [on July 10, 1913]. Táchii'nii (Red Running into the Water) is my paternal grandfather's clan, and Ashįįhi (Salt) is my maternal grandfather's clan. The man that I live with is of the Bit'ahnii (Folded Arm), born for the Ashįįhi Clan. We were married when I was sixteen years old and have lived in Monument Valley since then. I was still like a child when I came here. My family's home where I was raised was between Navajo Mountain and Shonto [Arizona], near the state line about a mile and half into Utah. My maternal grandmother was still living there, yet I do not know what her name was, but Asdzą́ą́ Náli (Lady Grandmother on father's side) was the name of the grand-mother who raised me. My paternal grandfather was Ashįįhi Ałts'íísí (Small Salt), and she was with him while I grew up there.

While I was only picking up parts of her introduction, I did recognize that her heritage derived from the Salt Clan, very likely indicating that she had strong ties with Navajo Mountain, a place well known for its con-nection with this clan. Ada, unlike some women we had visited, appeared eager to share her knowledge with us. As the conversation developed, she mentioned that she had a growing concern that many of the things she had been taught or experienced would be lost and that few of the young people now have a real interest or even understanding of many of the old ways. The teachings were slipping away, and it was hard to stem the flow. She held much of it sacred but found in her elderly years decreasing community support, fewer practitioners and knowledgeable medicine men, and an accelerating pace of life for many. Harvey, who chimed in occasion-ally in support of his wife's concerns, could see cultural practices becoming diluted. While he did not seem to have the same depth of knowledge about some of the things Ada discussed, he shared sidelights and some-times corrected her.

This led to an interesting experience. Our discussion was wide-ranging, at times dealing with the mundane, then dipping into a spiritual expla-nation as to how and why something occurred. As we progressed, Ada suggested we go into her bedroom off of the main kitchen-living room area so that she could share some things with us. Harvey remained by the fire. As Marilyn continued to ask questions, lend supporting agreement to what was being said, and recall some past events, I noticed that there were times when Ada lowered her voice and changed her tone markedly. Even though I wondered why she did this, I did not want to stop the flow to ask Marilyn what was going on. Aware of how Navajo people have a deep

respect for the sacred, how the holy people are always listening and reacting, how animals and other creatures can be offended if stories are told at
the wrong time of year, and how language has a power and force all of its
own—I began thinking that Ada was sharing something deeply spiritual.
What could it be?

Around 4 p.m., the sun was moving behind some of the large monoliths
close to Ada's home, indicating that we had better be on our way so that
she could finish her chores and get supper started. We promised that we
would return to continue our interview, paid her for her time, and thanked
her for all that she had shared that day. When Marilyn and I reached the
car and drove out to the main highway, I asked why Ada had lowered her
voice and spoken so softly, expecting one of my four explanations to surface. Not so. Marilyn said that the reason for moving into the bedroom was
that Ada had many teachings that belonged to her and not her husband.
Knowledge, something as tangible as a physical item, had specific bounds
of ownership. I paused. Why did she decide to share this information with
two relative strangers and yet exclude her husband? Marilyn suggested
that within Navajo culture there were proprietary bounds for this kind of
information, and yet in some ways, those strictures relaxed when dealing
with an outsider. This surprised me since most of my experience had gone
in the other direction, where information was not shared because I was an
outsider. Ada's main reason, however, was to share her teachings with the
upcoming generation.

Another lesson learned that day that I still wince at is my personal
feelings about taking people's pictures. In the back of my mind it seemed
invasive and made the interview more of a "production" than I wanted it
to be. Consequently, I do not have any pictures of Ada, Harvey, and the
setting in which we visited. I regret not having quickly snapped a photo or
two, but history will have to wait until one surfaces. For now, only Ada's
voice is left to teach.

ADA'S STORY, PART ONE

When I first came to Monument Valley with my husband, Harvey, his
mother and father, and his maternal grandfather called Hastiin Hawohee
(sound of a bird) of the Tódich'íinii Clan were living here. Then there was
his paternal grandfather, Hastiin Nálí, of the Bit'ahnii Clan. A man called
Dághaałbáhí who lived around here became another in-law to this clan.
These three men lived here. In Mystery Valley (Tséyáaniichii'), there was a
man called Hastiin Bitsii Łichíí'; I do not know his English name, but he

was of the Ashį́įhi Clan and was living here when I first arrived. These were
the elderly men—Dághaałbáhí, Hastiin Nálí, Hastiin Hawohee. Hastiin
Hawohee's grandchildren are the only ones that are living around here
now. There were no other people except in the Narrow Canyon area, where
a man called Hastiin Chaan Diniihi (Bowels in Pain) used to live. Near
El Capitan (Aghaałá—Much Wool; a rock formation) lived Tłízí Doo
Yiyáani and Hastiin Nilaai (Man Who Lives Near El Capitan). These are
the names of the Navajos who migrated around here and the El Capitan
area.

When I was five winters old, my mother died, and my father left for
his relative's area. My maternal grandmother was the only one who raised
me, my two sisters, and three brothers. One sister, who was a year older
than me, passed away in an automobile accident several years ago, as did
my oldest brother, who died five years ago. Thus, my two older siblings are
gone, and I, as the third oldest, now have two brothers and a sister.

We were raised well with plenty of food because we had sheep, which
our mother left to us when she died. We went after sheep because at that
time there was no other help with food. Sheep was our primary meat as well
as wild onions (tł'oh chin) and azahaleeh (literally, "put it in your mouth,"
a small plant that grows for a month in the springtime and is added to
soups, etc.), which I gathered while herding. My grandmother used these
wild foods in her cooking, which made her stews taste very good, especially
when she added corn. After spring arrived and things began to ripen, there
was chiiłchin (sumac), kai dootłízh (green greasewood?), tsidzé wóloo
(wood to make arrows), and sidze' (juniper berries), which are also flavor-
ful. All of these grow in abundance at Navajo Mountain. One month after
planting our crops, these delicious plants ripened. We enjoyed eating them
and so filled our pails and brought them home whenever we found some.
This was our food while growing up. During this time there was no sickness like stomachaches, which was fortunate because the closest medical
services were in Tuba City, where medications were given out. I was a very
healthy girl. I did not go to a hospital until I was in my late twenties or
early thirties once healthcare arrived in Monument Valley.

Grandmother had many young children to teach back then; her training was often difficult. She told us not to be lazy and to run to her even
though it was cold, because any physical discomfort was just in our mind.
By ignoring it and exercising, I would have endurance, and so she insisted
I run in the early morning or crawl bare-chested in the snow. "All of this
discomfort is just in your mind; you can get warm from this." If I followed
her teachings, I would be able to endure whatever confronted me in life by

providing a type of protection. So, I crawled partially clothed in the snow even when it was very painful, doing it four times in a row. This often felt like it was too much. Just as bad was shaking snow off of tree branches onto my naked body. It was cold enough to take your breath away and felt devastating. I also ran long distances until my legs felt like they were going to fall off. Each run I made, I had to increase the length of time, go to a different place, and always turn back in a clockwise direction. This was like running your course of life and taught us to think before we spoke, to cherish the good things in life, and to avoid self-destructive thoughts. Running hardens against the elements of life that confront a person, making one strong to encounter everything. There are things from the unseen that will bother a person. This is why we had these activities to give us endurance, I was told. Grandmother chased me around to do these kinds of tasks, but I did not talk about how I felt. I would never say, "Don't bother me. I'm sleeping," but did what I was told.

As I grew up, one of my main responsibilities was herding sheep, and so I learned everything there was to know about taking care of them. The same was true about handling horses, managing cattle, and learning daily skills. Grandmother told me that having life is all about taking care of the sheep, for they, like cattle, are money, while the horse is for traveling. This is what she used to say to me: "There are many things that are just nonsense and useless that will not bring money or other forms of wealth. This is how one walks in life; one's teachings sometimes might be frightening but are of great value." When I used to plant, I made offerings all the time. This is what I used to do, saying many prayers that served as a shield when I walked behind it, no matter where I went. In the summer, my maternal grandmother and grandfather moved on the far side of Navajo Mountain to the canyon, where we planted our gardens and tended peach trees. Water from the mountain fed these plants. We spent the entire growing season there and seldom traveled. The fall brought harvest time, and then, in preparation for winter weather, we moved toward Shonto and the canyons away from the mountain. This is what I was aware of at that time and acquired for life.

Making a living became increasingly important for me. I held fast to the sheep, cattle, and horses, but I also learned how to weave when I was eight years old, and by ten I was really good. There was no one my age who compared to my ability in weaving. I wove what was called the folded saddle blanket. At about the age of twelve or thirteen, I learned how to make Navajo wedding baskets from sumac and then moccasins with cowhide soles. When the hunters returned with deerskins, I removed

Navajo Mountain (Naatsis'áán—Head of Earth Woman) is an oasis in the red rock desert of southeastern Utah and northeastern Arizona. Corn, beans, and squash—staples of the traditional Navajo diet—were planted in terrain like this by Ada. (Photo by Stan Byrd)

the hair and tanned them. I then twisted the hides, softened them, and sewed the material into moccasins with long strips of deer sinew. Many of these shoes I sold to Anglo people. This was the start of my making a living, based upon the teachings of my people. During that time, there was little interest in becoming schoolchildren. One of my younger and an older brother went to school, but no girls. My maternal grandmother hid us very well. If I had gone to school, I would have really worked on many things, but now, the only thing I know is work around the home and caring for sheep, horses, and cattle. I was raised only with this.

Creation—In the Palm of Time

Navajo culture and life are rooted in the holy people, who established the rules and directions that guide us. This all goes back to the beginning of time on this earth. Beneath this world, there are four other worlds in which different creatures lived before they were no longer able to remain. They emerged through these different levels until they reached this, the Glittering World, where we live today. All of this information is very sacred, so it should be handled carefully. I have ceremonies performed for me in this way, and so I am protected. This is the way the teachings go. There are many stories to tell, but I will only discuss their tips, so what follows is just a small piece of what happened. There are stories upon stories, ones that go back to the beginning or palm of time, then through the gradual emerging into this world. Each of these narratives has others attached, all of which serve as the basis for our healing ceremonies.

In the beginning, there were four worlds beneath this one through which the holy people, in the form of creatures, emerged. The insect people were first to develop in the bottom world along with First Man and First Woman. Each of these realms had its own challenges and experiences that led to problems and eventual destruction, forcing its inhabitants to move upward to the next level. In the Yellow World beneath our Glittering World, there was an incident that profoundly affects us today. There occurred a separation of sexes due to a domestic dispute over adultery, jealousy, and pride. The men crossed a large river filled with supernatural power, and for four years remained alone without women. The men, however, had a male homosexual (nadlé), who by choice performed female duties such as cooking, carrying firewood, spinning and weaving wool, planting and caring for crops, and other skills that the men no longer had fulfilled because there were no women. Some made the nadlé their wife even though he was a man. We have these kinds of people today, and it is said that they will always exist in the population.

There will also always be those people who are handicapped. They are the ones who make life stable. When this kind of child comes into a family, the members must take care of him or her. It is said that those with handicaps receive far more protection from the holy people. When the emergence took place, both the nadlé and the handicapped came with the people and were highly respected—one for all of his skills and knowledge and the other for his special status with the holy beings. Women especially like to have a nadlé around to do difficult chores that require strength or protection. Through him comes the good life. This is what my maternal grandmother used to say.

When separated in the world beneath, both males and females turned to improper activities with different objects to satisfy sexual urges. From these perverse actions arose different types of creatures with destructive powers and abilities that created problems in the next world. The women gave birth to these monsters of various forms and abilities that preyed upon the people and forced two young men—the Twins—to obtain weapons from their father, Sun Bearer, a story to be discussed shortly. For now, the women were pregnant but had not yet brought forth these creatures. There

was, however, Coyote, an infamous trickster and troublemaker. His decep-
tion and scheming were well known, and he acted very much like a human.
At times he would try to kill himself, would sleep with his relatives, even
his daughter, and would steal whatever he could. Because he was known
for this kind of behavior, the people soon suspected him of taking a water
baby from its mother, the Water Monster (Tééhoołtsódii), and hiding it
in his clothing. The angry, vengeful monster flooded the world beneath,
forcing the people to evacuate. The water kept rising, which at first did
not alarm the creatures, but as it rose higher, they began to search for an
escape route. By growing different types of plants, the evacuees hoped to
reach the sky and safety. They tried many kinds of trees, such as pines, but
these grew too slowly, just a little bit each month. The water continued to
advance, and there was no place to turn.

The people searched about for a different solution and came upon two
men who agreed to help. They were found sitting in a round, open-sky
brush enclosure. The people explained their predicament and asked for
assistance. Before starting, they inquired as to their names, but both men
agreed that they could not identify themselves in front of each other. One
offered to walk away while the other remained to tell about the one who
departed. He said that his name was the Sun. Then he left and the other
returned, the people learning that he was the Moon, and he explained, "We
do not call each other's name in front of each other." At this point, these
two heavenly bodies in human form gave the people the seed of a hollow
reed (lók'aa' tsoh) capable of growing quickly into the sky. The Sun gave
planting instructions and volunteered to speak to the seed and directed it
to extend to its full height in four days. The reed agreed, and during that
time grew tall and wide enough for the people to use as an escape route to
the next world. Where the leaves of the reed had branched out, there was
enough room for the travelers to rest upon during their twelve-day journey
to the next realm. Birds, badgers, mountain lions, different types of ants,
and every other creature traveled and slept in groups, using their arms, legs,
and wings to move through the reed.

By the end of the twelve days, the creatures reached the top but were
blocked by the earth surface above. Badger came to the head of the line
and with his sharp claws dug and dug. He made good progress, but as he
was about to break through, the people cautioned, "There is no way we
should punch through. There is water on the other side of this roof, lots of
it. You, Cicada (Wóóneeshch'įįdii), will go up there because you are small
and do not blink." Cicada broke through the crust of earth and crawled
out on the other side, pushing the mud on the surface together around the

hole. Waves of water came toward him, then went around and past. Four times the water tried to wash away the earth, but Cicada continued to pile more protecting mud around the opening until the water ceased. Still, the Water Monster below knew that Coyote had its baby and wanted it released. Eventually, after reaching the next world, the thief relented and returned the child, and the waters subsided.

On the surface, four birds, each from one of the cardinal directions, challenged Cicada for his right to emerge and settle in their world. This happened four times as each of the birds presented a new test. The final challenge was when one of them passed an arrow through its mouth and drew it out of its anus. Cicada quickly answered that that feat was not all that special since there was already an existing hole at each end. He dared the bird (táłtł'ááh ha'alééh—blue heron) to perform what he now did, which was to pass an arrow from one side of his body to the other, appearing to go right through the heart; he next passed it through going in the opposite direction. Today, cicadas still have a hole in their midsection that allows them to do this. When the bird tried to perform the trick, it died. Cicada had won the right for the creatures below to emerge and become part of this world. This story teaches why the Navajo are so connected to their land. Whenever there is a war of words, saying that the earth does not belong to us, we strongly oppose it, since we have the knowledge that we have earned it through Cicada winning this contest. With this understanding, we are stable.

Following the emergence, there were other important events that affected the Navajo. Mother Earth and all of its animals, plants, birds, water, mountains, rocks—everything in human form—met in council to determine how the earth should be prepared for the soon-to-be-created Navajo people. At this time, each being received an inner spirit and an assignment as to its role upon the land. All of them bathed and placed cornmeal upon themselves, then ate a small amount of corn pollen, as part of the Blessingway (Hózhóójí) performed in preparation for life on earth. Now the things that they had been taught became theirs, and the knowledge of life began. Sacred words were pronounced upon all animate and inanimate beings before they departed to their assigned locations. These were the prayers, songs, and offerings that opened up their assistance to humans. With all of this came a variety of vegetation, different seasons of the year, offerings to the Sun and Mother Earth, and the sacred stones to give in thanks.

At one point, the mountains began to ignore the teachings and responsibilities they had been given and acted crazily like teenagers. They started to slide around, wander, and not care for themselves. In order to bring them back to order and calm them so that they could resume their important duties, the holy people crushed and mixed plants from the mountains into a blended tobacco, then had the mountains smoke it to settle them. Talking God (Haashch'ééłti'í) offered prayers on their behalf as he and the other holy people sat in the thought-planning hogan (naat'á hooghan) and sang the mountain songs. This called the mountains back to their senses so that today, we still use mountain tobacco to calm an individual who is acting out of control with self-destructive behavior. Now we are in the midst of craziness.

Following this, the rhythms of life resumed on the earth. Mother Earth and everything on it was ready to teach and assist the Navajo people as long as they showed respect and established a positive relationship with whatever was being asked for help. The creation of new life for people, varieties of vegetation, changes in the seasons, prayers to the Sun, and other assistance from every corner of Navajo land was now available. Young men belonged to the Sun and so offered prayers to it. Mother Earth is the same, desiring its own prayer offerings of sacred stones (ntł'iz). She said, "Those who are on me are all my children." The Sun also claimed that these were his children and that each day he required a life for performing the difficult task of crossing the sky to shine down upon the land. He also desired a prayer offering of sacred stones. Today, many of these devotions are no longer practiced, so our existence is not as it should be. These powers are called upon in the ceremonies, but are often forgotten in daily life.

As time progressed, First Man found a young baby girl in a cradleboard and brought her home. This holy being became known as White Shell or Changing Woman, who in twelve days matured into adulthood. Soon, her beauty caught the eye of Sun Bearer, who surreptitiously had sexual relations with her. From this union came two boys, Monster Slayer (Naayéé'neizghání) and Born for Water (Tóbájíshchíní). As they matured, they grew curious as to who their father was until finally the boys decided to go in search of him. After a difficult and perilous journey that tested their ability, they reached Sun Bearer's home in the sky, where they were tested once again before receiving the bows and arrows needed to kill the monsters roaming the earth, devouring people.

Some of the monsters, like Big God (Yé'iitsoh) and Gray God (Yé'ii Łibá), roamed about eating humans while others remained fixed, waiting to destroy those who came close. The Twins, armed with bows and arrows obtained from Sun Bearer, sought out and destroyed these creatures, leaving their remains upon the land in the form of rock formations. By

Different forms of holy people inhabit or work within water, plants, animals, and many other aspects of the natural world. In the winter, twelve of them appear as Yéʼii Bicheii who sing, dance, and pray to bless and heal Navajo people. (Courtesy Library of Congress, Photo #96721)

killing the various monsters, the Twins learned different prayers—such as ones concerning arrowheads, winds, and the mirage people—and of offerings—such as the sacred stones, which serve as a protective shield against things that harm. Only four of the monsters were allowed to live, because Monster Slayer saw that they would be of benefit to the Navajo people. Each pleaded for its life and continued existence. The Twins allowed Old Age with its infirmities to survive because it made room for upcoming generations, Poverty remained so that Navajos would work hard and care for the things they had, Lice required people to care for themselves, and Hunger fostered appreciation for food and the work to get it. While Old Age led to death, there would also be birth; Poverty led to objects wearing out but also the creation of new ones; and Hunger led to obtaining new and different foods. Thus, there will always be a renewal of things in the future. These are important motivations for people today, as explained in this story that is only told during the winter months.

After the killing of the monsters, the bloodshed and trauma associated with combat began to bother Monster Slayer. He performed different ceremonies to try to cure his depressing situation. Many of these rituals branch out in different directions and have a male and female form. For instance, there is the Fire Dance (Nightway) and the Mountainway, the Lightning or Shootingway, and the Holyway ceremonies. They are all very different. Some problems are cured by the Evilway ceremony, where evil forces are cast out. This ceremony clears away the sickness and bad powers from the past and restores a person to a positive life in the present.

When the Twins first visited Sun Bearer and he showed them his home and the lands surrounding it, they noticed his wealth that extended for as far as the eye could see. In one direction they saw wild animals of forest and desert, in another a large assortment of domestic animals, and in other areas different types of riches that are enjoyed in this world. Now that they had ridden the earth of its monsters, these young men wished to return to Sun Bearer and obtain this wealth for people on the earth. Their mother urged them not to go, but they went in spite of her wishes. The Sun at first hesitated to share his wealth but eventually relented and allowed some of his things to be brought to earth. The sheep's and horse's sweat on bits of dirt, pieces of wool, fur, eye water, and nose water were all packed for the Twins to transport back to their land. The same was true with cattle and the mountain creatures such as the bear and deer, as well as bison and the animals of plains and desert. Elements from them were prepared, carried to this world, and used to recreate the animals, which then received an inner spirit. Each creature received its assignment, its place to live, and its own specific songs, prayers, and offerings.

Our relationship to all living things should be harmonious and follow the instructions given by the holy people to show respect and concern according to their abilities and powers. If, for some reason, one is killed or abused in a disrespectful way, there will follow a sickness or physical problem, but it will also have a cure. For instance, a medicine person determines what is wrong, so may cut the branch of a tree and carve an image of the offended spirit. A special tobacco may be smoked in accompaniment with that animal's songs and prayers. This is the plan given to the Navajo, and we should live by it. This is also why the medicine from the clinic may not be powerful enough to use when something is bothering us. The only way to really effect a cure is to have a ceremony performed. The same is true when problems in human relations arise. Let's say that shortly after a woman delivers a baby, she has sexual relations with her husband, even though the teachings say that there should be a period of abstinence. She will get sick from this, but there is a medicine that will take care of that. There are also sexual diseases that people contract, which the elders long ago warned about. There are different herbs that cure these problems. The holy people have put them there and marked them for our use.

Another example of laws enacted at this time concern the mother-in-law taboo, where she and her son-in-law are not supposed to see each other once a marriage has taken place. This is a rule that comes from Big Star (Sǫ'tsoh), who said the two should not look upon each other. The mother-in-law is often referred to as an owl (ná'áshjaa') because she is always looking for issues, can twist her neck around to see, and bobs her head up and down inspecting things. Today, in-laws sit together when traveling and eat in the same room. In the past, it was said that this would make one's eyesight go away. If a short smoking ceremony is performed at the wedding or thereafter, the problem can be solved. When the mother-in-law knows that the marriage is confirmed, she will fix a smoke for her future son-in-law. She first puffs on the tobacco, then gives it to her son-in-law, who smokes some, then returns it to her. This is done four times. Once completed, there is nothing wrong with the two seeing each other. The taboo is lifted because the rules have been followed.

Establishing Patterns

Many of the things I talk about concerning early history, my own experiences, and traditions are based in the religious beliefs we received in the past. I will start here with the introduction of the Navajo people. Far past Gallup, there is a mountain called Tsoodził (Tongue Mountain or Mount Taylor). Nearby in its foothills is Wide Planting Field, where Navajo life as we know it began. Next, people traveled to Black Mesa, which forms the body of a holy being, then on to Dooko'oosłííd (Never Thaws on Top or San Francisco Peaks). From the east the Navajo learned the ways of life and the teachings of Changing Woman, who taught and guided them. Twelve people started back this way, traveling four days before returning to Mount Taylor. Next, they went to Black Mesa, where a large rock formation is said to be a hogan where all of the holy people met to discuss the life of the earth surface beings (humans). This is where Mother Earth and its creatures received their inner form and assignment mentioned previously.

From the inception of life, people are involved in patterns of existence established by the holy people. The inner being that stands within each one of us is made up of the wind. There are four of them: the White Wind (Nítch'i Łigai), Blue Wind (Nítch'i Dootł'izh), Yellow Wind (Nítch'i Łitso), and the Dark Wind (Nítch'i Dithił), which are sung about in the Windway (Chíshíjí and Diné Binítch'i) ceremonies. The former ceremony is associated with small twister winds and the latter ceremony with big, strong winds accompanied by heavy rain and fierce lightning. The Lightningway ceremony has both a female and male form from which human life received the electricity that powers it. Creatures on four legs live by these winds with the assistance of lightning. People exist through these things, too. The wind makes us move, and our path is the rainbow. The swirls in our fingertips are the telltale signs of this. When we were first born, the wind came into them and marked them with the coiling patterns on our fingers with which we live and are identified by the holy people. Everyone exists because of this wind. When a child is being born, the winds argue over which one is going into the body first. They say that it will be their grandchild and will live to his or her potential. The winds also establish a day that they will leave the body so that a person cannot live any longer than that appointed time.

There are actions to be taken in preparing for a baby to be born. When a mother is approaching the time of delivery but before the afterbirth (awéé' biyaała'í) has dropped, she should have a Blessingway ceremony. This woman and the people around her need to be careful of what they do. For instance, if her husband is working with horses and tying them up a lot or if he is tightening or screwing a gun back together or working on an automobile and there is no protective ceremony, the baby may become entangled with its umbilical cord around its neck or tightened into a ball that causes the mother problems in delivery. The holy people have prescribed plants and ceremonies that prevent or undo any of these problems. The untying ceremony (wooltą́ą́d), which is performed three times, untangles the baby so that it can come out normally. The hair tie of either the mother or father or the husband's rope is used in this ceremonial untying process. These prayers and rituals were first given during the palm of time when we came into the world. This is all part of birthing.

Once the baby is born, the afterbirth comes out and is fixed. If it is a boy, the afterbirth is formed into a very tight ball and placed under a young piñon tree that has good, full needles. The piñon tree is considered to be a male plant, and so a baby boy's placenta belongs there. If it is a girl, the afterbirth is put in a young juniper tree, which is considered female. This protects the individual on his or her life road to old age. It is said that at the emergence into this world, these two types of trees were once people. Upon reaching the surface, they walked out of the dark and got into mud surrounding the small plot of land. These trees were eager to become established in their new home and so sneaked away from the group and became stuck in the mud. They had not thought of what would be best beforehand,

The enculturation of Navajo values starts at birth and continues through adulthood. Among the teachings this young girl may have already learned are those of the hair bun (tsiiyééł), turquoise, jewelry, how to sit, modesty in dress, and importance of family and clan. Her first breaths, first laugh, and first menses are noted through ceremony. (Photo courtesy Harold B. Lee Library)

so were given rules that now they needed to follow. The piñon tree said, "In days to come, through me the world will be in harmony," while the juniper said, "I will be a home and be used for the benefit of mankind. Even with one of my branches, a person sleeps well through the night if it is cold." When the temperature drops, a Navajo can light a fire, using this wood to get warm. These are the rules by which these trees live.

After a baby is born, it needs to be cared for as it begins to learn. Once the infant is on its own, we do not know what it will go through as it walks into the future. The child receives a lot of sacred precautions while being born, but now it is up to the mother to remain in her holy state for four days and care for the infant. Although she has had the Blessingway ceremony before the baby is born, the infant receives its own corn pollen placed in its mouth shortly after its birth. Now the baby will have its own thoughts, be aware of what is around the home, have a desire for sheep and goats, and stay protected. The child will be introduced to and think about water, fire, and livestock.

Today, babies are born in hospitals and are quickly given bottles; that is why they cannot go far without drinking alcohol. They also eat from cans. Because of this, our voices are not heard. I keep warning mothers that these things should not be done, but my teachings are disregarded. Some of them say bearing children is not sacred, but how else would you walk? One can only move in a sacred manner. Every single day the wind is inside of us so that we can breathe. Every single day it moves us. If this was not holy, would it be like this? This is what I think. When the wind goes into the body, the little winds come out at the fingertips and feet. With this, one stirs as it pumps blood through all of the veins and heart. If this was not holy, could it be like this?

Training of the child is important, and so both the parents and grandparents take part. Some children are smarter and catch on to things quicker than others, but eventually everyone will figure out their purpose in life. As the stars move and the months go by, one will realize that all of the things around us are holy. If it was not, there would be no sun or stars that are also moved by the holy wind. Water would not flow, and nothing would come out of the springs. Everything would be closed up. As one investigates the world, it becomes apparent that we are all living in this way. Life is precious, and that is why we are awake at the crack of dawn. Children are always told to get up early, stretch, and run a long distance. That is what I was told to do when I was a child. My great-uncle or grandfather would come to the doorway, trying to see where I was. As you become more disciplined and understand the holiness of life, no one tells you what to do. You

The four-day kinaaldá ceremony is a time of intense instruction for a girl reaching puberty. Grinding corn is an important skill in food preparation, resulting in a large cornmeal cake (alkaan) that is baked underground and later distributed. A primary role of women is to know how to nurture family and friends. (Used by permission, Utah State Historical Society)

do it on your own. At dawn you are outside meeting and greeting the holy beings as they protect you. If this is done, even though life is hard, a person will live to an old age, having attained their full potential.

As a girl reaches puberty and begins to mature into womanhood, she has the kinaaldá ceremony performed for her. This is a form of Blessingway that prepares her to have her own children without complications in the future. She is also instructed in ways of acting like a woman—things to do and things to avoid. Women who are respected elders do much of this teaching during the four-day ceremony, and through the songs that are sung by the medicine people, she will be able to have children later in life. One of the tasks that this maturing girl performs is the grinding of corn on a mano (tsé daashch'iní) and metate (tsédaashjéé'). Over the first three days, she grinds large amounts of it that are eventually turned into batter for a large cake cooked in a corn husk–lined hole dug in the ground and heated with hot rocks. Early in the morning of the fourth day, the circular cake is cut into pieces in such a way that everyone attending can have some. This represents the training and well-being of the girl. Elements of Mother Earth are put into it, but it is also an offering to Mother Earth, when the heart or center of the cake is put back into the ground. During the ceremony people sing the home songs, which are also placed in the pit with the heart of the cake. Other songs are performed during this time, which people get to walk away with as a protective shield in life. They also cover and protect the children and livestock through the sheep, horse, goat, and sacred stones songs. These were sung in the no-sleep ceremony during the previous night. They bless the young woman in her life journey and as she has children. Livestock will now be readily available to her as she sets out on Mother Earth.

One of the many tools (habeedí) a woman uses in the home is the fire poker (honeeshgish) which serves as a shield and protection. There are both a male and female fire poker used in ceremonies by medicine men or in cooking by women. They were created at the beginning of time and given the responsibility to serve as protectors. This happened after the Twins had gone to their father, received their bows and arrows, and set off to kill the monsters. The fire poker became a shield, which when accompanied with Blessingway and protection prayers has the responsibility to safeguard its owner and their property. Since it has its own prayers, one can hold it as they pray and refer to it as a grandmother. When people leave their home for an extended period, a fire poker is left behind outside of the door. It is told, "I don't know when I will move back here, but until I do, you will take care of the place." A family might be gone for a year before returning, but once back, they pray with it again. To this day, fire pokers are still being used. Now I have really exposed myself.

Medicine men use them in ceremonies, but family members, especially women, use them all of the time when cooking. While she is preparing and heating food, she pokes the fire with it. Food particles left on her hands and on the poker are its nourishment. The bits and pieces of food left behind in the home after a person departs sustain the poker as it keeps the monster of hunger away. Once the cooking is finished, it is put aside before eating. Right after that the woman offers a prayer, perhaps about traveling in safety or that harmony may come her way, that the livestock will graze in peace, that the family might receive many earthly possessions, or that there will be nothing to fear. Even though a person may not have much, they will send their prayer this way. Another time for offering prayers is when a woman pushes the hot coals back into the fire. With this there is growth of generations; there is a home. I keep my fire poker under my woodstove, where the prayer is said.

There are other forms of protection that shield a person from harm, defend the home against evil, and bring wealth to it. The fire in a home is a tool of women and has the sacred name of Honbą́ą́h Nahookǫs (Moving near the Fire). It is told to take care of the home and keep the cold away.

This is how the prayers are said. By telling this, I have once again exposed myself. There are also the stirring sticks (ádístsiin) that are referred to as "arrows." Just as a man has his bow and arrow to protect his family and bring food home, the stirring sticks are also used to defend against hunger. They have their own prayers and responsibilities. The person using them stirs the scalding hot mush, then removes the sticks from the food and immediately gives a prayer. From this there will come harmony and rain and earthly goods. You also pray for your family and extended family so that the children will walk in peace with their mind straight and that they will remember you. This is what one prays for. There are other things for protection such as arrowheads, the sacred stones, and a stone ax (hał). All of these have prayers for your protection. In this way your days will be long.

One of the tools for women around the home is the weaving loom, composed of the be'ázhoo' (comb), bee akiniltłish (weaving batten), and the wool used for weaving. There are sacred names for the many different parts of the loom. Just before a rug is completed, it is given a spirit trail so that all of the good things that are woven into the rug will not be trapped and will allow for blessings in the days to come. For instance, there are rainbows from the weaving that are let out. The others are called k'os yish-chíín (children of the clouds) that border the rainbow, one being red and the other black. The opening represents time in the future while making a living today.

Just as women have their crafts to work on, so do men. Silversmithing is one of them that I have been around a lot. One of my great-uncles who lived at Navajo Mountain while I was growing up was very involved in this trade. When I was a little child, my maternal grandmother had me herd sheep in that region where he worked. I went with the animals just about everywhere in that area. There was a wash with water running down it where I found plates of yellow rocks that easily broke off. They looked like glass. I was told that this was called tsésǫ (star/glass; more likely, tsésts'agi—mica, isinglass, gypsum?) and that it was the same as silver. It broke in slices, and so I collected some pieces and put them in my pocket, hoping to do some silversmithing just as my great-uncle did. I brought it home and the next morning started to melt it, but was told that the sheep needed to be cared for and that I was to herd. My maternal grandmother agreed that I had found the right kind of stone to melt and that there was another type called fire rock (tsé kǫ) that was mixed with it but which could also be used to produce a yellow dye for yarn. When these two types of rock are melted and mixed together, exquisite silver jewelry can be made. I do not know what else my great-uncle used for ingredients when making jewelry. Maybe other people have since carried these rocks off, I do not know, but at that time no one was bothering it. I keep thinking that my husband and I should go over there and bring back some of my great-uncle's silversmithing tools. My husband's father had a silversmithing site in Mystery Valley, too, where it is said he melted rocks to make jewelry.

My great-uncle, when melting the rock, used a portable leather bellows to blow on the fire to get it hot enough. He would pour the melted silver into a mold and later use a hammer, files, punches, and many other tools kept in a wooden box. I do not know where he got them. There were four fixed logs that he used to work on. This was how I saw him making silver items. He fashioned a variety of objects—bracelets, engraved silver buttons, large conchos placed on belts, bow guards, and hat bands. The silver bracelets had many different designs and replicas of things he saw. He made pieces of jewelry that were straight and then put a design on the outer edge and added turquoise. Then there were belts. He made them wide and heavy with silver. The one taken from me by Virginia Carson Smith was made from this type of material. It was glittering white and beautiful. I have asked for it many times, but I believe she tricked me. It is probably still somewhere in Flagstaff. [Note: More on this story in chapter 6.]

Land

The land is extremely important to our people. It holds the stories, provides resources, and teaches lessons of life. Starting with the mountains, there are powers held by the holy people, wealth, health, and ceremonies that come from them that we call upon on a daily basis. The Four Sacred Mountains—Blanca Peak (Sisnaajiní), Mount Taylor (Tsoodził), San Francisco Peaks (Dook'o'oosłííd), and Mount Hesperus (Dibé Nitsaa)— are of primary importance and have many teachings. Much has been said about them. For instance, Mount Hesperus is one of the first mountains to be white with snow and so is associated in the prayers with sheep and stands for all of the four-legged creatures. Mount Taylor is said to be the doorway to Navajo lands, whereas Huerfano Mesa (Dził Ná'oodiłii) by Teec Nos Pos is said to be turning, gradually swirling in one place when one looks at it. This name indicates that. All of them received their titles and qualities through stories. There is Mount Taylor, which has a walking stick on its east side for elderly men and women and holds part of the teachings about old age. It is our mountain, which deals with our very lives. This is how it is told.

There are twelve mountains that the holy people placed in a sacred manner during the palm of time. Each has its own prayer and a ceremonial name, received when Monster Slayer and Born for Water visited their father, Sun Bearer, to obtain the weapons they needed to kill the monsters. One of the tests that Sun Bearer gave to determine if they were truly his sons was when he switched the mountains from their normal positions. The Twins needed to use their spiritual powers to discern the identity of each mountain and where it belonged. When the two young men had proven themselves, the mountains received their sacred names. The songs and prayers found in ceremonies use these names. When a person travels toward one of them, its name is used to call upon it for help and protection during the journey. You identify the place you are going and sprinkle corn pollen once you are close to the mountain. Because of their sacredness, the stories behind them should only be discussed in the winter when creatures that sting or harm, such as snakes, spiders, lizards, and lightning, are not around. Their teachings should not be discussed in front of these beings or else they might be offended and cause sickness or death. I will talk about those mountains and rock formations that are in the north and close to Monument Valley.

My maternal grandmother said that long ago the people used to migrate all over the land in search of food. The La Sal Mountains (Dził Ashdlaii—Five Mountains) received their name because they comprise five mountains. Grandmother said that it and Blue (Abajo) Mountain (Dził Ditł'ooí—Hairy Mountain) are related and that both were important places for harvesting piñon nuts. Travel in those days was only on horseback, and so some family members remained behind to care for the livestock while others moved to the harvest site and set up camp. The travelers packed as many food supplies and as much warm clothing as possible because the fall season could often turn cold. One year my ancestors, who roamed out there for piñon nuts, got caught in a large snowstorm and had to live there for some time before returning to their children at home. The same thing happened in the Henry Mountains (Dził Bizhi Adani—Nameless Mountain), all due to piñon nut picking. Those who could do so moved back to Navajo Mountain, but some of our relatives died there on the La Sals.

On top of Navajo Mountain (Naatsis'áán—Head of Earth Woman) to the west of Monument Valley lies the place where the Twins returned to the earth after visiting Sun Bearer. Two black rocks sitting on top are said to represent Monster Slayer and Born for Water. The mountain itself is the Head of Earth Woman, whose body is Black Mesa with a ridge that runs along it as the backbone. This body has everything in it. There are different four-legged creatures, many types of earthly possessions, sacred stones (ntł'iz), varieties of corn—white, blue, yellow, and variegated—and a lot of different wild plants. She is called the Pollen Range because of all of the growth and variety of plants she supports. If a person has a notion to acquire a great number of livestock, he can obtain them from this land. If there is a desire for horses or cattle, they will be received in abundance. This female figure, lying with her head at Navajo Mountain, said that on her surface, in the future, this would happen.

Blue Mountain and the rock formation known as the Bears Ears (Shashjaa') are considered to be connected as one. My maternal grandmother used to say that this mountain had many bears on it. They were sent to that mountain and now live there, but when the bears vanish, there will be no more harmony in life. This is one reason bears are not killed and just left alone, so that there would be life in the future. It is good that there are laws that protect them or they are placed in zoos. In the beginning, bears and mountain lions were used for transportation, it is said. They probably understood when they were talked to back then. People would say, "We need to go there," use their sacred name to summon them to their doorway, then travel to their satisfaction. Other nationalities were not able to do this because they did not know the sacred names. When the world deteriorates in the future, the bear and mountain lion will become our shield and we will go behind them for protection. This is why we are not going to leave our stories behind that allow us to walk the life path with these teachings. They are to be remembered because they are not just any old thing.

There is a male and female part to almost everything in the Navajo world, and so there are both a male and female rock formation that are paired with the Bears Ears—the one in Utah is the male. His children left him, so he remains behind, and his ears and nose are what is sticking out of the ground and visible. The people probably made prayer offerings there when traveling into distant places. For instance, servicemen make sacred offerings in these kinds of places as well as in the mountains. The power from these sites works as their shield when they go into battle; it saves them. With this protection they come back, no matter what big guns were shooting at them. Their life was saved by this power. These formations have a purpose when there is a group coming to harm the Navajo people, and it will be of great service in the future. This is why the Bears Ears and other formations are here. We have these places to make prayer offerings, and it is our right to use them. They were given to us at the beginning of time so that we can plead for our lives. Even when the very smallest thing affects us, there is a cure for that problem. We cannot live without our land and ceremonies as we walk upon the path of life. Thus, the mountains have everything needed for living creatures. There one finds different forms of rain, supernatural beings who take care of the water, and the ones who have gone before us, as well as all of the people who will make a life from it. There are varieties of corn and different types of pollen. All of these are set with the mountains. It has all of the prayer offerings in it. All of them have been given special sacred prayer offerings, and so from them come forth abundant harvests.

Not far from the Bears Ears is a formation of rock standing upright called Comb Ridge (Tséyík'áán—Upthrust Rock), which extends from Blue Mountain to the south for seventy miles. It was created at the time of the slaying of the monsters and serves as a shield or boundary, my maternal grandmother said one time when my daughter and I were picking piñon nuts and digging up a plant called nábįįh (?). When you are looking from where we were, there are red rocks that stand up in a row. Grandmother said that her mother taught that a long time ago this was part of a boundary created by the holy people as a shield of protection to defend Navajo people in the future from those who want to cause harm.

Near Comb Ridge sits Navajo Blanket (Dził Naneests'ee'ii—Mountain That Is Twisted, Grooved, Coiled), home of the Wind and a place where offerings can be made to this power. The wind is holy and sacred no matter where it is found. There is a mesa to the east, and when the wind is going to blow hard, it is heard there first. Where there are rocks that twist out (hada'adests'ee'), it is seen as another sacred place for the wind and should be respected. The Wind can take the lives of people and destroy their homes. The big winds [tornadoes and hurricanes] are very strong. When everything goes haywire, the big wind is given the right to take our lives. This is why it is feared. The small ones, like twisters, are messengers. Sometimes they move clockwise and other times counterclockwise. They are spies, it is said, and may also cast a spell. This type is called Young Female Twister (Ch'ikéé Naayisí) when giving it an offering. If it ever goes over you and takes a possession, you just let it go. Do not try to retrieve the object; just sprinkle corn pollen after it and say that the thing it took will have no meaning now. If it left a spell, however, it will not be effective. Otherwise, when the curse is given, the wind takes the sweat and dirt from one's body, then steals one's thinking and creates confusion. Sometime in the days that follow, when the people go in deceitful ways and there appears to be no hope, Big Wind has been given the right to take up their lives, just as it did with the Anasazi. If there is nothing wrong at your place, it will not come to your home or bother your livestock. Only when something is evil at your household will it do this.

West of Navajo Blanket in the Mexican Hat/Halchita area sits a volcanic neck of rock called Alhambra (Tsé Łizhin Ii'áhá—Black Rock Sticking Up from Ground) that was once a group of travelers. They probably stopped there when hungry and tired, then turned to stone. This is why, when one looks at these rocks from a certain angle, the people become visible. The same is true of what is called Baby Rocks, where a person took children from that area, sat down, and turned to stone. There are many stories like this of people on a journey who transformed into rock. Where molten [volcanic] stone stands, holy beings live. In many of these places, one can easily hear echoes, and even though the sound may be far off, it seems like it is happening right next to you. Another sacred place where holy people can be contacted is a young piñon or cedar tree. They were once holy beings, too. The piñon tree is male and the cedar a female, and each has prayers.

In Monument Valley there is an important rock formation called El Capitan (Spanish: The Captain; Navajo: Aghaałá—Much Wool/Fur). On the east side of this volcanic neck is a hole where Big Snake, one of the holy beings who traveled with Changing Woman at the time of creation, used to have his home. It is said that he traveled only at night on the wind and a rainbow before returning at daylight. During the springtime, when there was a new growth of plants, it would come out and live on the mesa. El Capitan served as the doorway for this snake. That is why the lizard and snake people are so abundant and consider all of Monument Valley as their sacred land. Monument Pass, at the northern end of the valley, has a lot of them there as well as many medicine plants such as tł'iish tsoh bibéésh (Big Snake plant used in Enemyway medicine), agizee (used for arthritis), and one for birthing called doo bich'į'achííhígíí (a plant that prevents pregnancy). If a person is injured, there is the Iináájí azee' (Lifeway medicine) that heals. All of these plants grow there. The medicine men who perform the Iináájí ceremony, use herbs in water that grow in this place. The white man called this disease adijiłii (?), which bothers a woman who does not take care of herself during her monthly. Her ankles, knees, back, or fingers will hurt unless she takes some of this herb that grows there. It can be found clustering in areas because it is holy around there, and so the land should not be disturbed in any way. Navajo people have medicine growing all over this place with numerous sites to offer prayers to holy people like Talking God (Haashch'ééłti'í), whom we call our maternal

This famous rock formation, named by Anglos as Totem Pole, is a place where medicine men made rain offerings. Its powers tie into nearby Sand Spring (Séí Bitó). One can understand why the sand dune over which this flock of sheep is traveling is called Herding Down. (Used by permission, Utah State Historical Society)

grandfather, Mother Earth, and jet (tséníłkáłí—black rock), all of whom can serve as a shield and a power.

Navajo people make offerings in many places for different reasons. This earth is our mother, where we first cried, made our first sound, urinated, grew, and slept. The darkness covers us to tell us to rest. Offerings can be made at these places as well as to Mother Earth, darkness, and the Sun, who says go to work. It is the same for the moon, who also shines light for us. All of these things have offerings that shield and protect from harm. Sickness remains at a distance from people who are protected.

There are four sacred rivers that circumscribe Navajo lands—the San Juan River being the one to the north. It also serves as a boundary and shield for protection. When one crosses, corn pollen is sprinkled in it to bring good health to the mind and body, and the transportation is used like a horse or an automobile. An offering and prayer summon the power in the river to protect the traveler until he or she safely returns. This is given with the left or male hand for protection, while the right or female hand is used for a second offering of thanks upon a safe return. Even when one is traveling among different nationalities in other countries, it is the same. Just as one gives prayers and offerings to rivers when crossing on or near Navajo territory, the same thing is done in foreign lands. If I were about to cross a river, a prayer for safety would be given. It might be something like, "I will travel in harmony wherever I go this day," with the foreigner in the land beyond being addressed through his sacred, ceremonial name. All of his goods, including money, are now placed in your hand. In this way there is wealth to be had.

There are many prayers that can be offered, but the one upon leaving the safe homeland is considered male, and the one returning is female; both are equally sacred. When rain is coming, the river crossing may make lightning. The San Juan River, along with the other three, was created when the holy people emerged onto the surface of this world and found themselves on a small plot of land surrounded by water. Four gods each went in one of the cardinal directions and with a large blade dug a trench that caused the water to drain off the land. One of the rivers subsequently formed by this action was the San Juan, male river of the north, while the Colorado, female river of the west, created another boundary. Behind Navajo Mountain the male river goes over the female, and they become one, providing a place where water is born. From there they go into the wide water [ocean].

The emergence of the Navajo people, the positioning of the stars in the heavens, and the establishment of some rules are all found in the game called tsidił (striking the sticks or tóna'ootsił—shoe game). The holy people placed rocks in a circle with small spaces in between and four larger spaces in the cardinal directions. These openings are referred to as rivers—the four that bound Navajo land. In the center is placed a larger rock off of which three cottonwood sticks about six inches long are bounced. One side of each stick is white, the other side black. They are held approximately a foot and a half above the rock, bounced off of it, then given points based on how the black and white combinations land. With each point, a player moves their small wooden marker clockwise around the circle of forty smaller stones. The individual who reaches the starting point [east opening] wins.

Coyote, the trickster, was one of the first to play this game. He turned the larger rock in the center into Big Star, then threw it and the smaller ones into the sky as lesser stars. One star that shined red he claimed as his, while First Man named Big Star. It was at this time that the others were also named. Big Star and one called Big Star Woman (Dilyéhé—Pleiades) follow the rules of in-laws. In Navajo culture, a son-in-law is not supposed to see his mother-in-law unless a special ceremony is performed. That is why Big Star comes out first and Big Star Woman does not come out until he disappears beyond the western horizon. As a warning, she pokes her cane up before she appears. Some of the little stars were said to be retarded beings, with twisted bodies. Then there is the Big Dipper (Náhookǫs) with its six stars and Pinching Together Stars (Sǫ'hots'ihi—Aldebaran and Hyades), two children playing together. As Coyote scattered or placed the stars, he did it quickly, spinning around in the midst of the creative process. Now we live with these patterns.

Wild Animals

Animals live with patterns that were established at the time of the creation. Whether wild or domestic, each creature has its assigned place to live, abilities, powers, sacred name, and role in this world. Whether on land, in the air, or in water, they have responsibilities and gifts that can be shared with humans as long as respect is shown and they are approached through prayer and offerings. Their power and teachings are gifts that can be summoned during a ceremony to heal an individual, protect a person, cure through physical application, summon other holy people, assist in learning, and help with everyday challenges. No creature, great or small, is insignificant. Indeed, size has nothing to do with the amount of power received in the beginning. As long as a person understands the story and teachings, how to access an animal's abilities, and how to not offend it, the creature offers positive assistance.

Since there are a wide variety of animals, a few examples will illustrate how the Navajo view and interact with them. Take deer, for instance. These are sacred beings, who at the time of creation had human forms and qualities. It is said that they acted and spoke just like people, and so there was an agreement between the deer and sheep. The sheep said that there would be twelve people who would raise them for their skin, wool, and food, so they agreed to act tame. But there would also be hardship in their footstep. The deer heard this and said, "I will also have twelve people follow my footsteps," referring to their hide being used to make moccasins, but they remain wild. These two types of animals were different and did not agree on working together. This is why, when cooking food or just handling the meat, the two kinds are not mixed. The domestic side is at odds with that which is wild. In this way they have established their likes and dislikes, and so neither one should be offended, even if they do not get along.

There are rules of how each animal is killed, their skin is removed, the limbs and heart are detached, and head with unused parts is disposed. When one is butchered, the eyes are kept in good condition. This is all very sacred and so should not be treated in just any old way. If a deer has urinated in the woods and it is found, it should not be disturbed because the plants there can be used as medicine. If a person makes a mistake when butchering a deer, that individual will be bothered in the same part of the body where the mistake was made, and it might even kill him. None of this should be treated lightly. Even though you might know every single thing about it in the sacred way, there can still be problems with mistakes. Some people who know the secrets of these practices may use this power to perform witchcraft.

Once there was a woman who fell in love with a deer. She knew the secret ways to move from human to deer form and then back. If you know how to perform this type of change, you probably can do it. This is how it is told. A long time ago, there was a woman who lived at home with her brothers. One day when they were out hunting, a male deer visited their home and courted this woman, who secretly became his wife. When he visited, he removed his antlers and spent time having the woman repeat certain formulas that he knew. In two days, the woman snorted and dashed off after the deer. For four days, her brothers hunted the couple until they found her. The men fired blunt tipped arrows so that they could bring her back home alive. Where she had been grazing were herbs she had urinated on that held medicinal powers. The men gathered these herbs that are now called dínee chil (Deerway medicine plant) used in the Deerway ceremony (Dine'é K'ehgo). Quickly collected, they were mixed, given to the woman to drink, put all over her body as a medicine, then taken home. For four years, the brothers' little sister remained at the camp, but because they killed her fawn that she had produced for her buck, she looked for every opportunity to escape and return to the forest. One day, her husband appeared and snorted for her to run after him, which she did, never to be seen again. There is a place called White Mountain (Dzil Łigai) where her people live.

There are also animals, such as the Coyote (Mą'ii), who has some good powers but is often associated with trickery and witchcraft. It is said that at the time of creation, a female sheep was the first of this type of animal to be formed. She soon had a lamb, which Coyote promptly ate. He proclaimed, "Don't be sad about this. I was the first to feast, so a person should pray to me, so that in the future they will receive wealth." There is a prayer given by an individual who has lost livestock like this, which provides more, just as Coyote promised. Although he is not smart in many ways and is a thief, this will take place. Later, when the holy people formed First Man and First Woman, they were given a similar makeup, knowing and creating things that were both good and evil. First Man and First Woman were coyotes who were not even Navajo, according to some people. At the very beginning, witchcraft came about with them so that now, when certain prayers are offered and actions taken, those powers to perform evil are unleashed. I do not know about this, but if a person lives so as to be able to use this ability, they can run at superhuman speed wearing a coyote skin.

The individual who knows about skinwalking in a dog or coyote skin understands the witching ways that are the exact opposite of the Blessingway, which starts with the good things from the mountains. This calls upon life to come in a positive way, bringing earthly goods (yódí) that are worn, sacred stones that are offered, a variety of livestock in abundance, and the mountain creatures. We call upon these things for the people by having these things bless their lives in the future. The person who knows and uses witching is doing just the opposite and is the "eater" of the Navajo. The witching ways destroy things and people who are good; the one who practices it shows no mercy for anyone. They kill people and cause great harm as they travel about in their coyote skin or as an owl. They call upon ghosts and use their power to perform evil.

I do not know how this is done, but I am afraid of it. I have been told since childhood that this was a dangerous thing. It is a tortuous trail that leads to nothing good, and so one should not ask about it. My interest has been only for what is useful for people. The good things in life are what one should carry for the protection of the grandchildren. I am protected by prayers, which are like hands that shield when the evil moves over you. These words work against this. I do not like the ways of evil. It walks at night like a ghost and uses different varieties of skins to travel, such as the coyote, owl, crow, blue jay, mouse, and snake. They are all part of the witching, and if something evil is upon you, they will attack. When a mouse chews on a person's things, it is not good because evil thoughts may be working against that individual.

People who know of witchery may send evil through prayers. When one is in good standing financially and their family is doing well, they may become a target for witchcraft due to jealousy. This is the time someone will most likely be witched. An owl might hoot or cross a traveler's path. One should not ignore this without having prayers and protection. There are standing rock formations that might have a slide, foretelling of future problems that need to be taken care of. This all goes back to the time of the gathering of prayers, when the holy people offered protection to be used when in need. There are prayers for echoes also. One should ask about these to keep a person safe in the future. I travel in this path, and this is what you are supposed to think. All of these things have special prayer offerings that are theirs.

The eagle came into this world for our protection. When Monster Slayer killed the two flying monsters known as the tsé nináhééhí, they had two offspring—one turned into the eagle and the other the owl. Before Monster Slayer released them, he gave each an assignment. The eagle's feather that falls when it is flying is a sacred life feather (iiná-ats'os) that can be used as a shield in the future when it is in one's home. The eagle says, "I travel in the heavens, and nothing can claim me. When my feather falls out and a person picks it up, they will have it as a shield." This is what it agreed to do to help the people by giving them this right. Whatever prayer offering is used in ceremonies, this feather may also be a part. Buzzards also appeared at this time. They were spies when they came down from the heavens, looking for decomposed bodies. They searched for things that were not good, only rotten. This was dangerous because decaying flesh is like cancer that was sent down. Whatever the buzzard ate could appear as cancer in the same body part that is found in an individual. Prayers can work against this bird and the "sore that does not heal" [cancer]. There is a ceremony that is potent in fighting it, with all of the properties of the special prayer offering and the cutting of an herb. This is also true with the other flying birds like the eagle, yellow tail hawk, and sparrow hawk. All of these have special ceremonies for ailments. If you do not know of the cure, you might one day suffer from these sicknesses, which could take your life.

There are other animals that appeared at the time of emergence but do no spiritual harm, although they should be avoided physically. Take Badger, for instance, who helped with the digging from the world beneath. It is a powerful animal that should not be bothered, but in terms of hurting someone in a spiritual way, he is not dangerous. The mountain lion is the same and causes no ailments. It is not into witchcraft. The skunk, it is said, is very powerful against anything that is there to harm. Both the skunk and the badger receive a sprinkling of corn pollen as an offering.

Although little wormy rodent creatures like the rat and mouse have witchcraft in them, there are others, like the squirrel and chipmunk, that do not. This is because they were part of the killing of the monsters as the fight was taking place. The designs on their fur came from these events, and so they are considered to be on the people's side and friendly to them. The same is true of the bear, although he is a powerful medicine person and often viewed as being grumpy. He teams up with porcupine, another creature from the mountains, so they work together. Even though the porcupine is small, it is said to have a lot of power, as does the bear, to cause sickness if not respected. This is why when a baby is conceived and the parents see a dead porcupine or harm one, the child will be bothered by the spirit of that animal after it is born. The infant gets sick with nosebleeds and other ailments. A nine-day Mountainway ceremony is the only cure potent enough to heal the child. This is the way it is.

The same is true with a man who kills a bear, dog, coyote, or snake if his wife has conceived but not yet delivered. The baby will be affected by the image of the animal that bothers the child while in the womb and after it is born. If one lets the creature alone, there will be no harm in seeing it, but if the father kills one, the baby takes the image and is bothered by it. There are ceremonies that heal this such as the Windway (Nílch'ijí), which has two different forms. One is the Navajo Windway (Diné Binílch'ijí), which has drawings on the patient's body, and the other the Chiricahua Windway (Chíshí Binílch'ijí), which treats problems with the heart and breathing. There is also the Lightning or Shootingway (Iináájí), which deals with problems of the heart caused by exposure to lightning and things from the heavens. If a person is having nightmares, pain in the stomach, or small sounds in the throat, the Evilway (Hóchxǫ'ijí) can address those issues. Many of the animals whose images cause sickness are from the mountains, and so a Mountainway (Dziłk'ijí) ceremony is performed to appease them. These ceremonies remove the harmful presence and replace it with one that is helpful. The patient is in the image of this ceremony. The holy people created all of these rituals during the time of the slaying of the monsters and so are very powerful. If the clinic does not cure a person, one of these ceremonies will. Even if the ailment seems like a little thing at the time, if it is not taken care of as soon as possible, the sickness will start to kill. After the ceremony is performed, the person gets well. An owl may warn one when traveling that they are about to see something that will be harmful. Sometime later, it really makes that person ill if there are not the proper precautions. If a person suspects that they have been influenced by one of these sights, it is best to have a ceremony done as soon as possible in order to live in harmony again. The warning lasts up to four days, after which, if a special ceremony is not performed, the offended creature will say you are theirs.

Take for example a person who offends a bear by not giving prayers or providing an offering, or if they shoot at it. The bear is considered one of the most powerful creatures and is said to control the different animals and medicines on the mountain. By bothering it, a person will begin to act crazily, have sustained nose bleeds, and suffer from disturbing thoughts and dreams about the mountains. Especially when it is starting to bother that individual, he or she will dream about these places because that is the domain of the bear. To effect a cure requires a nine-day Mountainway ceremony. During that ritual the holy beings, in the form of two Yé'ii Bicheii dancers with their medicine bundles and spruce branches as part of their clothing, come to visit and bless the performance. The spruce represents the bear's furry face as well as its connection to the mountains. This ceremony is the only one powerful enough to cure this ailment.

Domestic Animals

Domestic animals have their own powers and realms in which they operate. They are a form of wealth that can increase and provide protection and assist with their powers while enriching the life of the Navajo. To have knowledge about them brings blessings into one's existence, which are heightened through prayer when the animals are giving birth or being eaten, or at the conclusion of a meal. When one prays for their livestock, their offspring increase. This is true of all livestock who listen and heed prayers. They do just what you ask. Animals, whether wild or domestic, understand what is being said through the sacred words that are used and transmitted by the holy wind. Their holy wind or "spirit that stands within" communicates with the spirit of the person offering the prayer. They know each other. Even though there is nothing at your side, if you pray earnestly, the holy people will assist.

For instance, if you know the sacred name of the horse and use it, that opens up a spiritual communication. You would say that we are going to travel a long distance and that it should be patient and tolerant. This is the reason we are going there, and we will bring back certain items. This is what is told to the horse. Corn pollen is then sprinkled on it, placed in its mouth, then tossed in the direction of travel for a trail of pollen. Now the rider mounts and goes to his destination. If he is hunting, he will arrive safely, and in no time the deer will show up and be shot and butchered in the sacred way, its meat will be packed, and the hunter will start for home. It is from the prayers that have been answered using sacred names and language that this success comes. The horse and the deer understand their true names and respond to the responsibilities given to them. This is what the elders used to do. If you do not know and understand any of this, there will be nothing there for you to bring home.

Today, the automobile has replaced the horse when it comes to traveling, but it is treated and blessed in the same way. People still pray to it because the car works on the same principles as the horse. Wind, electricity, and the rainbow are what move the horse, which itself is composed of all the growing things on this earth. The automobile is the same—it moves with the help of electricity that runs through its veins [wire], it has a heart [battery], it depends on water [gasoline], and when it travels, it is moved by the wind. The concepts are the same. Before starting, one prays and scatters corn pollen to travel on and offers prayers in the same way, asking that the holy people assist in reaching its destination.

Dogs are another domestic animal with powers to help people. Long ago, there was a poorly made ceremonial basket that an old man used to mix plant seeds. In it, he kneaded the dough made of every color of corn. The basket became a small "food storage" (stomach) that had two rainbows running along its side. He made these into the sacred image of the dog with a rainbow around it and on its bottom side. There were also herbs cut for it. When the holy people put all of this together, the dog arose and started running around and howling. Eventually, it scampered off and found a place to dwell. From the beginning of time, the dog lived in a place called Tséyi. Talking God gave them to the Navajo to herd sheep. There was a great mixture of them with some black, others yellow, red, gray, and so forth. Still, they had the understanding and ability to communicate just like humans with their holy wind inside, only the skin was different. When a sacred picture of a dog is made for ceremonial purposes, it is said that the image goes back to its homeland at Tséyi (In the Canyon). The prayers offered for it tell them to return there. At that place it is like a human but a dog when with people.

The first dog did many crazy things like peeing all over the place, running around and howling, getting in people's way—all of which was bothersome. Some individuals began to have pains in their stomach that lasted a long time and were repeated often. They suspected that the sickness was connected with having a dog. At this time, the people were using woven baskets and clay pottery to hold their food when eating. They probably were not cleaning their dishes, and so the dog licked their plates and bowls before the people ate out of them again. As the humans became more suspicious of this animal for causing problems, they began to throw sticks at it, forcing it to run away. It did not return.

The people thought that perhaps the dog would come back and continue to eat all of their food. One day a stranger arrived and heard about the activities of the dog and how people thought that their stomach pains were connected. They did not like this creature. The man could not believe what he heard, declaring, "I was living among them, and together we hunted deer and rabbits, and they helped me. There were also two girls (in human form) that came to me and offered to take me home." He explained that these girls were really dogs, and that upon arriving at their hogan, the man went inside and saw male dogs lying about as well as female dogs with their exposed breasts full of milk. The man had brought some meat, which the girls took from him. He soon left to go hunting again, and at first did not want to return, but his mind kept thinking about what he had seen and of the girls he left behind. They liked him a lot and licked around his mouth and all over. He even placed his hands on them and found that they were not ticklish. Next, he put his hands all over them, and they did not even protest his touching. He liked this but still wanted to return home. On his way, the two girls found him again carrying more meat on his back. One of them ran up to him on one side while the second girl went behind, and both jumped up, bumping him in the cheeks. That really hurt. He yelled at them, picked up a stick, and whacked them with it. They began to cry and continued to do so all the way back to their home. This was when female dogs first got angry. The man left that place and went back to where he was living. This is how the story about the dog is told.

From this story, we learn that dogs were not made as humans, but more like coyotes. Many of them even look like a coyote or a fox. Their flesh is not like human flesh even though it is said that they were like people back then. The man, when he returned to his community, suggested that the stomach pains that they were suffering from probably came about because dogs ate human body waste. The people then recalled that whenever they left camp to relieve themselves, the dogs chased after them and ran to that spot. Today, Navajo people avoid eating anything that could have come in contact with a dog's saliva to prevent having stomach pains. If one gets them, they will grow, infest a body, and start to kill that person. As for cats, they have no evil in them. They are from the place where they walk with no sound and are called Kint'ah Neeyáanii (Raised in the City). They came from Talking God and are related to the mountain lion, just smaller.

Divination

The holy people have also provided ways for us to learn what has gone wrong and how to best help the person who is affected. This began in the palm of time when the gods decided to give humans the power to know things that had happened in the past, in the present, or future. During the killing of the monsters, the Twins used Big Star (Sǫ'tsoh—Venus) in star and crystal gazing. These two forms of divination are performed at night. It is said there was a supernatural being who goes into star gazing for

Dogs are an important greeter found at most Navajo camps and accompanying herds of livestock. Many people believe that they are conscientious shepherds who keep the flock together and protect against predators. Dogs are said to have the ability to detect unseen evil if it approaches a home.

the ones who look at Big Star, which shines all over the earth. This holy one carries lots of gossip. As one looks into the dark night sky, the medicine person will see Big Star shining like a flashlight. It will be pulsating, sending a message of what it has seen to the medicine person, who has to interpret what is being communicated. Once the answer is obtained, the light goes away. The star may also cover the subject in white light and may indicate who will perform the ceremony. The same results occur in crystal gazing, where an image or picture is found within the rock, showing what is causing the problem and telling how it may be cured. This is similar to being asleep and dreaming when an impression warns about something that will happen in the future. The image is real, and one sees this thing taking place. As you travel the road of life, your soul is learning what lies ahead. Many people do not understand that this is the way of prayer and not just some kind of nonsense. Prayers and powers used in star gazing are real. I have been very involved in that ceremony and understand it. The star knows the person performing the act, the one who makes an offering of prayers to the dark wind, blue wind, white wind, and yellow wind that reside in the four directions and carry the messages. Lightning is also involved, because we have it within us and it helps us to move and have life. This force becomes a shield that allows one to walk with protection.

Another more common form of divination is called hand trembling (ndishniih), which does not depend directly upon Big Star. The power from this comes from the Gila monster (Tiníléí). There are four types of this kind of lizard—ones that have red on their head that looks like the red on a snake, others that have yellow spots, one kind that has black spots, and another that has blue-green spots. During the palm of time, the first hand trembling ceremony took place. Gila Monster and Big Star formed an agreement. Following the killing of the monsters, the Twins became very ill and were about to die because of all of the bloodshed. The star and the reptile agreed to use their powers to prevent the Twins from dying and to help others in the future with things that threatened them. This is how the two forms of divination are related and continue to work together as one. When I was still young, it came to me through being ill. It felt like something had cloaked me. This is how I know this. The power understands what happened to a person or at a place. It knows everything. It is like you are tracking something and the power says that it will be like this henceforth, just as one learns from a radio what occurred. It is about the same thing. This is what I think.

If this ceremony wants a certain person, the power will make itself known. There will be movement of the hand for no apparent reason as it starts to tremble. Impressions are given to the mind that the power wants it to know, and perhaps a ringing in the ears will occur. To accept and receive this power officially, there is a prayer said to ordain an individual to receive it. A small offering and prayer are made, and the person transferring the power blesses with pollen key spiritual places on the body. Once this is done, a song is sung, and the man or woman receiving the power extends his or her hand, which begins to move. I was sick when I first obtained it. The power came into me suddenly, and even though I was very sick, the Gila monster helped me get well. It took over my body, pulled me up, and focused my mind on what was needed to heal. The power usually asks what is wanted, then indirectly shows something in the mind that must be interpreted for the cure. It is a type of investigation where images suggest what is needed, but the medicine person has to discern, through knowledge of the ceremonies, what is being shown. The power then confirms that what it has shared is understood correctly. If it shows two or more things, one must question about both. What kinds of ceremonies will be right for this ailment? Then it indicates what is needed. After the ritual, the patient will get well and again walk with happiness in life.

If the patient is in pain, the medicine person asks the spirit about the cause and where a cure may be found, the power indicating the answer. The plant should be given as soon as possible, but it is the power that tells how long it will take for the patient to get well. This might take only a few days or perhaps months. For example, after using hand trembling, I went to help a woman who had several surgeries to correct her illness. She was very thin, and although other herbalists had tried to help her, she had made no improvement. I thought I would give her a try, and after hand trembling, I went to a certain place to pick plants that I thought might work even though they grew far away. After making an offering to the herb, I mixed what I had picked with another herb (iinááji—Lifeway) that grew close by and placed them in water. I told this woman to constantly drink it for a month, and if she did, she would be walking the life of wellness again. Within that time, she had gotten well, and in two months her usually slow movements had changed to a lively energy. When I asked her if she was better, she replied, "Yes, I am well again. I drank the herbs for ten days and got better." Now she walks in good health.

There is another example of this kind of healing with a man who had a severe case of arthritis. Roy could barely walk, so I made herbs for him. "I used to drive," he said, "but now I can't. I can hardly get around." Sometime after his treatment, he drove to my home and jokingly announced that the women in his household, because of his condition, had assumed ownership of his automobile, but now that he was healed, he had taken it away from them and sat in the driver's seat. A man from Black Mesa who had a job working in the coal mine came to me saying, "I am in very bad pain at my waist and hip," and that he could not sit upright for very long. I mixed herbs for him, too. I stressed that he needed to take it easy and consume the herbs in a sacred manner for several days. He, too, was healed.

There were a number of times when I was involved in star gazing that the impression came to me that I should also use hand trembling. The power made it very easy for me to obtain this additional ability. When using it, a person really has to concentrate, thinking very hard about the images and impressions coming to them as they try to help a patient. The answer comes in the form of learning what the person did and why it is affecting them, then indicates what ceremony is needed for healing. It is like investigating. Because I know this ritual, people—even Mexicans—come from great distances for my help. Through this power, life goes on, protection prayers are extended, and the Blessingway ceremony assists. There are sacred supernatural beings for the Navajo who ensure that we will not be cornered. From far-off places like Gallup and Aztec, New Mexico, people come to me to perform hand trembling. This is how I am known, even though I do not go out and advertise and try not to go to other places unless it is absolutely necessary. Instead, people come from all over the reservation to see me.

At mid-winter all of these things and more are talked about without hesitation, because many of the creatures involved with these teachings are not active. Each one has a true or sacred name by which it is known. When it is used, the words in a prayer go directly to that being addressed so that one is not just talking into space. Once you know these things, hold fast to them because they are good. Now that wine and beer are available, our thoughts have become messed up. This is what I have observed. It is through these things that people have become crazy. For example, in the Enemyway ceremony, participants are creating new songs that are inappropriate. I wonder when the people will come back to their senses, but it is not happening. My maternal grandmother used to say there would be a time when the language of the enemy would be the only one spoken, pointing out that when it does occur, the harmony of living will pass and chaos will be everywhere. She warned not to let children lose their native tongue and for women not to wear pants or else things will fall apart. It is also not good for them to cut their hair.

Chapter Six

Ada Black

A Century of Change

Ada sat contemplating, choosing her words carefully. Often, she looked up when mentioning that she wanted this information to go to the young people and that much of it could serve as a shield of protection. Her reputation in the Monument Valley community ensured they would be respected. People recognized her as a quiet person, a medicine woman, skilled with herbs and in performing divination. Beyond that she was one of those individuals whom medicine men often invited to be involved in various aspects of a ceremony. While she did not conduct it, she knew what needed to be done, who should assist, and how to play that important support role to see that things went smoothly. Consequently, her personal knowledge expanded as she sang the songs, recited the prayers, and witnessed the power of healing. As our interview continued, Ada often addressed Marilyn as "her daughter," an honor that she appreciated.

Little did any of us realize that in less than a year and a half Ada would be killed by a freak accident. The winter of 1993 was markedly different from most. Snowstorms and rainfall in record amounts battered the United States, causing massive flooding or snow-related issues throughout. All of Utah, including Monument Valley, welcomed the much-needed moisture, but in the same instance wished it came in more manageable amounts. Ada, who at one point went with her son into a neighboring hogan, no doubt hoped for drier weather and increased mobility. The hogan, a symbol of the traditional life that she represented to neighbors and family, served as a safe refuge. Or so it seemed. These structures, if not maintained with a thick coat of dirt on the exterior, can become weakened, especially around the smoke hole/chimney opening at the top of the cribbed roof. Logs may loosen, dirt and bark can erode, and then structural stability will be lost. That is what happened. A few logs from the ceiling came crashing down and killed Ada, while her son was untouched. In a brief moment, her life was snuffed out, a prime connection to the past gone. Her family buried her within the four-day period, losing eighty years of experience and teachings, a fraction of which follows.

Ada's Story, Part Two

Anasazi

As I grew older, my grandmother warned me about the future and compared it to what happened to the Anasazi, some of the first people who lived on this land. They clustered together and grew in knowledge, inventing things through spiritual means and understanding that controlled many of the powers in the universe. It is said that they learned ways to use the wind, lightning, and forces of nature. They carved in rocks and alcoves, painted on pottery, desecrated stone axes and arrowheads, and used designs that symbolized these powers. Every way that is known by the wind came out in their patterns. Since they understood the wind's powers, the Anasazi turned this into the ability to fly, just as Anglos use these principles today in airplanes. That is why their homes are in the cliffs. They harnessed the same powers of electricity as seen in their paintings of lightning and rainbows used for flying or protection. Their ruins are all over the land, and broken pottery lies on the ground, painted with the holy symbols of the wind, lightning, and rainbows. The Anasazi became proud of their accomplishments, ignored the holy people, and turned the sacred into the profane by not praying and giving offerings. They were a blessed and gifted people caught up in their own greatness.

The holy beings watched, saw that this was not good, and met to discuss the problem. They were offended by what they witnessed and so decided to perform a wind ceremony that would destroy the Anasazi and leave a lesson for future generations not to be forgotten. The wind began to blow, sucking the oxygen out of the air, hurling fire and rocks about in Anasazi communities, and destroying their means of livelihood. Now there are only handprints and worn pictures, carved footholds and ruins, arrowheads and broken pottery to serve as reminders of what happened to them and why. The Navajos, like the Anasazi, have to keep their population under control and maintain a humble life through the Blessingway ceremony.

Our people did not bother these places, knowing that Anasazi spirits and powers were still in those sites and rock art. It was the white-skinned people who excavated their remains, took their pottery and stone objects, and exposed them to the world. Before that they were treated with respect; they should be left alone as a deceased people. We hold a high regard for them and do not disturb things concerning the supernatural. The white man has exposed them, removing the rocks that hid them and the sand that covered their houses. There were rocks that closed their entrances that are now opened. The Anasazi used to live in those places. Their bodies are found in sleeping positions with pots beside them, just as they had died.

When I was living at Navajo Mountain, there was a group of white people [archaeologists] who were digging in some ruins. A water reservoir was close by where they were excavating, with a flat surfaced rock and a white rock exposed in the ground next to a building and a stack of rocks. The stones had been used to make walls, and a pile of white sand rested nearby, while groups of rooms composed the site. These had doorways that led to different spaces. The whites were gathered there, putting things in gunny sacks and boxes. It was a harmful feeling that came with what they were doing to the dead and their possessions. It was a sight. I was six or seven years old at the time, herding the sheep back to water at the reservoir. There were piles of gunny sacks, some not even covered, with bodies sticking out, their heads still attached. It was a harmful sight to see, but I did. It is said their spirits will overtake and can kill a person unless they have an Enemyway ceremony to ward off and exorcise those evil forces. That night I had a nightmare concerning what I had seen that woke me up. I told my relatives about it, and they told me that I should not be looking at the remains of the Anasazi. The darn goats kept going back to that site, forcing me to go through it to round them up and get them out of there. They required me to go among the remains of the Anasazi. The white men were there for a number of days, maybe even a month. They brought many boxes and sacks to put bones in, then stacked them.

Some Anasazi rock art can be used for witchcraft. People say that those who know the Enemyway can do bizarre things with witchcraft against others. This uses the power found in it to curse instead of heal people, my maternal grandmother would say. It is believed that a person who is envious of another can call out an individual's name, draw their image, and curse it. This is why one does not bother rock art images or Anasazi dwellings; it is dangerous. Do not get involved in their places or with their objects or trace images because they are connected to and remind one of the bad things those people did. If one listens to what is told, they will be alright, but some who are foolish ignore these warnings.

Early Times in the Valley

After the gods destroyed the Anasazi, the Navajo and Paiute people lived in Monument Valley. There was a powerful medicine man named Hashkéneiniihnii who moved with his family to places like Tsin ahi-ihnáákaad (Wood That Stands Upright) and toward Béégashii Neel'á (Where Many Cows Are Raised) and on to Deez'aii (Mesa That Sticks Out). He had a son named Hastiin Atini, who, like his father, was a powerful medicine man. I did not know them but was told that both used their knowledge and power in a bad way, with witchcraft part of their means for obtaining wealth, according to my maternal grandmother. This is probably true because many of his offspring are dead. A long time ago, Hashkéneiniihnii used to raid white people and made himself frightening to them. This was why he received the name of Giving Out Anger, but I really do not know much about him. He and his son stole cattle from across the San Juan River in the Mormon settlements. It is said that one time when he was herding stolen sheep at the meeting place of the San Juan with Colorado River, he caused the waters to part. Hashkéneiniihnii and his son knew how to control the wind and so used it to separate the water so that the stolen sheep, horses, and cattle could cross. The water at that time ran so very high that one could see the backbone of the river, which was in a real rage. The two men started to chant to it, causing the water to gush upward. The horses crossed first, leading the sheep, then the cattle, and finally the warriors before the water rushed back in. They used evil ways when raiding their enemies and did crazy things. Much of this happened during the troubling times when there were enemies lurking around.

Navajos should not be afraid of the night because that was one of the few times that we were safe. The night cloaked us. This is what used to be said. The Utes were the first ones to fight us, then came the Mexicans to attack and scatter us, followed by Anglos and enemy tribes. There were even other Navajos who stole from us as the enemy hunted us down, gathered the people, and sent them to Fort Sumner. Some of our adversaries even go back to the time of the Twins and the killing of the monsters. For instance, the Paiutes who live around Navajo Mountain in the canyon called Ba-a-chini (?) are children of Kicking Monster (Tsédahhódzííłtátíí), whom Monster Slayer allowed to live if they remained there. This is not the best time of year [October] to be telling all of this because the ants are still out, the spiders still running around, snakes crawling about, and lightning possible. These things should not be discussed in front of them. To tell all about it now is a dangerous line to cross, so I will not do it in respect to the holy people. To do so could affect my whole family and extended families that are related. For one month around Christmas time, these stories can be shared. Then, you can tell about everything without the fear of your relatives; this is also true in the middle of the summer during the month of July.

My maternal grandmother said that the whole problem, ending with Navajos going on the Long Walk to Fort Sumner, started with our people stealing from the white men. This is the way she talked about it. "I was a little girl living on Blue Mountain just this side of Blanding. It is said there is a timber line right next to the canyon where many trees existed, right beside where there are now houses. In the distance there was another line of trees in which there was a lot of smoke from campfires where others were living. We thought these were Navajos who had moved into the area to graze their sheep and horses. My mother, grandmother, and I left our sheep at my uncle's camp in a place called Díwózhii Bikooh [around Hatch Trading Post in Montezuma Creek Canyon] to gather piñon nuts. While we were out picking, we had just finished our lunch when a man rode up on his horse. In a very anxious voice, he asked why the older women were not on the alert. The campfires in the distant wood line, he warned, belonged to the Utes who were out to kill and capture Navajos. He directed us to go somewhere that was inaccessible, then explained that a Navajo man named Ashkii Łizhinii (Black/Darker Boy), who had married a Ute woman, later killed her. The Utes wanted revenge, searching for groups of Navajos picking piñon nuts and killing them in retaliation. This happened a short while ago.

Now the Utes had gathered in larger numbers and were about to run into bigger groups of Navajos. My mother's mother went to the horses, quickly saddled them, and packed their things, saying they would return to Montezuma Creek. By this time, as a young girl, I was really afraid. The man who warned us said the Utes were about to ride this way and that we were all in the open in plain sight. I went to climb onto a horse, but was so badly frightened and weak that my mother grabbed me, placed me on her horse, and away we went through the woods and down the steep canyon slope. The whip was constantly on the horse. The two women were on

Navajo warriors were ever-vigilant against those invading their homeland in search of livestock, slaves, or trophies. These men have caps with eagle or hawk feathers, sinew-backed bows, arrows marked with lightning designs, mountain lion skin quivers, and rawhide or horsehide shields decorated with protective symbols. All of these elements speak of self-preservation and qualities desired by the bearer. (Painting by Robert Becenti)

foot, running behind the animal. My great-uncle appeared on horseback, coming from where he had been tending the sheep. He relieved me of my hard labor of controlling the reins of the horse, grabbed me off the saddle, and placed me on his horse behind him. My grandmother then laid blankets on the empty horse, mounted, and my great-uncle whipped it down the trail. It almost felt like flying, riding on the back of my great-uncle's horse. We were down in Montezuma Creek when some of the things tied on the horse fell off and I was thrown off. He told me to stay right there because my mother would catch up soon, then rode off. Mother was still chasing the horse that her grandmother was on, but eventually reached my great-uncle. Mother and grandmother were so exhausted from this flight that they just collapsed upon reaching camp.

Two days later, close to Blue Mountain, the Utes killed my uncle. The enemy then followed a trail that led them to our camp. The Navajo men joined together and fought across a large brush fence, but when the Utes attacked, there was no stopping them. They killed men and women but took the children and young girls as prisoners. Before the fight, the Navajo carefully planned to tie their horses away from the camp in a distant location. After the fight, some of the Navajos escaped and followed their foes as they moved on. That night, the Utes made camp, tied their horses at a distance, and built cooking fires. The Navajos watched and waited as their enemy clustered around the burning wood. At the right moment, the Navajos attacked, killed some of the Utes, recaptured their children, and stole some of the frightened and confused Ute girls, all under the cover of darkness. The enemy ran around as if they had been thrown in different directions at once. The Ute girls, who probably just followed the escaping Navajo girls, were probably frightened and took off after them. With this, the Utes went back to their country in the Cortez area but would later live around Blue Mountain." This is how my maternal grandmother used to tell about this time.

There were also those who later traveled to Fort Sumner and spent four years there. Our grandfather, called Tsii' Ná'ázt'i' (Headband), said he went there when he was four years old. But really, I do not have many in my family that went there. Almost everyone remained around here. It was said that those who went were given food, then killed. The government fed them for four years until the medicine men performed ceremonies and all were released. Those returning were given five sheep to start their herds and told to go back home. While there, some of the women became infected with venereal disease and wanted to know what cured it. They started to chew any plant with the hope it would heal. This is how the story goes, but it is not a good one. I don't like it, but that is why, to this day, people have gone crazy because their thinking has been affected in the wrong way. Some of those who did not go lived in the canyons and crevices of Navajo Mountain. My grandfather and grandmother did not leave their lands and lived comfortably while others suffered at Fort Sumner.

Influenza

Another difficult time for the Navajo people was when the Great Sickness [influenza epidemic of 1918–19] killed many of the people. A lot of this illness came to the Oljato area, with stories of whole families dying off. Nobody really talked about it until recently. The dawn foretold what was going to happen. The light was red, bathing the landscape in an eerie color and warning that a powerful illness was coming. At dusk, the fading light was also red. This happened in the spring and continued throughout the year until the fall, when the sickness arrived. My grandmother told me such things would happen. In the beginning the holy people designed this warning, telling of what was to come. Both the moon and the sun gave signs as they crossed each other's paths. The moon said, "I will be the sign of the Anglo" while the sun said, "I will be the sign of the Navajo." The Sun goes through an eclipse to show the People that a change is about to take place and put this in his law. He also said, "I will keep working, but in return a well-to-do Navajo man or woman, as well as the old people who have lived to their fullness, will die." This is why Navajos offer prayers to Mother Earth, who cares for us because we are like her babies, while the sky is our father. The sun and the moon said that our prayers should teach these things. Mother Earth, Father Sky, the Sun, and the Moon—with these a person will lead a harmonious life. It is said the prayers would be held in mid-spring, then in mid-summer, then in mid-fall, then in mid-winter. With these you will be blessed and protected from harm. For this reason, one asks for the earth's blessings. If these prayers are not given, people will die. Since the moon is for other, non-Navajo people, there are no prayers specifically for it. The earth blessing is the one that protects people from any kind of sickness.

My maternal grandmother used ceremonies to ward off the illness. For instance, at the break of dawn she offered white cornmeal, at noon it was mixed cornmeal, at twilight before the golden glow passed she offered yellow cornmeal, and at midnight it was blue cornmeal. She had separate pouches for each color. Sometimes at noon she also used corn pollen. It was said that when the sickness was coming, at the crack of dawn or at twilight, that the sky would be red. She knew what to do, and as the sickness spread throughout the land, she told us what to do. "Get up, get up, do not sleep." We offered our cornmeal to the rising sun at dawn. In the past, I did not really understand these ways, but now I do. If I had followed through with all of the ceremonies I am aware of, I would not have lost so many of my children. Now I see the right and wrong. It is easy to look back into the past and understand what happened.

Those who practice witchcraft cannot succeed against the power of earth blessings. That person who is cruel will give your soul to the earth by talking it into the ground, but if you have an earth blessing, they cannot succeed and you are protected. This is what my grandmother told me. The earth blessing prayer and the sky blessing prayer are offered to the four directions. All of these prayers are in a group of four; the stories of their origin should be known. As long as these are understood, a person will be protected, although there are some who do not believe this. If it is not true and holy, why are there stillbirths? The little spirits go into these babies, with the air coming out at the tips of their fingers and the top of the head, anywhere it can escape. The spirit moves the little body and becomes its voice. It is the holy beings [lightning] that move everything—the sheep and every kind of living species. That is why when the thunder first sounds in the spring, the insects come to life.

The Great Sickness took the lives of many Navajos, but it did not come our way. Our grandfather would prepare the sweat lodge so that at dawn the women could take a sweat bath. He heated the stones in a fire, placed them inside, gathered and mixed herbs, then boiled them in a porcelain pot to fight against the sickness. Once finished, we went outside and drank a cupful of herbs brewed in water. There is no food or medicine eaten inside the sweat lodge and no sleeping. When our bodies cooled down from the intense heat, we would go back in, repeating the process with herbal drink four times. The women performed this without men and the men without women. By the time the sun rose, it was time to take the sheep out.

Our family was very fortunate, unlike the people living in Oljato. I had no close contact with the illness, just diarrhea, and so we only heard about it. The reason we did not get the disease was because of prayers. It is like this when prayers are used. Plague-like diseases or infestations of insects do not come to your land. This is happening right now. North of us, there are caterpillars in great numbers that are eating many of the green plants. We do not have any here because we are protected by our prayers.

Trading Posts

One of the good things that came to Oljato and Monument Valley was the trading posts. John and Louisa Wetherill operated the first one [in 1906–10], a couple of miles south of the post that stands in the community today. This was built at the place where the water comes out of the ground. Nearby was a square house made of wood with logs that stood straight up with juniper bark stuffed in the cracks between the logs. Now, there are only rocks scattered around here and there. One of the main things sold at this post was coffee, one of the first items these traders brought with them in their wagon. The coffee beans at that time were not roasted or ground, and the sugar was a dark color, as was the salt. Soon other items like flour, lard, and basic foodstuffs moved across the counters of this one-room store. The Oljato (Ooljéé' To'—Moon Water) spring nearby had a small basin dug to collect water. One night under a full moon, an Anglo and Navajo man went to fetch some water and saw the reflection of the moon in the

The sweat lodge is essential for ceremonial and physical purification. Rocks heated outside of the structure are placed inside to the north and provide an intense dry heat for either the men or women inside. Four consecutive sessions, each filled with songs and prayers, cleanse the individual. (Photo by Kay Shumway)

pool. The Anglo said that it had come to draw its own water, giving the site its name. This is what the people living around there said.

I was still a young girl when my family moved to that area. A man called Hastiin Béésh Íi'áhí (Mister Windmill), who married my aunt, wanted to move there, so we went to shear sheep; the wool was taken in a wagon all the way back to our home near Shonto. The road was not as difficult as it would later become. A man called Tsé'naa'i (Enemy Rock) was going to do this for us. Because of him, we moved down from the mesa and sheared the sheep in the foothills. During this time, we went to the second Oljato trading post, the one that is there now. At that point, it was built with logs, both its ceiling and walls. It was made two winters previous [in 1921]. The names of the traders were Tsé k'ízii (Rock Crevice), Little Sheep (Dibé Yázhí), then Tsiis Ch'ilii (Curly Hair), Baa Jooba'ii (Caring Person—Stokes Carson), Biligáana Tsoh (Big Whiteman—Carson's son-in-law), then Virginia Smith (Carson's daughter), who drove off a cliff in Colorado. She really understood the Navajo language and used to call me "My Sister." The very first time she saw a belt I owned that was a family heirloom, she liked it. There was a place called Bééshłichíí'ii Haagééd (Copper Mine), where they were hiring people to work. There was lots of digging involved to clean up this place, and so they sent a big truck over here to obtain workers.

My husband, Harvey, wanted to earn money there but had no food to take with him, and so I pawned this concho belt for fifty dollars, even though its silver was from the old times and valuable. I think I loaned it for twenty-five days and went back within twenty. I did not want to do that at all, but I felt like I had to. Because this was in the springtime, we were shearing sheep and planting crops. This meant that money could be obtained by selling the wool, and so I saved the fifty dollars I owed. When I went to pay the money and redeem the belt, she said it would be sixty dollars due to interest. I returned with that amount in the late afternoon, but she said no and gave me another belt to take its place. I told her that the one she gave me might not be made of real silver and that I would not accept it. She refused to give it back to me. During this time people were mining copper in this area and had a piece of equipment that detects it. The belt she gave me read very high on this machine, buzzing away when it was close to it. By now, the sun was going down, and so I told her I would return in the morning and that I wanted my belt back.

We were not living very far away, and since my children were close by, I wanted to know what they thought of this whole incident; I showed them the belt she had given me. I do not know why I did that and think now that I should have left it. In the morning, because of some things going on at home, I did not get to the post until around ten o'clock, although I had told her I would be there earlier. She had already left for Flagstaff to conduct trading business. Once she returned to Oljato, I confronted her about taking my belt and treating me this way. I said I was not going to let go of it because it had been passed from generation to generation in my family. Every time I went there, I reminded her that she needed to give it back, but she never did. Shortly after this, she drove off a cliff, and even though I voiced my concern for the belt, nothing came of it. I still have the other belt. [Note: Virginia Carson Smith from the Oljato Trading Post lost her life as a passenger in a vehicle that plunged down a Colorado mountainside in 1985.]

Many of the traders were kind to their customers. When people arrived at their post after a long journey in the wintertime, the trader would pour a hot cup of coffee and give a slice of folded bread or crackers with something on it. All of the men and women who ran trading posts did these kinds of things, were very generous, and good-natured. Money was scarce, and so they extended credit on flour and other necessities. The traders knew everyone back then, and so even though you had nothing, they would allow you to pay in the future for anything you wanted on the counter, like coffee, flour, salt, sugar, or shortening. Payback came twice a year—in the spring with the shearing of the sheep for wool or in the fall with the sale of lambs. During other seasons, a person might work for a trader or someone else for money to pay him back. We never went into debt that could not be paid off, and we are still like that. It is good to pay every month so you don't owe people.

The traders also helped with big family events like ceremonies, providing food and candy for free. When they gave it, they would call us by kinship terms such as my sister, brother, grandfather, grandmother, mother—whatever term they were comfortable with, since they really understood the Navajo language. They expressed their relationship by saying, "My sister, I will help you with whatever you wish," and then pack it for you. They also attended the event and may have had a Navajo ceremony performed for them. One might say, "I had a bad dream," then have a medicine man provide a cure or else say, "I am traveling a long distance to go and purchase food, and so I want a blessing for the journey," then get one. He would have a good trip, and upon his return, express appreciation for the blessing.

White men introduced alcohol on the reservation, and this was not good. Some actually made it here by putting grapes in a container and

Leone "Mike" Goulding serves Navajo customers standing in the Goulding Trading Post. Wide counters, shelves against the wall, a scale for weighing, a stove in the bullpen where customers wait, and a door facing east were hallmarks of many of the roughly 260 Navajo posts found on and off the reservation. (Special Collections, Marriott Library, University of Utah)

letting them spoil to make wine. At first it was moonshine, where Navajo workers off the reservation purchased it. They called it "cow" (béégashii) and the individual container "azisłigai" [literally, "a small white bag," actually a feed bag used to give grain to horses, but in this context, where a person would hide or carry a small pint bottle]. In our area of Navajo Mountain, we did not have much of it because no vehicle could travel to where we lived, so it only came in by horse. Once I moved to Oljato, alcohol became more plentiful. One of my brothers and a friend who had gone to school with him decided to go into business and make it. They obtained a keg and copper tubing, while the trader called Little Sheep allowed them to set up around the trading post. Somewhere near the store there was a thin smoke pipe they got from the people in the area working on water projects. Once they had made a batch, they took a small glass container and passed the brew around, while the trader sold it. The ingredients were easy to obtain—sugar, wheat, and corn boiled in a big pot— soon everybody was doing it. This was during the time when the Civilian

Conservation Corps [CCC] was here working on reservoirs and wells in Narrow Canyon and down past Oljato.

In 1925 Harry Goulding started his post in the main part of Monument Valley. He was known as Tall Sheep (Dibé Neez). At first, he moved around from place to place, living in a tent. During this time there was only one Navajo home in the area, which belonged to Asdzą́ą́ Neez, who later moved to Kayenta. Goulding and his wife, Mike, helped us a lot with food and credit as did the trader in Oljato. This white man was very kind. When it was hot, he would say, "Wait. It is hot," and give us food as we waited for the day to cool off. During the cold season, he served a hot meal. People herded sheep for him while he paid others to haul firewood and then shared it. At that time, Anglos were very kind, but now they are dying for wealth.

Livestock Reduction

The way we paid our bills at the trading post was through the wool, hides, and lambs from our livestock. Everyone owned animals—some had many sheep, goats, and horses, others only a moderate number, but all provided part of the Navajos' livelihood. A few years after the CCC programs started, the federal government, through the Soil Conservation Office, became concerned about overgrazing of the land and there being too much live-stock. The government sent men to reduce the herds. There were Anglo and Navajo range riders who fanned out across the country to determine how many animals each family owned. The range riders first identified the number of horses by putting paint on them and giving them injections. This was in the fall, but by mid-summer of the following year, they began rounding them up.

We got tricked. We were returning from working in the cornfield and about in our front driveway when the range riders drove up behind us. At that time, we only had two mules, two horses, and a donkey. They painted the mules that were pulling our wagons, the horses used for herding sheep, and the donkey. We did not say we had more. They gathered the untamed and tamed horses and took them away. The sheep and goats were next; we lost half of all we owned, which was eighty animals. They killed the goats and took the sheep but did not really bother the few cattle. In the spring, the government issued permits for what we had left. The range riders took half of the herds of sheep and goats. Each year they did this, removing part of our livelihood.

I was about seventeen or eighteen years of age when this happened, but I did not know what they were saying because everything was in English. The police arrived late at night in their vehicle and arrested my husband's stepfather, Ólta'í Nééz (Tall School Boy), who was a chairman on the livestock committee. The sheep were corralled for the night, the police threw him in the car, locked him up in jail, and later reduced his sheep and goats. At first, they took his horses and he did not resist, the police doing anything they wanted to them. But when they started on the sheep, he protested, and that was when he was jailed. Although he explained to them that those animals were the only source of livelihood for us, it made no difference. Men such as Hastiin Jani (?), Hastói Adláanii (Man Who Drinks), and Ólta'í Nééz—a total of twelve from our area—went to jail together as well as some from Kayenta. They all resisted livestock reduction. After this, with only us to protest, the government did what it wanted, and we did what we were told.

I remember the killing of the goats near our home. The officials hauled our goats away to two sheep corrals by the mesa. They told the people to butcher the animals and that the government would only take the skins. The meat was for the people who slaughtered the goats. The Anglos sent out messages to people to gather there and help kill and prepare the animals for food. Navajos came to help. When my husband and I arrived, there was meat strung along the corral fence and skins piled in the midst of all of this. As soon as someone stripped off the skin, it was added to the pile. There were small, young, beautiful goats there, causing one person to exclaim, "What great sacrifice! I wish we could put them back in our corral." The People were concerned about the waste of meat and how it could have been used if the slaughter had been handled properly. Instead of spreading it out over a period of time, this mass killing ensured that much of the meat went to waste. Angry words flew about, but the butchering continued until there were only two or three animals left. Other corrals and similar scenes in the Oljato, Goulding's, and Kayenta areas fanned the flames of resentment.

At one point, the officials ordered my husband to kill goats, but he refused, telling them to do it themselves, before he started home on foot. I had come with some friends and sat in their automobile watching events unfold. An official told them to go into one of the corrals and start killing animals, but they refused. He threatened to take the Navajo man off of the rolls of the CCC project in which he was employed unless he did what he was told, to which he replied, "The heck with all of this. I am going home."

I agreed and asked them to take me also, which they did. I got to ride, my husband ended up walking, arriving home at sunset.

A second time we received word that there was going to be another slaughter, but this time at Goulding's. There were many women now living in the Monument Valley area who were invited. An automobile came for us, and since my husband was around, the officials wanted him to be there, too. He was working in the CCC Program at the time, so he and his fellow workers were needed and expected. Harvey initially refused but the next day relented, and we went to the site. When we arrived, meat was again hanging on the corral fence as before. Women were scattered all over the place butchering. The goats' throats were slashed, placed by a woman, and allowed to bleed out as the animals churned about in the dust of the corral. Some were old goats, which displeased many of the people. Men hauled the remaining ones away, then shot them with rifles. Workers stacked the dead goats, creating a tall pile of bones that would be there for years. In Oljato the same thing happened, but there they drove them into a box canyon before shooting the animals. Right next to the rock where this happened, there remained another large pile of bones. The Navajo people involved remembered for a long time how they had been wronged. There was one man named Tódích'íiniidííl who fled to Blanding and lived in that area for about three years. When everything quieted down, he moved back to Monument Valley but never surrendered his livestock to reduction. The range riders never counted his animals or got any of them, but he also did not receive a grazing permit. Those who stayed behind and lost livestock did get one.

Early Innovations

As Monument Valley became more populated and better known, new experiences and technology began to change our lives. This area is famous for moviemaking; the only one I was in was filmed in Moab. For two days of work, we were paid twenty dollars, and for five it was eighty-nine dollars. We did not receive that much money because part of our pay was in food and the gas it took for a bus to pick us up in Monument Valley and bring us to Moab. While filming, we lived in big tents that were pointed at the top with floorboards on the bottom. Some of the people stayed out in the open or in their pickups, while others had campers on their trucks and brought their own food and bedding. We stayed within our own group, and one woman had her child. In the evenings there was bathing close by. As for the work, I did not have a very exciting part, just standing around

One of the first cars (Maxwell) to enter Monument Valley, piloted by Dolph Andrus and accompanied by W. H. Hopkins and H. Stanley Hinnricks in the fall of 1916. First-time Navajo observers had a variety of explanations as to what an automobile was, but it did not take long before it began replacing horse and wagon. (Used by permission, Utah State Historical Society)

in a crowd. In another scene, what they had us do was ugly. Supposedly, a person had died and was being buried. That was ugly, even though the body was covered when it was carried around. We were told to stand in line at this funeral. I did not like what was going on, so I remained in camp.

One thing that has really changed our life was the introduction of motor vehicles. I remember the first one I saw was when I was a young girl living north of Shonto in the summertime. There was a great sound, and I wondered what it could be. When I saw it, the machine looked like a wagon with headlights sticking out, wagon-like wheels, and axles that protruded and were just screwed on. It was burning coal with a chimney sticking out the back end. People said it was the burning of the coal that made it run, and so all of that smoke coming out gave it the name of anus smoke. It was not called chidí at that time, but anus smoke. A few years later the name changed, and the term chidí stuck. Once the vehicle moved past me, it made its way to Shonto.

At first Navajos said that these vehicles were looking for children because the person driving it was often picking them up for boarding school. This is what the first car I saw was doing, and a month later, the children were taken away. One was my brother, and the other was my uncle called Rough House (Kin di Ch'ízhí). They went to school in Bear Water (Shashbii'tóodi). We were living very close to the mountain with the sheep at the time when the government picked up the children and took them away. During those times, there were no good roads, only poor-looking paths, so these vehicles made a great noise as they traveled over the rough terrain. The people would say, "There it goes," even though they were frightened and not sure exactly what it was.

Although the airplane did not really come in until recently, medicine men were singing about them in the squaw dance (Enemyway) songs. One of them told people to look up and see it flying. I have never flown in one, but my husband has. It took off from Goulding's and flew over us and the rock formations of Monument Valley before returning to the airstrip. Another time, he flew from Kayenta to Albuquerque. There was a second Navajo person flying with him who kept missing his breath. My husband laughed at him, and he got angry.

Uranium Mining

From the late 1940s through the 1960s, Monument Valley was the scene of a lot of uranium mining. Harvey was heavily involved in these operations. In fact, at one point, we owned a mine that he worked in. It started when we went to Window Rock several times to meet a white man who asked to see certain types of rocks and be told where they were found. He offered to handle all of the paperwork, provide the equipment needed to mine the ore, hire and pay workers, and give us a percentage from the uranium rocks after they were weighed and measured for radioactivity. It took five days to get the contract approved, then the white man started working on our property. At first two big trucks arrived, then several more to haul the material away. Where they went, I do not know, but I do know that I was paid only a little bit. The mine operated from early spring of one year to midwinter of the next. Work stopped due to some places caving in and my husband's eyes feeling the effects from the job. Other mines began to close down until eventually all did. But for about twenty years, Harvey worked extensively in the mines of this area, many of which—seven or eight—were operating on top of some mesas as well as in the valleys.

Mining at that time was dangerous. Even though he did not go to school, Harvey was good at drilling and dynamiting rocks and so was often picked for that job. He drilled holes about twenty-five feet apart, and even though people warned that rocks might fall on top of him, he continued with his work. Nothing like that ever happened to him. There was one site he worked in near Narrow Canyon that was sixteen feet down that scared him because it looked like the rock was layered and could easily collapse. Fortunately, there was no problem for him, and he tried to do as many jobs above ground as possible. There was one man crippled from falling rock and two others who died when the ceiling and walls collapsed on them. After these fatalities, the owner closed it down, but there were other accidents in neighboring mines.

From the start of mineral development around here, the mines continuously employed him. One of the jobs he had was operating the łééžh yisolí (sand blower). This meant he went into dangerous places where rocks might fall. Another time, he worked at the top of the cliff on the north side of Oljato Mesa, running a metal hoist that brought the ore to the valley floor. There was a big bucket tied to a metal cable with a thinner metal cable to guide the load to the bottom. The white men struggled to work this system, but for Harvey, it was easy to run it smoothly. When these types of jobs were added to his responsibility of blasting rock, I became increasingly concerned. I told him, "We have plenty to eat. We have sheep and cattle. Do not go," but he went anyway. Now he has problems with his eyes from lighting dynamite. The sparks from the thin, black fuses exploded into his eyes and singed them. There was also sand from the blower that blinded him. One side of his eyes turned gray and really hurt. At one point, they flew him out in an airplane to have doctors look at him, but he never received any payment for his injury. They told him that they would send money, but he never received it and feels like he was lied to. Time is passing. Between the ore that we were not paid for and his injury payment not received, they are in debt to us. They made a living, while we live with suffering as we continue to get old. We keep thinking we might receive a chunk of money and are now in need of many things like firewood, but there are only the two of us depending on each other. During those years of mining, he worked in different places, held a variety of jobs, and had many employers. His pay ranged between thirty and sixty dollars given every two weeks.

A typical workday started early in the morning and sometimes went for twelve hours. If there were several big trucks that needed to be filled, his work might take into the evening or night, and we would receive overtime pay. It looked like he was making a lot of money, but it was less than what the goods at the store cost. The white men were cheating us. They were probably thinking how they could get more, and since I did not have it on paper, there is no record now. If I had known what the papers were for, I would have kept them. I did not know, so I do not have them. It was up to him to do the work, and he did his best. The only thing that mattered was how much rock was hauled away. The pay he received was not enough, but he worked for it anyway. He would leave around five o'clock in the morning, even if there was no moon, hurrying off to his job with a flashlight. In rain or snow or cold, he went so that he could continue to work without thinking about the money. When asked why he worked for such small pay, he said he felt it was his duty. At the same time, at home he had to haul firewood and water with our wagon, but we never had any problem. I packed his meals to take to work and did everything to support his efforts as well as performing my responsibilities at home with small children, taking care of the livestock, and planting a garden in the spring. He had his work and I had mine, but I did it with a baby in the crook of my arm. I never heard of any women working in the mines. Life and work around the home kept us there.

We grew much of our food, and I made a variety of lunches and dinners for him. For instance, I boiled corn, added some meat, and wrapped it in bread. I might make ash bread one day, dry bread or fry bread another time, but each was nicely made. The meat came from a butchered sheep, was thinly sliced, then ground. This is the way I packed for him. If he was working at a far distance, I provided lots of food to last him a long time. Five days later he returned, and I would begin making more lunches for him. Washing his clothes was another task. Sometimes he took them off, and other times just slept in them. If he had a change of clothing, he put them on, but other times he was so tired that he just fell asleep in what he was wearing. Saturday was usually wash day. By this time, Bluff City [Utah] was the only place that had a laundromat, and so if I did not wash them at home, I went over there. I asked the people who worked with him for a ride and took his dirty clothes. It required time to get this done, but there was no laundromat in Kayenta.

After my children were in school, I wanted to earn money, so I worked with uranium ore at our mine close to home. A person named Béésh Kalí (The One Who Cuts Metal—Charles Haskin, a.k.a. Spin) from Farmington, New Mexico, gave me bags with zippers on them, so on Saturdays and Sundays, I picked through the rocks the big trucks had dumped, found the yellow ones, placed them in a wooden box I carried, then eventually loaded them in sacks. Once full, I leaned them together. Even though I worked hard, I never received any money for it and think they should have paid me. Maybe they do not even remember me. Haskin just took the rocks away.

These Navajo miners, eating outside of their workplace, like so many others of this time, were unaware of the problems of uranium's radioactivity. Primitive sanitary conditions existed at most sites, while the traditional practice of using certain types of clay as food extenders compounded health issues. (Special Collections, Marriott Library, University of Utah)

There were a couple of mines not far from here that had yellow rocks that we used for food. One year there was a lot of rain in the summer and snow in the winter that gave rise to abundant vegetation. A plant with red berries called haashch'éédą́ą́' (wolfberry) also has a root used in cooking. At first, I did not know it could be eaten, but Harvey's mother and sisters and uncle's wife consumed a lot of it. They boiled it with the uranium, now said to be dangerous, but we were not aware of it at the time and ate it as food. The rock was said to be a special mud (hashtł'ish) that was ground with a mano and metate, while the water used to boil it was also consumed. I was herding sheep at the time, and they were living out in the valley. As I brought in the sheep, I rode by their place on my horse. There were often different types of food set out, including meat and haashch'éédą́ą́'. I spooned some up, tasted its sweetness, then ate lots of it. Many times after that, I continued to eat this special mud that tasted like milk.

This food extender was like the white mud found in the mines, used as a sweetener. Lots of people worked there, and many died from it. Harvey's uncle and his wife passed away, as did his mother. They probably did not take any preventative measures, but I offered earth prayers to the rocks where the mine is. In this way it does not bother you. We both have reached old age even though we really ate a lot of it. Before the mines in Monument Valley opened up, we used to gather the white clay from a mine called Dlééshbí'tó' (Clay's Water) close to Comb Ridge. It provided very white clay that came from a vein of rock that had a seep with the water trickling down. The people dug out the clay and took it with them. The uranium and the clay were used in the same way even though one was very white and the uranium was very yellow.

There was also water pumped from the mines, lying around in pools that the sheep drank in the Oljato area. The pipe carried the water to the surface as people worked below. Although animals went there to drink, we did not use that water, but people did eat the sheep. Our water came from a windmill that had a drum attached to it. Since that time, we have learned about the dangers associated with radioactivity from uranium. There are other people throughout Monument Valley that were either hurt by accidents or by exposure to radioactivity. Some had sores on their legs that took months to heal. After I treated them with herbs, they became better. Harvey, now, does not go anywhere. He cannot even ride a horse but just stays home. We heard that there is an application for help for those who worked in the mines and are bothered by sickness coming from the uranium. People came to visit us about this, and I told them part of his story.

I believe that one reason we are still alive is that, as Navajos, we have prayers. Although people say that the yellow rock is dangerous to health, it is different if you have the ceremonies. We have really eaten a lot of the yellow rock, but before doing so, made offerings to it using sacred stones and tséłchíí' (light red/orange coral), tádídíín dootł'izhii (blue pollen), and tééh tádídíín (water pollen). This is how the shielding takes place. You first call the place's name, then Mother Earth, First Man, and Mountain Woman. These three are in a group that receives the offering. Whatever you have eaten from there, you say, "Here. I am making an offering to you," and ask them to be a shield. "With this I will live a long life. You will remember me, and you will hold off the monsters from me." This is how a prayer is started and grouped together. This can also be offered to rocks that have slid down toward you, but you have to be quick about this. Once you have seen the rocks fall down, you blow toward it. Stone Woman, or whomever you are doing this for, will not harm you. This can be done before noon. If it happened a day or more before, you just blow to it, but the next day an offering is made toward it with the sacred stones that are separated, which now becomes part of a protection prayer. It is the same with mining when working with the rocks. A person might get sore and have aches and pains in their body. That is when a protection prayer may be offered. From that point on, there is nothing wrong, after they go to sleep. If you do not have the prayers, then you will not have the cure or the protection. We have the prayers and so are still alive. Even though we ate the yellow rock, we have not had any sickness associated with it. This is what I think.

Later, Harvey worked in the Salt Lake area drilling in a copper mine. After that he worked for the railroad, setting metal tracks on the ground. This was high in the tops of the mountains. The job did not pay very much. He worked up north for about five years and went into strange places as the railroad tunneled through the mountains with other Navajos working beside him. The company provided food while the laborers slept on their bedding in rail cars pushed to the side of the tracks. Sometimes they ate as the train moved down the track to the next work site. That was a very different job for him.

Today in the Valley

We live here in Monument Valley, which has seen many changes over the years. We used to live where the Ranger Station now sits. There were a few trees growing next to our small hogan and shade house, but there was no water nearby, and so we took our sheep to Bullsnake Spring (Diyóósh Tó) down in what is now the tribal park. There were no other people living around there and only a few on Douglas Mesa, in Narrow Canyon, and near El Capitan. Our livestock grazed all about on this open range; we did not see many people unless there was a ceremony or some type of activity that drew them together.

Now things have changed, and I wonder about the future. I do not know anything about writing, and I have no reason to get out in public. Instead, I remain within the boundaries of our property with my livestock, home, planted fields, and work. It is plain to see how I am living and the worthwhile things I do. I think to myself that I am improving my life. Many of the things my children and grandchildren have learned in school, I do not use, but that is how they get their jobs. Since they get paid for it, they like the way it is. None of my children are working at the Ranger Station, but I do have a grandchild employed there. I hope they will continue to work there for a long time; the only thing that hinders them is that thing that they put to their mouth [alcohol]. Once they start to drink beer or wine, it ruins their work at their job. If they do not get involved with it, they will lead a very productive life. I do not want someone to haul in liquor to sell to the people because it ruins everything.

Tourism in Monument Valley has been growing and growing. Some of the development that comes with this is good, and some is bad. What if in the future a tractor is brought to start clearing the area and buildings are put up? I think that would not be good, but at the same time we need a store and places for tourists to stay and eat. In return, our children who did a fine job will cook food, make beds, and work as tour guides to earn good pay. It would be of great joy to see such a sight. There may be those who feel the urge to become managers of these stores or motels. These are the roads I think of for them. Kayenta is like that with homes being built and the town growing out. But this can also bring in things that are not appropriate, like alcohol and crime. Still, white people coming to see Monument Valley is good. We do not want them to move here and do the terrible things that come when people live in large groups. Perhaps our children and grandchildren will return to their senses and remember their home, automobile, and livestock. They will figure out where they stand in life and return to the earlier values they had when growing up. That is what I did. They will evaluate what they did when they reach old age and think differently about how they live their lives.

One thing that has always been an issue in Monument Valley is water. Our livestock has existed with hardship in getting enough of it. We have had to haul it in for our sheep and other animals, and I do not even own an automobile, an important tool for our livelihood. The water that flows underground is sent to the Monument Valley Hospital and Goulding's grocery store. The motel uses it for cooking, bathing, and other things; I wish that someone would help me get water. I have asked for assistance from our chapter officials, but they are not strong in their office. Our council delegate does not talk to others to solve the problem, and he does not think. Many issues face us here, but that is just the way it is. It would be good for our children and grandchildren to have some money put aside for them for the future. There should also be regulations against people who want to build really fine houses in the area. A lot of clearing, grading, and construction disturbs the ground. The earth provides all of the herbs needed to heal ailments. Those plants should have a place so that they can continue to help. In the future, people and all living creatures depend upon them to provide every type of healing upon this earth. I have made many herbal remedies for many people, and now they are in good health.

Life is full of challenges and changes, and then it is over. I have seen two elders die from old age—my maternal grandmother and my husband's mother, who was very old but still able to walk around. Every last one of her hairs had turned white. My maternal grandmother, on the other hand, had a more difficult time. This happened three years after I had moved to Monument Valley with my husband. She was at the very peak of old age. Her skin was extremely wrinkled, there was water in the folds, and it was said that if you touched her very hard, the skin would burst and the water would squirt out. This is how it is when one dies of old age. I am beside myself because I left my grandmother during her elderly years when she was extremely old and needed my help. She was also very intelligent and the one who shared so much information. The woman who raised me was not a teller of things. My maternal grandmother used to say that the information she taught should not be told to just anyone because the stories are like a shield that protects us as we walk through difficulties. They are not foolish tales, but are there to provide guidance as to how to live correctly. She encouraged me to enjoy everything that life has to offer, like bracelets, concho belts, sheep, cattle, and horses. Because of this, I spent a long time learning from her.

This knowledge is good so that my grandchild and another grand-daughter that came to me through clan relations can understand these things. I do not want these teachings messed up, because today's life is confusing a lot of it, and it is not getting any better. Our children's children are learning only in the Anglo language, the girls are wearing pants, and the young people do crazy things to their hair. Navajo hair is said to be the dark clouds filled with water that is falling to the ground and is very sacred and powerful. When one's hair is cut, it is cutting the dark clouds off that person. Little wonder it does not rain. A horse's mane and tail are viewed in the same way. These are put there to assist us on our trail of life. Therefore, we are not supposed to harm horses. They are made of every-thing—air, rainbow, lightning, and thunder. When they were first formed, these elements were placed into them. Even the movement of the ears signals growth. This is what grandmother used to tell me.

Our present day has turned things away from these teachings and is horrible. If only the wine and beer could be stopped for a year, perhaps the people would come back to their senses. There would be no stealing, spouse abuse, or fighting among the people, and violence would slow down. This would be a thankful thing to do. Our children's scars will heal, and those who live in uncertain ways would change and live differently. The number of thefts and automobile accidents will lower by stopping the flow of things that make people crazy. They will come back to their senses. If it is possible to spread the word of the teachings and way of life I have shared, I would be very grateful, and our visit would not be a waste. With this I hope things go back to the way they were and that I have made a difference.

As I have said, I never went to school to learn how to read and never made a mark on a paper. I stayed home and learned of what was to be done there, like herding sheep and work around the house. These are the only things that I grew up on. What I have learned in my lifetime is what I have made my home of. I was able to bring things there through weaving rugs, basketmaking, fashioning moccasins, planting crops, and taking care of livestock. Whatever I made, I exchanged for money and purchased from the white man. Even though I did not go to school, I have seen everything and feel rich in experience. It is like that; now I have told about the things that I am.

Navajo women of all ages enjoying the traditional game of tsidił. While Monument Valley can boast of its rich history, there is also a bright future. Will the young people of today embrace their heritage as willingly as those pictured here did in the past? This decision belongs to each generation. (Drawing by Charles Yanito)

NOTES

Introduction

1. Charlotte J. Frisbie, ed., with Rose Mitchell, *Tall Woman: The Life Story of Rose Mitchell, A Navajo Woman, c. 1874–1977* (Albuquerque: University of New Mexico Press, 2001).

2. Charlotte J. Frisbie, *Food Sovereignty the Navajo Way: Cooking with Tall Woman* (Albuquerque: University of New Mexico Press, 2018).

3. Kay Bennett, *Kaibah: Recollection of a Navajo Girlhood* (Self-published, 1975).

4. Bradford Keeney, ed., *Walking Thunder: Diné Medicine Woman* (Philadelphia, PA: Ringing Rocks Press, 2001).

5. Lori Arviso Alvord and Elizabeth Cohen Van Pelt, *The Scalpel and the Silver Bear: The First Navajo Woman Surgeon Combines Western Medicine and Traditional Healing* (New York: Bantam Books, 1999).

6. Emily Benedek and Ella Bedonie, *Beyond the Four Corners of the World: A Navajo Woman's Journey* (Norman: University of Oklahoma Press, 1995).

7. Ruth Roessel, *Women in Navajo Society* (Rough Rock, AZ: Navajo Resource Center, Rough Rock Demonstration School, 1981).

8. Gladys A. Reichard, *Spider Woman: A Story of Navajo Weavers and Chanters* (Albuquerque: University of New Mexico Press, 1934, 1997).

9. Maureen Trudelle Schwarz, *Molded in the Image of Changing Woman: Navajo Views on the Human Body and Personhood* (Tucson: University of Arizona Press, 1997); Maureen Trudelle Schwarz, *Blood and Voice: Navajo Women Ceremonial Practitioners* (Tucson: University of Arizona Press, 2003).

10. Louise Lamphere, *Weaving Women's Lives: Three Generations in a Navajo Family* (Albuquerque: University of New Mexico Press, 2007).

11. Carolyn Niethammer, *I'll Go and Do More: Annie Wauneka, Navajo Leader and Activist* (Lincoln: University of Nebraska Press, 2004).

12. Donna Deyhle, *Reflections in Place: Connected Lives of Navajo Women* (Tucson: University of Arizona Press, 2009).

Chapter 1

1. There are many excellent versions of the creation story and beginnings of Navajo culture, including the emergence and the events surrounding Changing Woman, Monster Slayer, and Born for Water. Here I have included, in alphabetical order, some of the most readily available examples. See Stanley A. Fishler, *In the Beginning: A Navaho Creation Myth*, Anthropological Paper no. 13 (Salt Lake City: University of Utah, 1953); Pliny Earle Goddard, "Navajo Texts," in *Anthropological Papers of the American Museum of Natural History*, vol. 34, part 1 (New York: American Museum of Natural History, 1933), 127–79; Berard Haile, *The Upward Moving and Emergence Way: The Gishin Biye' Version* (Lincoln: University of Nebraska Press, 1981); Jerrold E. Levy, *In the Beginning: The Navajo Genesis* (Berkeley: University of California Press, 1998); Washington Matthews, *Navaho Legends* (Salt Lake City: University of Utah Press, 1897, 1994); Franc Johnson Newcomb, *Navaho Folk Tales* (Albuquerque: University of New Mexico Press, 1967, 1990); Aileen O'Bryan, *Navaho Indian Myths* (New York: Dover Publications, 1956, 1993); Mary C. Wheelwright, *Navajo Creation Myth: The Story of the Emergence by Hasteen Klah* (Santa Fe: Museum of Navajo Ceremonial Art, 1942); Leland C. Wyman, *Blessingway: With Three Versions of the Myth Recorded and Translated from the Navajo by Father Berard Haile, O.F.M.* (Tucson: University of Arizona Press, 1970); and Paul G. Zolbrod, *Diné bahane': The Navajo Creation Story* (Albuquerque: University of New Mexico Press, 1984).

2. Gladys Bitsinnie, interview with author, March 26, 1993.

3. Sally Manygoats, interview with author, April 8, 1992.

4. Ada Black, interview with author, October 11, 1991.

5. Sally Manygoats, interview.

6. Betty Canyon, interview with author, September 10, 1991.

7. Sally Manygoats, interview.

8. Sally Manygoats, interview.

9. Dave Holiday, interview with David M. Brugge and Bernadine Whitegoat, January 7, 1961, Doris Duke #691, Doris Duke Oral History Project, Western History Center, University of Utah, Salt Lake City, Utah, 3.

10. Gladys Bitsinnie, interview.

11. Gladys Bitsinnie, interview.

12. See Louisa Wade Wetherill and Harvey Leake, *Wolfkiller: Wisdom from a Nineteenth-Century Navajo Shepherd* (Layton, UT: Gibbs Smith Publisher, 2007), 65–89.

13. Sloan Haycock, interview with author, October 10, 1991.

14. Gladys Bitsinnie, interview.

15. Lorita Adakai, interview with author, March 8, 1984.

16. Charlotte J. Frisbie, *Food Sovereignty the Navajo Way: Cooking with Tall Woman* (Albuquerque: University of New Mexico Press, 2018).

17. Sally Manygoats, interview.

18. Jenny Francis, interview with author, March 23, 1993.

19. Anna Black, interview with author, April 8, 1993.

20. Anna Cly, interview with author, April 8, 1993.

21. Jenny Francis, interview.

22. Velta Luther, interview with author, April 8, 1992.

23. Gladys Bitsinnie, interview.

24. Anna Black, interview.

25. Sally Manygoats, interview.

26. Kitty Atini, interview with Fern Charley and Dean Sundberg, in *The Navajo Stock Reduction Interviews of Fern Charley and Dean Sundberg*, (Fullerton: California State University—Fullerton Oral History Program, 1984), 2.

27. Sally Ralph Gray, interview with author, August 6, 1991.

28. Velta Luther, interview.

29. Lucy Laughter, interview with author, April 8, 1992.

30. Sally Manygoats, interview.

31. Anna Lora King, interview with author, April 8, 1992.

32. Frank Mitchell, "Blessingway," Version II, in *Blessingway: With Three Versions of the Myth Recorded and Translated from the Navajo by Father Berard Haile, O.F.M.*, ed. Leland C. Wyman (Tucson: University of Arizona Press, 1970), 385.

33. Stella Cly, interview.

34. Nellie Grandson, interview with author, December 16, 1993.

35. Jenny Francis, interview.

36. Gladys Bitsinnie, interview.

37. Stella Cly, interview.

38. Nellie Grandson, interview.

39. Charlotte Johnson Frisbie, *Kinaaldá: A Study of the Navaho Girl's Puberty Ceremony* (Salt Lake City: University of Utah Press, 1967, 1993); Maureen Trudelle Schwarz, *Molded in the Image of Changing Woman: Navajo Views on the Human Body and Personhood* (Tucson: University of Arizona Press, 1997); and Maureen Trudelle Schwarz, *Blood and Voice: Navajo Women Ceremonial Practitioners* (Tucson: University of Arizona Press, 2003).

40. Pliny Earle Goddard, *Navajo Texts*, Anthropological Papers of the American Museum of Natural History, 34, no. 1 (New York: American Museum of Natural History, 1933), 148.

41. Slim Curly, "Blessingway" Version I, in *Blessingway: With Three Versions of the Myth Recorded and Translated from the Navajo by Father Berard Haile, O.F.M.*, ed. Leland C. Wyman (Tucson: University of Arizona Press, 1970), 172.

42. John Holiday and Robert S. McPherson, *A Navajo Legacy: The Life and Teachings of John Holiday* (Norman: University of Oklahoma Press, 2005), 368.

43. Stella Cly, interview.

44. See Ruth Roessel, *Women in Navajo Society* (Rough Rock, Arizona: Navajo Resource Center, 1981); Kay Bennett, *Kaibah: Recollection of a Navajo Girlhood* (Self-published, 1975); and Charlotte J. Frisbie, ed., with Rose Mitchell, *Tall Woman: The Life Story of Rose Mitchell, A Navajo Woman, c. 1874–1977* (Albuquerque: University of New Mexico Press, 2001).

45. See Alexander H. Leighton and Dorothea C. Leighton, *Gregorio, the Hand-Trembler: A Psychological Personality Study of a Navaho Indian*, Reports of the Ramah Project, no. 1 (Cambridge, MA: Peabody Museum of American Archaeology and Ethnology, Harvard University, 1949); also, Robert S. McPherson, *Dinéjí Na'nitin: Navajo Traditional Teachings and History* (Boulder: University Press of Colorado, 2012), 13–43, which has an extensive list of sources in the endnotes.

46. Gladys Reichard, *Navaho Religion: A Study of Symbolism* (Princeton, NJ: Princeton University Press, 1950), 99.

47. Reichard, *Navajo Religion*, 99–100; Charlotte J. Frisbie and David P. McAllester, eds., *Navajo Blessingway Singer: The Autobiography of Frank Mitchell, 1881–1967* (Tucson: University of Arizona Press, 1978), 163; William Morgan, "Navaho Treatment of Sickness: Diagnosticians," *American Anthropologist* 33 (Summer 1931): 390–92.

48. John Holiday, interview with author, September 9, 1991.

49. Marilyn Holiday, discussion with author, September 23, 2007; Jim Dandy, discussion with author, September 24, 2007.

50. Harry Walters, personal communication with author, January 28, 2012.

51. Clyde Kluckhohn, *Navaho Witchcraft* (Boston: Beacon Press, 1944, 1970), 22.

52. Gladys Bitsinnie, interview.

53. Kluckhohn, *Navaho Witchcraft*, 59.

54. See Robert S. McPherson, "Murder and Mapping in the 'Land of Death,' Part I: The Walcott-McNally Incident," *Utah Historical Quarterly*, vol. 18, no. 3 (Summer 2013): 249–66.

55. See William Haas Moore, *Chiefs, Agents and Soldiers: Conflict on the Navajo Frontier, 1868* (Albuquerque: University of New Mexico Press,1994), 124–36.

56. Ada Black, interview with author, December 15, 1991.

57. Nellie Grandson, interview.

Chapter 2

1. Susie Yazzie, interviews with author, August 6, 1991, and November 10, 2000.

Chapter 4

1. Richard Hobson, *Navaho Acquisitive Values*, Reports of the Rimrock Project Values Series No. 5 (Cambridge, MA: Harvard Museum, 1954, 1973).

2. Hobson, *Navaho Acquisitive Values*, 4.

3. Charlotte J. Frisbie, ed., with Rose Mitchell, *Tall Woman: The Life Story of Rose Mitchell, A Navajo Woman, c. 1874–1977* (Albuquerque: University of New Mexico Press, 2001), 84.

4. Nedra Tódích'íi'nii, interview with Fern Charley and Dean Sundberg in *The Navajo Stock Reduction Interviews of Fern Charley and Dean Sundberg* (Fullerton: California State University—Fullerton Oral History Program, 1984), 12.

5. Robert S. McPherson, *Viewing the Ancestors: Perceptions of the Anaasází, Mokwič, and Hisatsinom* (Norman: University of Oklahoma Press, 2014); and Robert S. McPherson, *Navajo Land, Navajo Culture: The Utah Experience in the Twentieth Century* (Norman: University of Oklahoma Press, 2001).

6. Sloan Haycock, interview with author, October 10, 1991.

7. Berard Haile, *Soul Concepts of the Navajo* (Saint Michaels, AZ: Saint Michaels Press, 1943, 1975), 88.

8. Anna Lora King, interview with author, April 8, 1992.

9. Joseph E. Persico, "The Great Swine Flu Epidemic of 1918," *American Heritage* 27 (June 1976): 28.

10. Alfred W. Crosby, *America's Forgotten Pandemic: The Influenza of 1918* (New York: Cambridge University Press, 1989), 228.

11. Benjamin R. Brady and Howard M. Bahr, "The Influenza Epidemic of 1918–1920 among the Navajos: Marginality, Mortality, and the Implications of Some Neglected Eyewitness Accounts," in *American Indian Quarterly* 38, no. 4 (Fall 2014): 484; Persico, "The Great Swine Flu Epidemic," 84.

12. Gladys A. Reichard, *Navaho Religion: A Study of Symbolism* (Princeton, NJ: Princeton University Press, 1963), 19; Ada Black, interview with Bertha Parrish, June 18, 1987.

13. The color red signifies a number of beliefs in traditional Navajo thought. Gladys Reichard points out that when it is reversed from its normal role in sandpaintings, it can represent evil associated with lightning or storm. On the other hand, "white apparently differentiates the naturally sacred from the profane—black or red, for instance—which through exorcism and ritual, must be transformed to acquire favorable power." Gladys A. Reichard, *Navaho Religion: A Study in Symbolism* (Princeton, NJ: Princeton University Press, 1950, 1974), 182, 187. Thus, the red dawns and sunsets warned of the approach of evil, as opposed to having the white and yellow light associated with the normal beginning and end of day and the directions of east and west respectively.

14. Ada Black, interview, 1–2; Rose Begay, interview with Bertha Parrish, June 17, 1987; Tallis Holiday, interview with author, November 3, 1987; Fred Yazzie, interview with author, November 5, 1987.

15. Scott C. Russell, "The Navajo and the 1918 Pandemic," in *Health and Disease in the Prehistoric Southwest* (Tempe: Arizona State University, 1985), 385; Fred Yazzie, interview.

16. Gilmore Graymountain, interview with Marilyn Holiday, April 7, 1992.

17. Franc Johnson Newcomb, *Hosteen Klah: Navaho Medicine Man and Sand Painter* (Norman: University of Oklahoma Press, 1964), 144–48.

18. Tallis Holiday, interview; Fred Yazzie, interview; Rose Begay, interview.

19. Pearl Phillips, interview with Bertha Parrish, June 17, 1987.

20. Frances Gillmor and Louisa Wade Wetherill, *Traders to the Navajos: The Story of the Wetherills of Kayenta* (Albuquerque: University of New Mexico Press, 1934, 1979); Samuel Moon, *Tall Sheep: Harry Goulding, Monument Valley Trader* (Norman: University of Oklahoma Press, 1992); Robert S. McPherson, *Both Sides of the Bullpen: Navajo Trade and Posts* (Norman: University of Oklahoma Press, 2017).

21. Klara Kelley and Harris Francis, *Navajoland Trading Posts Encyclopedia* (Window Rock, AZ: Navajo Nation Heritage and Historic Preservation Department, 2018).

22. Stokes Carson purchased the Oljato post in 1938, becoming the first in a long line of owners. Since this goes beyond 1940, these subsequent owners will not be discussed here. Those interested in the later years should read Willow Roberts, *Stokes Carson: Twentieth Century Trading on the Navajo Reservation* (Albuquerque: University of New Mexico Press, 1987), 99–111.

23. Nedra Tódích'íi'nii, interview with Fern Charley and Dean Sundberg, in *The Navajo Stock Reduction Interviews of Fern Charley and Dean Sundberg* (Fullerton: California State University—Fullerton Oral History Program, 1984), 11–14.

24. Nedra Tódích'íi'nii, interview, in Charley and Sundberg, *Navajo Stock Reduction Interviews*, 13.

25. Lula Stanley, interview with Fern Charley and Dean Sundberg, in *The Navajo Stock Reduction Interviews of Fern Charley and Dean Sundberg* (Fullerton: California State University—Fullerton Oral History Program, 1984), 5.

26. Sarah Begay, interview with Fern Charley and Dean Sundberg, in *The Navajo Stock Reduction Interviews of Fern Charley and Dean Sundberg* (Fullerton: California State University—Fullerton Oral History Program, 1984), 5.

27. Gladys Bitsinnie, interview with author, March 26, 1993.

28. Sloan Haycock, interview.

29. See Robert S. McPherson, "The Chidí and Flying Metal Come to the Navajo," in *Navajo Land, Navajo Culture: The Utah Experience in the Twentieth Century* (Norman: University of Oklahoma Press, 2001), 84–101.

30. Anna Lora King, interview.

31. Jenny Francis, interview with author, March 23, 1993.

32. Gladys Bitsinnie, interview.

33. For more on Navajo livestock reduction of the late 1920s and 1930s see Kenneth R. Philp, *John Collier's Crusade for Indian Reform, 1920–1954* (Tucson: University of Arizona Press, 1977); Richard White, *The Roots of Dependency: Subsistence, Environment, and Social Change among the Choctaw, Pawnees, and Navajo* (Lincoln: University of Nebraska Press, 1983); Ruth Roessel and Broderick Johnson, eds., *Navajo Livestock Reduction: A National Disgrace* (Tsaile, AZ: Navajo Community College Press, 1974);

Donald L. Parman, *The Navajos and the New Deal* (New Haven: Yale University Press, 1976); Lawrence C. Kelly, *The Navajo Indians and Federal Indian Policy* (Tucson: University of Arizona Press, 1968); and L. Schuyler Fonaroff, "Conservation and Stock Reduction on the Navajo Tribal Range," *Geographical Review* 53, no. 2 (April 1963): 200–223.

34. To understand the cultural impact of livestock reduction from the Navajo perspective, see McPherson, "Navajo Livestock Reduction in Southeastern Utah, 1933–1946: History Repeats Itself," *American Indian Quarterly* 22, nos. 1 & 2 (Winter/Spring 1998): 1–18.

35. Annual Report, 1930, Bureau of Indian Affairs, Navajo Archives, Edge of the Cedars Museum, Blanding, Utah, n.p. (hereafter Navajo Archives).

36. Annual Report, 1934, Navajo Archives.

37. Annual Report, 1934, Navajo Archives.

38. Garrick Bailey and Roberta Glenn Bailey, *A History of the Navajos: The Reservation Years* (Santa Fe, NM: School of American Research, 1986), 197.

39. White, *The Roots of Dependency*, 312.

40. John Holiday, interview with author, September 9, 1991.

41. Maria Chabot, "Some Aspects of the Navajo Problem," New Mexico Association of Indian Affairs Report, 1941, in Museum of New Mexico, Laboratory of Anthropology, Santa Fe, NM, 6.

42. Stella Cly, interview with author, August 7, 1991.

43. Lucy Laughter, interview with author, April 8, 1992.

44. Nedra Tódích'íi'nii, interview, in Charley and Sundberg, *Navajo Stock Reduction Interviews*, 20.

45. Kitty Atini, interview with Fern Charley and Dean Sundberg, in *The Navajo Stock Reduction Interviews of Fern Charley and Dean Sundberg*, (Fullerton: California State University—Fullerton Oral History Program, 1984), 5.

46. Betty Canyon, interview with author, September 10, 1991.

47. Lucy Laughter, interview.

48. Sally Manygoats, interview with author, April 8, 1992.

49. See Colleen O'Neill, *Working the Navajo Way: Labor and Culture in the Twentieth Century* (Lawrence: University of Kansas Press, 2005); Jay Youngdahl, *Working on the Railroad, Walking in Beauty: Navajos, Hózhǫ́, and Track Work* (Logan: Utah State University, 2011); and Wayne K. Hinton and Elizabeth A. Green, *With Picks, Shovels, and Hope: The CCC and Its*

Legacy on the Colorado Plateau (Missoula, MT: Mountain Press Publishing, 2008), 221–51.

50. See McPherson, "Digging the Bones of Yé'iitsoh: Navajos in the Uranium Industry of Southeastern Utah," in *Navajo Land, Navajo Culture*, 158–78.

51. Jenny Francis, interview.

52. Bessie Katso, interview with author, March 26, 1993.

53. Anna Black, interview with author, April 8, 1993.

54. Doug Brugge, Timothy Benally, and Esther Yazzie-Lewis, *The Navajo People and Uranium Mining* (Albuquerque: University of New Mexico Press, 2006).

55. O. F. Oldendorph, "Monument Valley: A Navajo Tribal Park," *National Parks Magazine* 40, no. 227 (August 1966): 4–8; "2,000 Attend Valley Park Dedication," *San Juan Record*, May 13, 1960, 1; "Navajos Dedicate Tribal Park Gateway," *Denver Post*, May 9, 1960, 31; Marsha Keele, "Monument Valley Park Celebrates 25th Year," *San Juan Record*, July 28, 1983, 1; Statistics on file in San Juan County Economic Development Office, County Courthouse, Monticello, Utah.

56. Guy Cly, interview with author, September 9, 1991.

57. Jenny Francis, interview.

58. Gladys Bitsinnie, interview.

59. Bessie Katso, interview.

60. Nellie Grandson, interview with author, December 16, 1993.

61. Sloan Haycock, interview.

62. Sloan Haycock, interview.

63. Stella Cly, interview.

64. Betty Canyon, interview.

65. Nellie Grandson, interview.

66. Sally Manygoats, interview.

Index

Brugge, Doug, 133
Bullsnake Spring (Diyóósh Tó), 201
Bureau of Indian Affairs, 125
Bureau of Land Management (BLM), 125
buzzards, 170

Calling God (Haasch'éé'ooghaan), 52, 78
Canyon, Betty, 16, 30, 129, 137–38
cardinal directions, 14, 109, 149, 166
cars. See automobiles
Carson, O. J. "Stokes", 121, 123, 189, 213n22
CCC. See Civilian Conservation Corps
Chaan Diniihi, Hastiin, 144
Chaco Canyon, 122
Ch'ah Adinii (No Hat, Mister), 125
Ch'ah Łibáhi' (Gray Hat), 19
Changing Woman (Asdzą́ą́ Nádleehé), 35, 52–53, 76–77, 94, 109, 150, 153, 164. See also White Shell Woman
Chased by the Mexicans (Naakai Ch'íhoníłkaad), 55
Chee, Hite, 138
ch'įįdii-tah (ghostland), 117
chiiłchin (sumac), 23–26, 66, 93, 144–45
children, jobs of, 22–23, 29–30, 61–64, 65–68, 145–46, 159, 204
Chinle, Arizona, 19
Chiricahua Windway (Chíshí Binílch'ijí), 171

Chíshí Binílch'ijí (Chiricahua Windway), 171
Chíshíjí (a Windway ceremony), 153
Christianity, 38, 73–76, 100, 102–4, 137
Cicada (Wóóneeshch'įįdii), 148–49
Civilian Conservation Corps (CCC), 130, 192–94
Clay's Water (Dlééshbí'tó'), 200
clothing, 22, 28, 60–63, 71, 80
Cly, Anna, 25
Cly, Guy, 133
Cly, Stella, 32, 36, 128, 136
Collier, John, 126, 128
color significance, 14, 118, 185, 212n13
Comb Ridge (Tséyík'áán), 124, 163, 200
cooking, 32–34, 144, 158, 199
Copper Mine (Bééshłichíí'ii Haagééd), 189
corn, importance of, 23, 26, 30–31, 34, 64–66, 68
cornmeal mush, 23, 34, 36, 98
corrals, 126, 127
Cortez, Colorado, 57–58, 185
Cottonwood Rising Out of the Valley (T'iis Haaz Áhá), 58, 60
Coyote (Mą'ii), 14, 148–49, 166–68
coyotes, 15, 138, 169, 171, 174
crystal gazing (déést'íí'), 4, 37, 39, 50, 75, 84, 174–75
Curly Hair (Tsiis Ch'ilii), 189

Dághaałbáhí, 143–44